Earth
Angels

Earth Angels

*Engaging
the
Sacred
in
Everyday
Things*

Shaun
McNiff

Foreword
by
Thomas
Moore

SHAMBHALA
*Boston
&
London
1995*

Shambhala Publications, Inc.
Horticultural Hall
300 Massachusetts Avenue
Boston, Massachusetts 02115

9 8 7 6 5 4 3 2 1

First Edition

Printed in the United States of America on acid-free paper ∞
Distributed in the United States by Random House, Inc.,
and in Canada by Random House of Canada Ltd

Library of Congress Cataloging-in-Publication Data

McNiff, Shaun.
    Earth angels: engaging the sacred in everyday things / Shaun McNiff;
    foreword by Thomas Moore.—1st ed.
        p.   cm.
    ISBN 1-57062-048-2 (pbk.)
    1. Angels.   2. Spiritual life.   3. Creative ability—Religious
aspects.   4. Self-actualization (Psychology)—Religious
aspects.
    I. Title.
    BL477.M395   1995   95-3900
    291.4—dc20   CIP

For the family and the angels of our household

I am the necessary angel of earth,
Since, in my sight, you see the earth again
—Wallace Stevens, *The Auroras of Autumn*

Contents

Foreword

It's often the case that as we gain something, we're not aware of what we've lost. In the past century we have gained enormously in a certain kind of knowledge about the world and in many ways of controlling and harnessing the materials of the world. What we've lost is enchantment, the realization that we humans are not the only beings in the universe who have personality, presence, and even subjectivity. We've grown accustomed to thinking of the entire non-human world, including animals and things, as inert, lifeless, personless, and inanimate—this last quality meaning literally "without soul."

One of many consequences of this prevailing attitude toward the world and philosophy of life has been a loss of conscience about the way we treat the nonhuman world. Take the train, as I sometimes do, into New York City and look at the rusted, broken, decaying things that have been abandoned along railways, in ditches, and in some backyards. Go into any city in this country that is built along a river, and try to find a place to stretch out on the ground and let the river massage your soul. There are some brilliant exceptions, but in many cases you will instead find warehouses, factories, junkyards, and train tracks preventing you from being by the river, and not only will you be deprived of necessary sights and sounds of water, but you may get angry at those things.

It's clear to me that we treat things badly because we have forgotten that they, too, have a soul and are therefore precious. Our relationship to things is often one of sadistic master instead of kindly relative or friend. We fail to realize that things, too, are sensitive, whether they are the things of nature or things made by human craft. Worst of all, we seem as far removed as possible from the ancient notion that the world soul and our own soul overlap, share the same substance, and suffer the same fate. When we maltreat the world of things, we are doing ourselves immeasurable harm.

When I studied medieval philosophy, discussions about soul and spirit, personhood and individuality, psychology and ethics all seemed quite abstract and detached from everyday concerns. Now, having become more focused on ordinary life through existentialist philosophy perhaps, phenomenology, Freud, Jung, Hillman, Sardello, and current poets of nature like Gary Snyder, Wendell Berry, and Mary Oliver, to say nothing of old traditions of nature in poetry and philosophy, we are in a position to reimagine our relationship to our homes, the things we have around us, nature, and the culture at large. We treat them all with renewed appreciation and even reverence.

It's at this point that I see the importance of this new book by Shaun McNiff, written in such an accessible way, from personal experience and from years of teaching art and therapy. An appreciation for the soul of this world of things requires that we get close to them, even in our thoughts about them, and that is what McNiff does here. He introduces us to many things and reveals secrets about his relationships with them. This book is about affairs of the heart, not in relation to humans, but to things.

Shaun calls himself a "keeper of the studio," a vocation I appreciate very much. A keeper is a curator, someone who houses and watches over, but doesn't treat in any therapeutic sense, the things in his care. We have finally learned, at least to some extent, that as humans we shouldn't enslave each other, but we have yet to learn that we shouldn't enslave things. We can keep them, admire them, use them, protect them, and contemplate them, without losing our care for them. To the person who cares for things, the whole world is a studio, a place for study—not analysis, but attention.

Another principle of Shaun's that I like very much: "There is a

landscape of the mind that has to be fed by the actual landscape."
The whole notion of world soul and human soul implies that there
is an incredibly intimate dialectic taking place, in the best of circumstances, between the outer world and the inner world. When I
use the term "human nature," I always think of nature as land and
animals and plants, imagining that I, too, have flora and fauna in my
inner jungles and farms and hills. I see them in my dreams and
know that there is some kind of mirror effect taking place. I don't
know which is glass and which natural substance, maybe each is
both, but I do know that I need to meditate by a river or a lake or
an ocean if I'm going to "keep" the waters of my soul, my fluidity
and depths. But I also have to be concerned about my own nature
if I'm going to take care of nature outside myself, if I can even use
that term. Nature is both me and not me at exactly the same time.

I'd like strongly to affirm Shaun's interpretation of the Epicurean value of "educating the senses." I have no doubt that we have
reduced experience to our mental life. We think of education as a
mental exercise, and we even undergo therapy as though it were a
way toward self-understanding. It's about time to broaden our notion of education, realizing that we have widespread illiteracy in the
realm of the senses. Otherwise, how could we fill our cities with
ugly buildings, and allow airlines to shut off all avenues to sensation
as we travel the airways, and let businesses keep us away from rivers
and lakes, and spend our days and hours of leisure in front of a
television screen? Clearly, we need remedial education in the
senses, to begin with. We need to learn how to live from the heart,
the hands, the stomach, and the feet. And, close to my heart, we
need to educate our ears so that we will no longer tolerate the soul-
wounding noises that dominate modern life.

I was once asked on national television if I had a guardian angel.
Without thinking, because I had only a split second to consider the
matter, I blurted out: "Of course, I have a guardian angel!" I think
that if we could follow the suggestions of Shaun McNiff in this

volume, we might be educated not only in the senses, but in a living, nonsectarian theology, and only theology can talk adequately
about angels. Medieval theologians used to say that philosophy was
the servant (ancilla) of theology, so maybe we can approach a new
appreciation of angels by developing a philosophy of enchantment,
sensation, beauty, and love of this world such as the one sketched
in this book.

THOMAS MOORE

Acknowledgments

In keeping with the theme of this book, I need others in order to create. Thanks to my wife, Catherine Cobb; Vincent Ferrini; Steve Levine; my children, Liam, Kelsey, Elysian, and Avery McNiff; Sandra Thoms; Herbert Rogers, S.J.; and other friends for their conversations which generated many of my thoughts. Special thanks to Thomas Moore for his foreword. Tom and I see ourselves working within a tradition, and our common mentor is James Hillman, who always incites and guides my thought. Rudolf Arnheim has been another major influence, teaching me for over twenty-five years how to look and to witness life. I am especially grateful to Kendra Crossen, who caught on to my sense of earth angels when I first proposed this book. As the project took shape, she kept sending sparks of encouragement and stimulating images. And lastly, thanks to the Penguins for the inspiration of their song, "Earth Angel."

Through the Eyes of Angels

Fill your spirit with the spirit of the world.
                                                            —Marsilio Ficino

A new way of looking ....

Angels are a way of looking at the world, infusing life with creative vitality and renewing our sense of the sacred. I am more concerned with seeing things with an angelic sense than with the literal discovery of angels.

Locating angels exclusively in the supernatural world banishes them from niches in neighborhoods and the workplace. My emphasis is noncelestial, but like most people I'm intrigued with airy spirits. I've got nothing against them. The problem lies in overlooking spiritual or subtle expressions of physical things, the earth angels available to the most ordinary consciousness. This way of looking might bring renewal, but it is not new. It lives through a tradition, deep waters flowing from antiquity, forever revitalizing themselves through changing forms.

Because I live in a world of physical images, I am drawn to this aspect of the angel. My meditations on angels have been shaped through years of clinical work with the arts, where it has become clear that images offer spirits to the people who make them or look at them. Like the images of the arts, angels come and go with the rituals we perform. Helping people access the medicine offered by the arts has kept me rooted in the material realm of soul's expression, where the images constantly call out for attention and for deeper and more imaginative interactions. I have come to angels through the aboriginal creative expressions of ordinary people in my art studios, where I have been taught many lessons about the soul's hunger for imagery. When these epiphanies appear in dreams, meditations, or the arts, we are faced with options as to how we will engage them. The rationalists explain them away as discharges of excess energy, whereas I prefer to welcome them as intimate figures of our inner lives.

I have been caught by surprise by the huge public interest in angels and find myself in the position of offering yet another angel book. But I hope the idiosyncrasies of my personal search will offer something different and useful to the discourse.

The guidebook reader asks, "How do I do it? How do I find the angels?"

I suggest looking at the most basic assumptions of your life, the things you take for granted, the stories you tell, your imaginings and desires. I will try to show how re-visioning the most common aspects of life yields an influx of imagination and angels. The richest veins are in the most unlikely sources. What we do not see is typically lodged in places where we do not want to look, or in those things we think we really know. Parents and childhood memories always evoke the earth angels. Tell the outrageous, embarrassing, and strange stories of your childhood, the ones you would never dare publish, and watch how people love to hear these things. It worked for Freud.

When we locate the angel "above" humans and closer to God, we are operating within a perspective that sees God as transcendent rather than immediate and present in everything. Rather than take sides on this ancient debate, I accept both. But this book is written from the latter perspective, which has been overlooked. I am concerned with the particular ways in which the divine presents itself through the forms of the world and their subtle expressions, what I call earth angels.

We really cannot operate within the realm of angels without affirming the divinity from which they emanate. I envision the divine source of all life as a mystery whose names include God, the numinous presence, the Creator, and other equally holy words. Jane Harrison described history's different experiences of the divine as images of desire.[1] This does not suggest falseness. The desire for the divine is the core, the *appetitus naturalis,* the *instinctus divinus.*

In addition to addressing the spiritually oriented reader, I want to approach angels in a way that engages skeptics, materialists, cynical artists, suspicious depth psychologists, and the average person. Anybody who can perceive through the senses can experience the angels I will be evoking. They do not require extrasensory perceptions of any kind, but they ask that we reconsider how we relate to things. Angels are the "intermediaries," the perceptual images and imaginings that exist between myself and the physical world.

The arts and religion come together through angels and soul's natural desire for images and intimate relations with persons, places, things, and spirits. The spiritual reverie makes endless configurations. I liken images to angels, and this connection between physical things and their spiritual expression is the purpose of this book. The temples of the spirit are expanded to include our homes, workplaces, likes and dislikes, and other uncommon places for locating the divine.

Because angels are so closely associated with individual imaginations, I will try to evoke their presence by writing a personal book. My dialogue with the figures of the imagination will, I hope, support yours as others have inspired me. The creative spirit is a community of influences in which the angels of our expressions stimulate one another.

Reflections on angels help to deepen connections to the physical world. Conversely, I have found that giving careful attention to the physical details of a person, object, or landscape evokes the angels through feelings of depth. Sustained attention to the particulars of a thing passes through resistance and opens the soul. "Depth" often has more to do with staying in compassionate and attentive contact with the presence of another than with revealing "deep" secrets, which may take us away from the immediacy of the present engagement. Deep down is always right here and now. The angel can be imagined as the energy that exists between things and that furthers the process of relating.

Like a dream, the angel comes in its own time. It cannot be rushed or controlled. We prepare ourselves by readying the psychic household for guests and displaying welcoming signals. If we want the spirits of the dream, we have to participate in their world. The same thing applies to creative expression. Like dreams, the arrivals of art cannot be planned in advance. If we begin to write, to paint, to move or make sounds, the creative images will appear. If we designate shrines and places of meditation in our households and focus attention on them, the angels will present themselves. We woo the images with these affections and never take them for granted. It is a lifelong cultivation of imagination, and we find that the well-being of our souls is closely attuned to the way we interact with material things. We are beginning the long psychic recovery from centuries of nature abuse fueled by the religious command "Love not the world and its things."

The angels are returning to the world as interest in spiritual figures grows daily, and from history we see that a cultural influx of angels always bring a renaissance of imagination. In our personal reveries we view the world through the eyes of angels, but we have debased this divine intelligence, forever declaring, "It's just fantasy, only imagination. It's not real."

Angels are classically defined as intermediaries, carriers of messages from one world to another, experienced concretely here as connecting what we see and do not see, or as joining things in a new way. But the angels are much more than conduits. They are an influx of the creative spirit in our lives, and in the most personal sense they act as guardians of the soul and guides to its mysteries. I try to stay attuned to the pulse of the angel by looking more attentively and creatively at what is already taking place in my life. In this sense I am an avid conservationist of ordinary things. The angel brings me home to the life I am living and cannot see.

It is against my nature as a teacher to tell a person "how to do it," so I can't claim that this book is a guide in the conventional sense. We find out for ourselves by examining our lives, the images our psyches make, and the phenomena of the world. They will reveal whatever we need to know if we can learn how to engage them and trust their wisdom. The creative journey lets our visions find *their* path through the world. We follow their lead. They know the way.

In my experience, the path of the creative spirit is not clearly marked. When it does appear, it emanates in instants, fragments, and insights. Yet somehow the pieces find a way to form a whole, a broader vision tied together with the threads of feelings that keep returning and asking for a response. This is the way of creative work, of imaginal reality, so familiar to creators who eschew the clearly delineated paths of their predecessors and instinctively forge their own—or, better yet, those of their visions and images. The creator follows the uncharted way of the angel, always a step ahead of the reflecting mind.

I will try to demonstrate a creative way of looking in daily life, perhaps even seeing the ordinary as a wild and unusual place, the unexplored fields of our souls. I define the "field" as our immediate environment seen through the eyes of imagination. We can walk through kitchens and backyards with the imagination and enthusiasm of a Sierra trek. The arrivals of creation, what I call the earth angels, are apt to come quickly and obliquely. The artist knows all too well how the creative epiphany may show itself and disappear like a bird in flight.

Dreams illustrate how glances and even unconscious perceptions are transformed into psychic images. They also confirm the importance of commonplace objects in psyche's household. There is a discipline associated with cultivating a rich dream life, and similar methods are used to enhance household spirits. We learn to watch and witness the soul's movements, striving to be more aware of its wants and ways. We take time to reflect on habitual acts, doing a routine thing as though it were the first time and experimenting with new ways of being in familiar places. These meditations let imagination fly through our habitats and revitalize the commonplace.

My demonstration may incite your discovery. Suggestions for practice are offered as hints. They are presented as possibilities and incitements, not as exercises to be strictly followed. I don't think the angels approve of cut-and-dried techniques either. I demonstrate to give a sense of how you can create your own methods of engagement. The realm of earth angels is one of subtle intimations about what we do not normally see.

By mentioning angels, I evoke religion, and most people either have very definite ideas about this subject or tend to stay away from it, preferring to speak of "spirituality." The words *soul* and *spirit* have an ability to move between sacred and secular worlds, and judging from the current popular involvement with angels, these figures have been similarly detached from exclusive ties to religious beliefs. But rather than skirt religion, I want to renew its imagination. It seems crazy to express an interest in sacred things while rejecting religion, a repression that only increases its shadow power. I prefer to re-vision religious experience in keeping with the way it manifests itself in my personal life. I start with myself and try to show how I experience the earth angel, with the hope that this will be useful to you.

I have spent my life committed to a sacramental vision of the arts, in which creation is viewed as a mode of healing and transformation, as the spirit of community, and as a way to deepen our relations to things. As D. H. Lawrence said, "This is how I save my soul."

I believe the divinity moves through us via creation and that images can be viewed as angels.[2] Although concrete things emerge from creating, the movement and feel of the action cannot be recorded empirically. It can only be suggested and glimpsed. Describing earth angels is like trying to explain what happens in dance or listening to music. The movement is always ahead of reflection, and words exist in a completely different world than the bodily and aural expressions. Therefore, nothing in the imaginal realm can ever be literally described. Rather than perceiving this as a weakness, we can embrace it as defining the poetic reality where metaphors link worlds and where pure images are appreciated without any attempt at metaphoric translation. The images stir and inspirit. At best this way of communicating can be considered angelic—subtle, hinting, and never literal.

Yet there is also a very basic physicality, or groundedness, to my sense of earth angels. They are accessible everywhere and express themselves through the asphalt and details of the material world. They are the angels of material reality.

When I look at physical things through the eyes of the angel, I am perceiving through my spiritual being, which resonates with theirs. "It takes one to know one." Soulfulness is felt through compassionate perception and never through analytic distance. Creation is an open meditation in which we receive the influxes of others and then act in cooperation with them.

In spite of the complete split between matter and spirit in Western culture, our philosophical traditions have sustained the idea that the two can be present in the same thing. My reflections will try to rekindle our natural human appreciation for the souls of things and places.

Earth angels are embodiments of an interplay between soulful matter and creative spirit. For me, soul is an inward motion toward depth, a magnetism that pulls me into its being. I speak of "the soul of a thing" as its kernel, heart, or pulse, whereas spirit flies out from it, like breath or a breeze, an aura, esprit, the spark that ignites my imagination. The way soul and spirit insist on penetrating one another is as interesting to me as their distinctions. This book hopes to fly between the two, approaching angels through the imagination of material things. Its methods are closer to those of a skeptical realist than to a clairvoyant who summons spirits, or perhaps it is located somewhere between the two. The materialistic orientation may actually help to expand our sense of the angel and further the work of imagination in daily life.

Our creative vitality will be enhanced as we deepen our appreciation for the spiritual expression of things, focusing less on ourselves and more on them. My antithetical moves are meant to serve creation and the revisioning of spirits. As the spectrum of creative expression is increased, we will feel a corresponding expansion within ourselves. Our egocentric theories miss the paradoxical and indirect movements of the condition we call creativity, wherein the most solitary creator never acts alone, but moves in partnership with other spirits.

Creativity also suffers from a cultural aggrandizement that makes it increasingly inaccessible to people. This is why the ordinary and habitual things of daily lives are vital agents of the soul's renewal. They are the earth angels who deliver a new message about the nature of the creative spirit.

I hope this book helps to reverse, twist, and ultimately expand our ideas about creativity. I focus on *them*, and this liberates me from the boundaries of self-consciousness and habitual action. We create together as partners. I am not their passive agent, nor do they function in this way for me. We depend upon each other, and my creative expressions affirm my faith in them, my love for them, and my longing for the images forever emanating from our cooperation. As I become more appreciative of the subtle expressions of things, they transform my ways of being with others in the world.

I take liberties with ideas, which can themselves be angels, and I am inclined to reframe the way we look at things. The eyes of the angel can be described as offering fresh and novel pictures. My notion of the earth angel can be viewed as a complete fabrication, but it also feels like a very ancient notion, something that continuously insists on being recognized for what it is. The idea presses on me because the common understanding of a spirit is so limited. My sense of the angel is a survival of the Hellenic *daimon* and Roman *genius*, the prevailing spirits, characters, and expressions of people, things, places, and periods. It is also very close to the familiar spirits of native cultures everywhere.

My earth angels are the spiritual counterparts of every thing. I am intrigued with how these "others" shape the people who look at them. Since the things of the world are agents of my formation, I want to know them more compassionately and deeply.

I have repeatedly said to myself, "Why get caught up in all of the contemporary hoopla about angels? You're an artist concerned with tangible things, acts, and the essential spirits of creation. Angels are a distraction, something else altogether. Let them stay in the heavens, living on as immortal beings. Don't get involved in the celestial pop craze, our most recent spiritualized denial of darkness, uncertainty, and sensual living."

But the idea of the earth angel has a hold on my soul. It won't let go. I believe there is good medicine in the idea, something the soul desires. It is a reaction against the one-sided prettiness, the beautifully dressed and always golden visions of angels in the popular imagination. My earth angels can be perverse demons as well as loving guides. Because I trust the psyche's wisdom, I repeatedly discover that the afflicting demon helps me see where I have gone astray. My sense of the earth angel is in this respect a return to an ancient view of spirits that does not make rigid boundaries between good and bad ones. It is a matter of nuance rather than the simplistic dichotomy that persists in our contemporary angel culture. The earth angel is a force, or demon, urging me on.

The soul will always desire and treasure beautiful things, but the one-sided imagination of elegant angel shops obscures the earth spirits who are suffering because of our treatment of the physical world. The golden angels are inversions of the way we actually see our city streets and sprawling malls. We cannot see the spirits living in these environments, so we fabricate alternatives. The challenge for me lies in the appreciation of the earth angel in all its forms. The places that repel my sensibility may have the most to offer in deepening my involvement with the earth and all of its manifestations. James Hillman keeps reminding us how the Greeks felt that our most serious offense is not paying attention to the gods who are present in every aspect of the physical world. Everything is full of spirits, and the malady of our era is the alienation of the individual soul from the souls of things—all things.[3]

The idea of earth angels also helps treat our soulless attitudes toward the physical world. My sense of the angel endows physical things with psychic significance. The two worlds ensoul one another through their ongoing interaction. The figures of our inner lives have forms influenced by the expressive qualities of the material world; and the spiritual nature of external things is enhanced by our reflection on them.

The forces of the creative spirit do not stay fixed within tidy boundaries. They impinge upon us, and one another, and they fly about in a sometimes maddening way. As a man in Connemara once said to me, "Can't fence anything with wings." I assume this applies to the earth angels contemplated in this book. Its pages fly from reflections on daily life in the West of Ireland to Gloucester, Massachusetts, where I contemplate the spirits of snapshots, paintings, stone walls, household shelves, dreams, childhood memories, furnishing a room, and mowing the lawn. Although this diversity may be fragmented, it is a necessary condition of my inquiry, which strives to make connections between separate things. The inconsistent mix is itself a primary manifestation of the earth angel's being.

The psyche is a cooking of diverse substances freely interacting with one another. The earth angels are the winged spirits that move about in unexpected ways, flying from one place to another, from one idea to the next, making the new connections we call creation. They are energies moving through us, the forces of the creative act, fleeting instants, and lifelong companions.

My vision of a soulful materialism is foreign to almost everybody's idea of an angel. I long for deeper relationships with physical things. The objects themselves seem to ask for this. They have been neglected, misunderstood, and viewed as lifeless artifacts, existing to be used and ultimately cast aside in a materialist world serving people. But according to my contrary nature, "the toxin is the antitoxin." Material things contain the spirits of their salvation. We can help the process along by reframing our relationships to them, appreciating their expression, life, and creativity. When we begin to see how the spirits of things affect, and actually form us, our relationships with them will be transformed. They will change us if we can deeply contemplate their natures. This intimate dialogue is basic to consorting with angels.

I am intrigued with the angel in the microwave, my grandmother's portrait, the plant on the windowsill, the computer on which I write, and things that go contrary to my aesthetic sensibility. I am also concerned with spirits that live outside consciousness in homes, offices, and neighborhoods. In this book I will try to offer simple descriptions of my experiences with these ordinary things with the hope that they will stimulate your imagination. This contagion of spirits is the way of the earth angels.

I will also talk about demons and how the things that disturb us have much to offer. This realization helps to keep us grounded and protects against fears of roving spirits who want to harm and overwhelm us. Over and over again my work shows that the imaginal figures appearing in dreams, meditations, and art works never come to hurt us. If they feel overwhelming or imposing, that always has something to do with the necessity of their messages. They need to use these tactics to get our attention, to soften the rigid psyche and help it open to the messenger. My work in training psychotherapists has kept me close to the purposeful and transformative ways of our psychic ills. This sense of the helpful malady is what really distinguishes the earthy and soulful angels from their more celestial cousins.

Because materialism and disturbing situations are so antithetical to our popular sense of spiritual well-being, they may have the most to offer its revisioning. When a depressed person goes shopping to lift his spirits, we tend to think of buying things as an avoidance of feelings, a superficial and fleeting substitute for a more direct confrontation of his condition. In keeping with the deep rift in our culture between matter and spirit, mail-order catalogues, automobile showrooms, and TV advertisements are assumed to be far afield of spirituality. Nothing in our era is more ripe for inversion than these ideas that keep spirits divorced from daily life. The person may be depressed because he is so deeply alienated from material things and their aesthetic infusions.

My sense of earth angels is in keeping with the ancient idea that the divinity is present in everything. I don't argue the whereabouts of God, and I don't think of myself as a pantheist, which is just another limiting label. I am simply fascinated with how things express themselves and offer us a more inspired, interactive, and imaginative view of the world. Throughout this book I will give descriptions of how objects throw off rays, auras, and medicines to those who relate to them within the ecology of soulful living. Although my focus will be on material things, because we are so unlikely to see them as carriers of spirits, I will also envision dreams, psychic images, and the inner forces of creation as earth angels. The bedrock of my view is that all of these images are the fulfillment of the soul's desire. The soul desires images, many of them, and they are the earth angels that fly through our psychic lives.

A silver Mercedes convertible ......

> What is your soul, what is my soul? It is not some evaporated spirit. Ah no. It is that deep core of individual unity where life itself, the very God, throbs incalculably. . . . This angel business, this spirit nonsense! Even spirits, such as really exist, are potent sensual entities.
> —D. H. Lawrence

The average person, Joe Skeptic, who hears how mystics see every idea or perception as an angel, wants to know how this way of looking differs from his.

Joe says, "When I look at a tree, that's what I see, nothing else. No angels, spirits, or fairies. I see a trunk coming up from the ground, branches, leaves, and the space around them. That's it."

I reply, "I see those things too. Perhaps no differently than you."

He says, "Then where are the angels?"

"If I reflect on the tree and look at it with the eyes of imagination, then something different starts to happen. Can you imagine the spirits of the tree, or its soul?"

"No," Joe says.

I ask, "What about a silver Mercedes convertible? Does that image make you feel something?"

"It sure does."

"What happens when you think about it?"

"I see myself driving on a winding road, in the country at sunset. It's warm outside so I've got the top down. I feel the wind all around me."

"What else?"

"The car's new, so it smells great. It's all leather inside and the wheel has a great feel, the seats too, and the dashboard. It's beautiful, elegant."

"Anything else?"

"The sound of the engine. That's the best thing of all. It's powerful, but you can barely hear it."

"Why do you feel passionate desire for the Mercedes and not the tree?" I asked.

"Because I want the car!"

"You don't have one?"

"Right.

"Do you see it clearly in your mind's eye?"

"Yes. It's probably more real than the real thing."

"Because you want it so much?"

"I sure do," Joe says.

The silver Mercedes is an image in Joe's imagination. It also exists in the physical world, although it is not present before him at this moment. If the car were here now, the actual thing would interact with the images in his mind. His perceptions of the automobile would also generate feeling and further images of the imagination. The angel of his heart's desire is both physical and imaginal. We can probably say that unless you have these two elements, you won't experience the angel. Like angels, images appear in varied forms— the visible images of perception, images created through the arts, and the invisible images of reveries and dreams, which grow from material perceptions and, as many feel, sometimes exist independent of them.

Joe lives amid imaginal spirits, but his perspective on them is different than mine. He thinks literally about the car, and I approach it imaginally. The different qualities of the car that flew out to Joe can be described as its spirits, whereas the soul of the car is the core of its being, a gathering of its characteristics.

I can hear Joe now: "What are you trying to tell me? Do you

mean you really wouldn't like to have a silver Mercedes convertible?"

"You caught me, Joe. I would. Yes, I confess, I would enjoy it. You are more honest about these things. I suppress many material desires. But right now I am more interested in the imaginal Mercedes. There is a big difference for me."

"What do you mean?"

"The actual thing is an object of desire that stimulates images of the imagination."

"It sure does. I'm still driving on that country road."

"Now you can take that same desire for the car and transfer it onto the tree in front of us."

"Why bother?"

"Because the feeling of desire, the passion and love for all things, is ultimately the purpose of my life. It makes me feel good, just as good as the fantasy of driving down a road in a Mercedes with the wind blowing on my face."

"We're different."

"Absolutely. The imagination is our most individual faculty. I enjoy hearing you describe your desire for the car. It expands my limited sense of life. But it's hard to see people torturing themselves and hurting others to get these things."

"But I still want the car."

"I don't want to try and make you into a monk. The world needs all kinds. And we need objects of desire, the visible and invisible ones. The world economy wouldn't function very well if people stopped wanting things."

"Do you mean to tell me that you can really feel passion for a tree?" Joe asks.

"Yes," I say. "When I reflect on its qualities, I am feeding my desire for the experience of imagination for its own sake. It is a desire that is different from possession. It has more to do with living imaginatively."

"Sounds like you prefer dreaming about the car to actually own-
ing it."

"Perhaps. I know people who have everything and they have
lost desire. They are afflicted with a failure to thrive, even though
they're surrounded by all of the things they previously wanted.
Their desires become more perverse and unusual because they still
want things they don't have."

"I think I'm beginning to see what you mean," says Joe. "Why
not have fantasies about the things we already have?"

"Right, and bring more imagination and desire to our interactions with ordinary things available to everyone."

I don't think the advertising industry will promote that idea.
It's no angel for them. It's fascinating, though, how the ad people
really understand this business about objects of desire. I've got no
problem with commerce. We could not share this experience of the
imagination without the actual Mercedes and our direct experiences and memories of cars. The Mercedes of the imagination is an
earth angel.

Joe asks, "So how do you see angels in a tree?"

"I look at the tree with imagination, in a kind of meditative and
personal reverie. Images emerge from the interaction. You can also
call them spirits or angels. They are not literally present, but they
are alive within the context of my contemplative dialogue with the
tree. The same thing happens when I look at a painting of angels
on the wall, an artistic image that deliberately portrays spirits. The
experience of the angel requires an interplay of imagination and the
senses. The physical thing does not necessarily exist as an angel
until it is experienced imaginally. Every time I engage a painting in
my house, our relationship changes, and different images or spirits
emanate from our interaction. This is the way I approach the interpretation of the physical world. It is an ongoing dialogue with the
angelic nature of things through the poetic and loving intelligence
of the heart. There's no real difference between the way I relate to

the tree and the way you imagine the Mercedes. If we just look at what you are doing and the pleasure it gives you, then it is clear that possession of the car is just another part of the imaginal experience. Once you actually own the car, everything could change."

"I might even get tired of it," Joe replies.

"That does happen with the persons and things closest to us. The medicine of renewal comes through the imagination and constantly looking at things in different ways, with desire, or at least with aesthetic appreciation."

I've found that the key to enjoying an activity is the mindset I bring to it. If I approach the long walk as a tedious obligation, it will fulfill my expectations.

I can change the significance of the bus ride I take every day, by approaching it aesthetically. I can do this completely within my imagination as I sit and open to reverie, or I can actually begin to document the trip artistically by keeping a poetic diary focusing on each day's ride or writing a story from the perspective of the bus and its repetitive odyssey. By personifying the bus I get a completely different perspective of the world. This is what I mean by infusing life with imagination and increasing its influence on daily life. The bus might tell stories about the people it transports, the qualities of neighborhoods and streets, the weather, and the variations in an otherwise consistent routine. By re-visioning the bus as a pundit who wisely reflects on its environment, or as a poetic observer, I open new perspectives on the world.

If I have negative feelings about taking the bus, I can be assured that there is plenty of psychic energy involved in my relationship with it. Personifying the bus expands my compassion for its experience. The demon bus, the thing I loathe to ride, is transformed into a psychic helper who shows me how to look at things differently. Stuckness, boredom, anxieties, and even depression involve a certain failure of imagination. I see over and over again how the healthy and creative person has an open, flexible, and engaged attitude toward things. This ability to shift attention and accommodate to situations probably has something to do with the origin of the term "well-adjusted."

So when the bus demon or angel (I see little difference between the two) becomes a personified figure in my imagination, it serves as a guide to the transformation of how I view my present situation. This is what artists and writers are doing all of the time with their experiences.

Children's literature can teach us how to personify buses, trains, houses, animals, and objects. Imagination flourishes in that genre, and it is no wonder that so many adults long to write and illustrate children's books. The angels and spirits of creation are thriving in that art form. Children give parents the opportunity to fulfill their own longings for a rich life of the imagination.

I can make drawings at the bus stop and from my seat on the bus, and build the sketches into large paintings, or I can document the experience with photographs, record street sounds and conversations, and then create a bus stop performance. The most lowly and tedious experiences from daily life seem to have the most potential for these transformations. But we have to take time to appreciate them and see the angels in the incidents.

Ordinary things that annoy us are loaded with spirits waiting for transformation. After scraping and painting my house last summer, I realized that I missed the opportunity to turn every phase of the experience into a work of art. I wished that I had taken comprehensive "before" photographs as well as pictures documenting my tools in action and the various apparatuses I used to reach the peaks of the house. But I can do all of this through imagination and memory and still reap the benefits of the transformational feelings. Writers have great freedoms because their image-making medium is not restricted by time and place.

I just realized how it is usually people in the most restricted situations who discover the wonders of the imagination. The hostage who mentally replays his favorite game of chess, his favorite restaurant meal, and other details of his past life; the prisoner who recites the plot of a novel to his cellmate from memory. Over and over again we discover the riches of the ordinary imagination when confined against our will. The artist Don Burgy told me how his vocation of the imagination came to him when he was a child and bedridden for a year. When there is nothing, imagination enters and opens the doors to its treasury. In poverty, the angels always flourish. This is why artists and creative people flee from the anesthesia of habitual life.

The powers of imagination are intimately connected to longing, and from the history of the world's monastic disciplines we see how the life of imagination becomes the object of its own yearning. Vows of poverty paradoxically make way for the wealth of spirit.

Foreign places also stimulate imagining. A friend told me that one of her most delightful images of earth angels focuses on a German supermarket full of attractively packaged goods, experienced like a museum display. She said to me, "When I walk through an American supermarket, I see food, but in a foreign store, there is visual stimulation divorced from knowing what is in the package, or from instantly knowing what the item is, as we do with familiar brands. There is a sensation of fresh impressions and the feeling of curiosity, excitement, infinite possibilities. One of my most treasured travel mementos is an Arabic Pepsi can. Of course, I know it's Pepsi because of the design, but the word *Pepsi* in Arabic makes me reexperience the strangeness of being in the Dubai airport and the exotic aura of the Middle East."

Pepsi written in Arabic gives a radically different twist to one of our most familiar cultural images. The can signifies our different ways of looking at the world, and for my friend it is a material link to a personal memory. It carries feelings and imaginings, earth angels issuing from its being.

The way imagination flourishes in restricted and foreign places suggests that we can bring these attitudes to everyday situations. I can look at the local store displays with foreign eyes and reflect on the strange ways of familiar things, or savor the simple pleasures of daily life by imagining what it would be like to lose them.

Can the imagination have the things of the world and still maintain the intensity of its longing? I ask myself whether it is possible to find angels in a well-stocked wine cellar or in a room full of antiques, existing within our own homes. I believe so.

Joe Skeptic can materially possess the silver Mercedes convertible and maintain his longing for it. Every action, thought, and physical thing has a spiritual nature or angel. The conversation with Joe reveals how the actual car stimulates the imaginal reverie. Once he owns the car, he can still approach it as an object of desire and never take it for granted.

The principles of *tantra*, which means "expansion," can be applied to our relations with things. Most Westerners associate Hindu tantrism with esoteric sexual practices, but the teachings of the *Kama Sutra* are not limited to sexual relations. I will venture to say that Eros was present in Joe's feelings toward the Mercedes convertible. He might not like me talking about him in this way, but I sense that he is the kind of guy who would instinctively relate to his precious car with a wide range of gestures, whereas I tend to approach machines through unimaginative and confined movements. I am more likely to interact with a tree, or my garden, with delicate variations of feeling. Aphrodite shines for me there and not on the hood of the car. The energies that pass between the car and me are restricted. Few things in the world serve me so completely, and yet for some reason I give it the most minimal attention and care.

I can see Joe having a far more expansive relationship with his Mercedes, wiping it down every day, polishing and vacuuming it once a week, changing the oil and filter himself, observing subtle changes in engine sounds and tire pressure, keeping the trunk neat and clean, spraying rubber freshener on his radials, parking it carefully to avoid dings, changing plugs, making sure the shocks are perfect so that his ride is always smooth and no unnecessary damage is done to the car, cleaning the engine, and generally having his life structured within the intervals of these rituals. He is able to adapt himself to the life of a machine, which requires a significant commitment. Ah, I see now that I am so busy with other things that I don't want to let the car into my personal time. The tree asks nothing of me. There is a part of me that might even resist being given a silver Mercedes convertible because of the way it would change the structure of my life.

Aside from maintenance, the various ways in which Joe might interact with the car activate different energies. I imagine it making many changes in his social life.

Let me offer some possibilities. He loves the feeling of people turning to look at him when he drives with the top down, and he has become aware of the subtle glances that less demonstrative types cast out of the corners of their eyes when he passes them on the highway. The car becomes an extension of himself, and it is the agent of new ways of being with people. They stop to admire it outside his house or when he pulls into the gas station or the parking lot at the supermarket. As people lavish this interest on the car, he feels it coming into him, and it is a good sensation. There is a sparkle in their eyes, a passion and enthusiasm, a desire to engage that was never there before. What difference does it make if it is the car or him that is the stimulus, because he is getting the attention. He actually likes it better this way. There is something delightful about indirect admiration and the way positive regard for the car affects its caretaker. He remembers how invisible he felt in his old car.

Many of us fear that if our objects leave, our identities will go with them. It seems that only the advertisers understand how we are defined by our relations to things and the company we keep. On the whole this need for things cultivates soulful and interdependent living. None of us exists alone, and alienation is the inability to appreciate the things around us and our interplay with them. But just as our involvement with other people may become too dependent at times, we can become overly reliant on things and expect too much from them.

The car can also influence Joe's spiritual contemplation. I see him sitting next to the Mercedes, reflecting on its presence or just luxuriating in the feel of the wheel and the views from the driver's seat while parked at the beach or the park. There are so many different qualities of his desire for the car, which becomes a beloved partner, a means of transport that is not restricted to physical movement. As he unites himself with the car, Joe travels and glows with its spirit. He loses himself in its being.

It is remarkable how the presence of a thing can change the structures of our lives.

These imaginings about Joe and a beloved thing establish a basis for comparison and expansion. Can we bring the same qualities of attention to things that we already have, especially after their novelty has faded? Can we long for things with which we are totally accustomed? Joe's feelings are contagious, and I feel that I am living within the condition of desire as I listen to him. The relationship with a specific object of affection opens to a universal state that shows different faces, or angels, to individual people. Any image can serve as an intermediary between me and the archetypal energy of desire. Once I realize that desire is out there in the world ready to attach itself to any object of contemplation, I feel the ability to locate it anywhere. I am less likely to affix desire to any one thing as I see how concentration on a particular object multiplies the focal points, just as Joe's reverie stimulates mine. The love objects expand far beyond themselves and emit auras and rays that touch everything in their paths. So the recognition of the angel of desire in any thing spreads desire to any place imaginable, and especially to the things that exist within the orbits of our daily lives.

Desire is an expression of the personal imagination, but it is simultaneously divine and totally outside us. It is fascinating how Wallace Stevens would keep saying that "poetry is not personal," and then say at another time that "it is the personal in the poet that is the origin" of the poem.[4] I feel that this contradiction is the essence of desire. Paradoxically, the specific individual, and deeply personal experiences, transport the person into an archetypal or pandemic condition. The global state of love emanates from particulars: the new spread my wife put on the bed, the wallet and sunglasses my son left behind on the kitchen table, my daughter's sheet music on the piano, the dog's leash hanging on a hook after we lost him. Each of us is going to open to emotions through different things.

But there is also an angel of contagion. When I listen to Joe, my desire is activated even though I do not necessarily share his personal interest. Although the angels of love and desire are often generated by glances at things, my reflections on Joe and his imaginal car indicate that some relationships need maintenance, time, and sustained imagination. Because certain things are always going to appeal to us more than others, I may never apply the same quality of imagining to cars that he does. But he has stimulated me to revisit the way I interact with my VW.

There are so many angels out there in the world, and I cannot feel responsible for them all, and they don't need me for this, but my car is an intimate figure in my life that may benefit from more attention. I also don't have the mechanical interests that Joe and other people have. Yet it does feel good to think about my car and expand the imagination of our relationship.

Persian mystics felt that the thoughts people have are more powerful than the people themselves, and that "every thought *has* an Angel."[5] Joe's thoughts about the silver Mercedes convertible stir my imagination because they are so foreign to my own way of relating to things. I will carry the thought of his vision with me the next time I unlock the door to my car.

"Not I, not I" ....

The fire muttered softly, the oil-lamp counted seconds drop
by drop. . . .   —Colette, *The Innocent Libertine*

The world's many cultures have imagined angels, and their ancestors, the Greek *daimones*, as intermediaries and messengers who go between the human and the divine. Can the pickles on the shelf of a quaint store or the Mercedes in the show window actually function as agencies through which divine intelligences are transmitted to human beings?

My sense is that the most unlikely things deftly play the intermediate role because of the way they protect and maintain the mysterious nature of the angel. If the creative spirit operates in the guise of wordly things, then the essential rule for those wanting to experience earth angels is: Think imaginatively about ordinary things, giving special attention to the details of your life, with the realization that angels congregate when we leave our usual perspectives on things, and ourselves, to contemplate otherness.

Paradox is essential to the angel's identity. It is in me and not in me, of this world and not of it, in the pickle jar and not in it. I imagine the angel as a connecting force that sustains an ongoing creative interaction among things. It moves around and cannot be fixed to a single place. When an object or a person is isolated from the interplay of creation, there is a loss of soul, and the angel is the mediator who treats the separation.

A broken bottle can be as evocative as a celebrated painting to the person who contemplates it as an expression of a numinous world. Through my imagination of the pickle jar, I minimize distinctions between human and divine things and see the angel taking shape between things when they interact. I have often felt that thought emerges from the process of talking. When I speak to another person, something new emanates from the exchange. Typically, the thought cannot be attributed to either person, and it comes to life through what they make together. There is a loss of self-consciousness, and I feel as if I am a participant in a process. This happens whenever I am immersed in writing a book, making a picture, painting a fence, or cleaning a floor.

When the angels of creation flourish, we feel as if we are in the company of others. Things act through us instinctively and without premeditation, an effortless vitality described by D. H. Lawrence with the words "Not I, not I, but the wind that blows through me."

The idea for an essay comes from a line I read in the magazine on the table; my painting is transformed by the picture my eight-year-old daughter draws alongside me; a poem is created from a feeling I get from a telephone conversation.

Let me give an example of how the spirits work through us in daily life. When my daughter was sixteen, we moved into a new community. She is only with us during the summer, and for the first month she stayed largely to herself, even though the neighborhood is full of girls and boys her age.

I knew the parents of a girl her age, so I said, "Why don't we just walk over to her house and say hello? If you meet her, you'll get connected to all of the others."

My daughter replied, "No, Daddy. Kids don't do it that way. We have to be doing something together, and then we get to know people."

A few days later one of the parents who knew about our situation called and told me that her daughter would like to invite mine to a social event with a group of her friends. The intercessors appeared spontaneously and connected my daughter to the free interplay of community spirit. My attempts to help were calculated, stiff, and impatient. This is not the way angels work. When my daughter said, "We have to be doing something together, and then we get to know people," she was describing how creativity involves immersion in an activity through which things come together in new relationships which cannot be planned. Things happen spontaneously or daimonically, as if a force is acting through us.

But I must first commit myself to the painting, the book, or the sport with a fluid and relaxed discipline. The angels of creation need more than a casual relationship. It is a paradoxical training in which we learn how to let something act through us, trusting its ability to find the way. This is a place where art and religion meet.

When I try too hard to fix a painting, it becomes overworked. When the creative process is flowing, I paint the picture and don't paint it at the same time. Something moves through me and paints the picture. I am not passive, but I am also not completely in control. I collaborate with the energies of creation moving from one thing to another. It is similar to being in a group. Even when we are supposedly working alone, creation is a participatory experience in which I interact with a flow of spontaneous arrivals. Rather than try to describe this process technically, according to the six or seven "stages" of creative expression, I find the personified vision more accurate and closer to the feeling of creation.

The *Koran* (8.17) elegantly articulates the paradox of action: "It is not you who throw the dart when you throw it." You paint the picture or meet new friends, but something other than you moves the process when it is inspired. You dance, and the angels dance through the agency of your being. The creative spirit manifests itself through these reciprocal relations.

Herman Melville restates the same questions about agency in Ahab's famous soliloquy in *Moby Dick:* "Is Ahab, Ahab? Is it I, God, or who, that lifts this arm? But if the great sun move not of himself; but is as an errand-boy in heaven; nor one single star can revolve, but by some invisible power; how then can this one small heart beat; this one small brain think thoughts; unless God does that beating, does that thinking, does that living, and not I."[6]

Creative persons know how forces move swiftly through them during periods of inspiration. This movement is imagined as a winged figure. Its nature is flight. Angels are personifications of these feelings and energies. They are images of fleeting sensations and expressions of our longing for the mystery they serve.

Modern self-referential psychology has reduced everything to the person. When I see movement in a painting, it is considered to be a condition that I project onto the picture. We have lost our aboriginal sense of otherness and the naive ability to appreciate the expression of things, the way they convey energies or feelings lodged within their structures. All of the figures in my painting, poem, and dream are considered to be parts of myself. No wonder the angels vanished from the world for most of the twentieth century. There was no room for them, no space, because it was all occupied with ourselves, our complaints and obsessions.

The twentieth-century mind was sure that the "I" alone lifted its arm, threw the dart, painted the picture, made the dance, and had the dream. The possibility of other contributors, agencies and sources of movement were not compatible with its perspective. As a matter of fact, the consideration of any source of expression other than the immediate person was considered mad.

A bus can talk to a writer or storyteller, but never to a person who is under psychological review. The microscope of mental diagnosis sees things within the limits of its lens. Whatever does not fit the ruling paradigm is considered mentally unsound. We are left with a psychological fantasy in which everything we imagine is ourselves. It is burdensome and expressively oppressive. Nothing has the freedom to move freely through us anymore. Every thought has to be ethically correct and censored to avoid offense. The wild images, the last frontier, are being domesticated. What would D. H. Lawrence think? The angels and demons have lost their freedom to speak. We're caught up in ourselves and have no sense of the wind that wants to pass through us.

Seeing connections ....

I asked my wife, "Do you experience earth angels?"

She replied, "They are people and things that I love and
adore—my children, my cat, things that make me feel connected to
the earth. Each thing is in a different category. They are not all the
same."

"They connect to different aspects of your experience," I said.

"Yes."

"They carry different spirits."

"The perfume bottle you brought back from a trip, that's different from the cat. The perfume bottle is sentimental and connects
husband and wife. The cat is a comfort. She is a being in the house
that demands nothing. I find her in odd places—on top of the piano
in the sun, or with her head between the balusters on the staircase."

After all of my philosophical inquiries into the nature of angels,
I got my best and simplest definition in a passing conversation with
my wife—angels connect us to the earth and its many spirits. Seeing
earth angels is seeing these connections. They are the soulful qualities of relationships.

Angels also thrive in what appear to be the most impersonal
connections to things. For example, the inner figures of the dream
are often related to peripheral contacts we have during the day: the
parking lot seen from the corner of an eye, the photograph on a
newspaper page that was glimpsed and not even read. These images
from the physical world are the "intermediaries" between ourselves

and psyche. Or if we abandon the mediating function of the angel as someone who goes between worlds and view ourselves as immersed in an all-encompassing spirit, then these figures are companions in the psychic field. Every thing is a carrier of significance.

The angelic way of looking at the world notices connections between things, otherwise completely overlooked. Life is to the dream as the person is to the angel. Rather than reducing dreams to life experiences or trying to keep dreams as a pure realm, uncontaminated by life, we can imagine the two as needing one another. Life gives body to the dream, and dreams give soul back to life. The person who sees the dream as simply an excess of energy is consumed by the perspective of scientific materialism. In order to support the view of despiritualized matter, a person has to deny the existence of subtle and intelligent connections between dream spirits and events in the physical world.

Dreams teach us how to appreciate the necessary cooperation between spirit and matter, the reciprocal spiritualization of earthly things and the materialization of the imagination. This is the interactive zone of earth angels that dreams illustrate so well.

Right now I am reading the works of C. G. Jung, and in a dream *I hear his name being called out in the granite Gothic library at Fordham University in New York, where I went to college.* The dream helps me recall that Jung gave his first American lectures at Fordham. I also remember how I kept coming across his books in the library while researching my humanities papers. I was always referencing Jung, although he was not directly taught in any of my courses. And later in my life I never was involved in formal Jungian training, but I made personal connections to the tradition through my work with James Hillman. The dream helps me see how long Jung has been cooking in my soul through subtle and indirect relations. My psyche keeps calling on his name. In the dream, his name is spoken in the granite library, a great hall of Gothic imagination, and Jung was an imaginative scholar and writer of many books who also carved granite as a form of soul work. My dream helped me see how the spirit of Jung's work has always been moving through me daimonically. Our psychic lives are a rich ecology of connections "calling out" to be seen.

The extraordinary qualities of dreams help attract our attention. But the same type of thing happens as we work in our kitchens or drive our cars.

I asked my poet-friend Vincent Ferrini, "What is an angel for you?"

"An incident," he said.

The Latin *incidere* means to fall upon, to happen. An incident is a distinct but apparently minor occurrence that is linked to something else. The incident refers to the angel, the something else, that falls upon us.

Vincent went on, "I was just driving in my car and something was wrong with a tire. I got out and saw that the rubber was chewed up. I was seized by anxiety because I don't have any money. But then everything shifted. The accident became an angelic incident that made me look at things differently. Once I got myself out of the way of the experience, everything began to flow."

Things keep moving, even the tire. The event simultaneously arrests and stimulates a remaking of life.

Vincent continued, "Anxiety and ego get in the way of the angel. You've got to point out why we don't see them, what interferes."

If I look through the eyes of the angel, I see the creative force moving through everything. Incidents are awakening events. Disturbances are especially useful because they force us to make contact with things. Vincent had to deal with his tire, his car, his dependence on them, to realize his liberation from them. The "breakdown" of the car cracks the habitual shell and lets the numinous presence enter.

In addition to breakdowns, separations force us to reconsider the nature of things. If something is no longer present in an accustomed way, we feel the presence of its spirit through the absence. Vincent had been away from his house for a week when I called. He spoke of how he missed his typewriter. "It's my angel wings," he said.

The angel is a pouring of spirits into a thing that keeps its physical identity but simultaneously becomes something else. The angelic world is a place of multiple and complementary functions. The literal use of the typewriter is combined with its spiritual or imaginal value to an individual soul. Everything is always itself but also becomes yet another entity through a person's conception of it. The sacred or poetic way of being in the world cultivates these extrasensory qualities. Earth angels, in keeping with the Baroque representations of their celestial kin, are superfluous, an excess of emotion, an overflow of spirits, the states of inspiration, the life of the imagination that is an infinite bounty streaming from the most ordinary things.

I recently had a conversation with a woman who helped me see the subtle relationships between things that usually pass unnoticed. I took my daughter to a swim meet at a conservative club where people don't typically engage in conversations about spiritual figures. A woman whom I have known for years but with whom I rarely speak, came up to me when she saw me reading Sophy Burnham's *A Book of Angels.*

"Can I ask you why you're reading that book?"

"I'm writing a book on angels and creativity."

"Oh, so you're doing research," she said. "My sister gave the book to me months ago, but I haven't opened it yet. I figured I will get to it when I'm ready."

I described how I was trying to approach angels as qualities of things. As I spoke, I realized that it was the book that brought us together. It expressed something that drew her to me.

I went on to talk about how I am trying to reflect upon angels

as the soul of a thing, which takes on a life within our creative meditations, something other than the literal presence of a spirit.

I said, "People insist that the spirit is 'real,' standing right next
to them, and 'not imagination.' It does not have to be this way.
Whether or not it is actually present is irrelevant to me."

Literalizing the angel disparages the imagination, which is the
primary faculty or intelligence of the spiritual consciousness.

I continued, "I can accept what people say about spirits actually
standing next to them, touching them, and guiding them away from
dangerous situations, even though I do not have these experiences
in my life. I am sure a physicist or a banker will see the creative
spirit in ways quite different from me. Although the things of the
world express themselves autonomously to everyone who contacts
them, our individual faiths and visions will shape how we see the
angel, who is an expression of the soul's desire for intimate and
individuated experience. The angel appears within the frame of
how we imagine the world."

She said, "I run into people who give me the answers to what I
have been working on in my own mind. They complete my process
without having any previous connection to me."

I listened without saying anything about how she was doing it
for me at the moment.

"I am at a point in my life where I am more open to people and
experiences. My husband left me, and at first I was bitter and
closed. But now I see that I have so much more space in my life for
things to affect me. I watch how others who have been left by a
spouse isolate themselves from life and control their environments
with anger. It has taken time, but now I am seeing important connections between things and messages everywhere—at the supermarket, the antique store, the traffic intersection. I am not in
control and that's okay, because if I was, I wouldn't be receiving
these gifts. I take the time and I have the interest in what I previously overlooked. I just got asked out to lunch by a woman whom

I have not seen for eight years. I had an argument with her, and my husband told me that I ruined the possibility of friendship with her and her husband. Do you see the uncanny connection? My husband has just left me and she calls out of the blue. I can't explain why these things happen and I really don't care why. I'm just fascinated by the connections."

My idea that the angel appears in the usually overlooked incidentals of daily life was being affirmed by a woman who appeared like an angel to talk to me. She affirmed that the angels are links between things, forces that connect through indirect and "subtile" relationships.

Things to do ....

This and subsequent practice sections are intended to stimulate possibilities for creative reflection, so please don't follow my suggestions too strictly. Take freedoms with everything I say. Improvise, bounce off from what I propose, go contrary, or read these exercises as meditations accompanying the text. Practice in a way that suits your interests and those of your environment. You can go out into "the field" and do some of the suggested activities, try them in your imagination, or make a combination of both. Hopefully, my discussions of everyday angels have connected to *your* experiences. I am less interested in creating new things and more concerned with evoking a deeper appreciation of what you already do. These practice ideas are intended to help you look more creatively at your life as it is.

• Go to any object in your house and imagine the environment from its perspective. Personify the object and tell it how you feel when you look at it, touch it, listen to it, or move with it. Poets talk to things all of the time. Their sense of mutual creation is not limited to the spirits of people.

Shift your perspective and act as the object's speaker. Let yourself be crazy and say unusual things. We fear madness, which is really only the inability to distinguish between imaginal speech and a conversation with another person. In *A Midsummer Night's Dream* Shakespeare makes a stone wall into an important character that is intimately addressed and that speaks. The wall describes how the lovers Pyramus and Thisby whispered through its crannies. Then Pyramus enters and says, "And thou, O wall, thou sweet and lovely wall, / That stand'st between her father's ground / and mine! / Thou wall, O wall, O sweet and lovely wall, / Show me thy chink, to blink through with / mine eyne!"

Reflect upon how the wall feels when Pyramus addresses it as "thou" and contrast this to the way we usually think about material things.

If you are able to lose yourself in creative dialogue, you will spontaneously access points of view and expressions that you would never voice through your more habitual and controlled conversations. Imaginal dialogue is poetic speech. It comes through us angelically in flashes of inspirations, glimpses of things we do not usually see, and a tenderness of language that flows from the linking of our spirits with those of the thing with which we are engaged. In our normal conversations, even with people that we love, we don't usually contemplate and affirm the subtle qualities which are their angelic spirits.

Although the contemplation of objects helps us to be more aware of other people, this is not the sole purpose of these poetic actions. Imaginal dialogue makes us more aware of the world as an animated place where everything expresses itself to those who are open to the communications of spirits.

• Reflect on objects you have lost over the course of your life. Which ones would you love to have again? Is there one thing in particular?

• Goethe said, "We see only what we know." Try looking at things as if you know nothing about them. You will probably become much more aware of their formal structures, colors, textures, and the way they sit in their environments. They will speak to you directly through their physical qualities.

• Re-vision the problems of the world from the perspective of things. The things might speak more forcefully than you. For example, two Brooklyn women gathered shoes from people whose lives have been affected by gun violence, and they plan to arrange 38,000 shoes on the White House lawn (later they will give the shoes to charity). Their ritual is imagined as a silent march. A man sent the shoes he was wearing when he heard of his son's death. A woman whose husband was shot in the spine sent the rubber-soled pair he wore to get a grip on the metal foot rests of his wheelchair during the last month of his life.

Things act together with people. The expressions of guns are being countered by those of shoes.

• What things do you touch most frequently each day? What have you touched for the longest period of time in your life?

I just sat with a friend who smokes a pipe and I noticed how nearly half of one side of the pipe had been worn away. I said, "It looks like you have spent some time with that pipe."

He said, "It's my favorite. It got this way from years of being tapped on the side of the fireplace when I empty it out."

• Think about any person and watch how images of things you associate with the person appear in the mind's eye. Do the same thing with places, a particular month, a year in your life, a period in history.

• Imagine history as a successive life of things.

Look at your own life from the perspective of the things with which you were engaged. What objects have remained relatively constant (e.g., cotton sheets and pillow cases, towels, No. 2 yellow pencils, blank sheets of paper, silk ties, jewelry, antique furniture, silverware, Oriental rugs, fireplace equipment, garden tools, things of nature)? What types of things have changed the most (cars, bicycles, office equipment, telephones, appliances, kitchen designs).

What objects embody the changes in your life and your different periods? Don't think of the things as symbols representing something else, but try to accept them as beings in their own right that have accompanied you in life. Because they were present at a particular time, or used in a certain way, they carry memories of these things.

• Is there a particular place that you consider more sacred than others?

What were the sacred places of your childhood and youth? Were there imaginary places that you visited in your dreams and fantasies? To what extent are the spiritual values of your adult life in keeping with the qualities of these early images?

• What were the most sacred or precious objects of your childhood? Are there differences of value between then and now?

• Put something aside that contains what you hold sacred today—a closed container with notes or things—to be reopened in one, two, five, ten, twenty, or twenty-five years.

• Imagine the future from the perspective of the places and things that you treasure today. Record your desires for the future and keep them to mark the soul's longing. Maintain a diary of desires and not just a literal transcript of events. Watch how the images change and stay constant.

If you want to meditate on the spirits of people and places that you love, or even those with which you have conflicts, keep a journal of images that you connect to them. Write poems as meditations on the qualities of people, places, things, and events. The spiritual powers and significance of images and things will increase in relation to your focus on them.

2
Intimate
Rites

Early memories of ensouled things ....

I asked myself how it was possible that men should have blinded themselves to the point of seeing the Earth as nothing but a dried-up mass and to the point where they go looking for Angels above them, or somewhere in the emptiness of the Sky, and find them nowhere.   —Gustav Theodor Fechner (1861)

Since childhood I have been involved with the spirits of tangible things. I remember my first trips to my father's office, brimming with his lawyerly artifacts—files, books, desk, papers everywhere. When I entered, I stepped into a distinctly different world whose spirits flew out to touch my senses and imagination. Alone in what then felt like a huge room, I imagined myself as my father, visualizing the acts and thoughts of a lawyer, the client sitting across from me, or on the phone needing help. The thick manilla files were packed with life and the configurations of his handwriting, the movements of a silver fountain pen leaving tracks in black ink. Those things and the way they were arranged, gathered together, or separated on his desk, expressed a vital life that carried me into the imagination.

His walls were covered with pictures, and to this day when I visit his office, I love to look and inhale their expressions. There is a tinted photo of the city square at the end of the nineteenth century that evokes the historic spirits of the place where he works and the transgenerational life emitted by its buildings and streets.

On the wall opposite his desk chair, there are four sets of pictures of my brothers and sisters and me. The series starts with the bottom row when there were five children, and moves upward in rows of six, seven, and finally the eight of us. The pictures convey each child's chronological place within the family—youngest to the viewer's right and the oldest—me—always on the left. They have been there for thirty years, and time has effected the arrangement's aura. In earlier years I may have taken them for granted, but now I see them as an office icon invoking the spirits of a family and its history. The pictures have a life in the present, but they also take me back to imagining the four different periods during which they were taken.

My father fills his home and office with personal artifacts—things that belonged to his parents, his deceased brothers, my deceased sister. My mother is in a nursing home and is overcome by the advanced stages of Alzheimer's disease, so he carefully keeps the objects that carry the history of their marriage. He said to me recently in his home, "This house is full of memories. At my age that means something. When I walk past a picture or a chair, or that plaque on the wall, they convey memories."

I never imagined that my pragmatic father, from whom I appeared to distance myself twenty-five years ago when I left law school and a job in his office, might be one of the primary influences on my poetic and spiritual involvement with earth angels. As I look back to my childhood, to those days when I was driving alone with him in the car, I remember the textures of his Pontiacs, the feel of the seats, the views through the glass, my imagining of what it would be like to have the wheel in my hands and my right foot on the pedals, the radio, the careful rhythm of his driving, so many sensations—the colors, the different seasons.

I remember what it was like to go to the golf club with him for the first time. I savored the smells and the sweeping green vistas cut through the trees. I remember the wooden floors outside the locker room perforated with spike marks, the men inside changing and showering, and the huge pregnant stomachs on top of muscular legs that were commonplace in the 1950s, all of the fancy cars outside, and the feeling of inferiority I felt when my father pulled into the circular driveway in his "second car," an aged and plain 1951 Chevy that I would love to own today.

What was once lowly is now raised to a lustrous place in my memory. I often dream of that car and its rounded lines, simple interior, and manual shift on the steering wheel column. I also remember my father walking out of the locker room one day in gray Glenplaid pants, the remains from a suit that he no longer wore, when the other golfers were dressed in their Izod-Lacoste slacks and shirts. He was different, and I felt embarrassed because of the distinctive spirit of his appearance, to which I was so sensitive. He was one of the best golfers in the region, and I was proud of his skills. As soon as he hit the ball, I forgot about his pants.

It is amazing how these spirits work their way through families. When my son was in the fourth grade and wearing combat pants to school, I came to pick him up wearing a beret. He saw me before I saw him, slipped out the back door, and walked home. Some of the outfits I wear walking my daughter to the school bus in the morning make my father's pants look like a modest deviation from the norm.

Earth angels are the spirits of things—locker-room showers, steering wheels, berets, and old pants—and memory tends to exaggerate their expression. Even the most nonspiritual types cherish memories. If we tap into a good recollection, images swarm like angels within the frame of a Baroque painting.

The fir porch at my father's club has long been replaced by a more efficient modern floor that will not be chewed by spikes. But something is missing. There is a loss of soul in the floors, a loss of texture, a loss of something distinctively "golf," the wear, and the visual records of the interactions between feet and boards. There is an old-fashioned club that I visit where they maintain the fir floors. Whenever I look at them and walk on them, they carry me back to those first impressions of my childhood. The earth angels are for me lodged in these details of our lives, incidentals usually overlooked. The angelic dimension is the infusion of imagination into things that otherwise pass unnoticed, and it is also receptive to what comes to us from outside ourselves. Dreams are a treasury of earth angels because our controlling mind has gone to sleep and psyche is open. So if we want to access the spirits of the day world as well as their nocturnal counterparts, we have to learn how to relax our grip on the controls.

The angels come through imagination and its reverie. As I describe images connected to my father, the personal artifacts of my mother enter my thoughts. I am especially drawn to her bedroom dresser. It was the focal point of her feminine mysteries, and so different from my father's simple and utilitarian display. When I was bored, I went into their room and contemplated her arrangements of brushes, combs, jewelry boxes, pictures, perfume bottles. The jewelry box was packed with treasures. In those days most women wore clip-on earings, so I could put them on, together with a lavish necklace, and stand before the mirror transformed. My tranvestite play did not feel like an abnormal desire. As with the initiation of shamans, putting on the artifacts of a woman helped me feel her presence inside. Jungians will say that the little boy was getting to know his anima image, the female soul that lives within him, and of course Freud would have something to say about his "Oedipal" longings.

As I look back, I feel how these explanations obscure the imagination of the things themselves. I was fascinated with the objects and *their* powers of transformation. We are so busy referring everything back to ourselves, or worrying about what something says about us, that we miss the spirits of things. By reducing these memories of childhood experiences exclusively to our unconscious conflicts, we've banished the angels and stifled the ecology of imagination. We have to learn how to step aside and let them proceed.

When I opened my mother's dresser drawers, I immersed myself in artifacts foreign to my boyish ways. There were sections for nail-polishing paraphernalia, areas where silken things were carefully folded, sewing threads and needles, lipsticks, makeup, and more jewelry. In addition to perusing these sanctums by myself, I enjoyed watching her use her feminine tools of transformation. I was especially intrigued by the 1950s garters and their metal and rubber snaps onto which nylon stockings were attached. It felt like magic when she came down the stairs dressed for dinner, in a velvet dress, high heels, and a cloud of perfume. No wonder I wanted to try it all out myself. I was acutely attuned to her subtle ways and the spirits of the things connected to her. The distances I felt between the two of us increased my involvement with the artifacts. They were the intermediaries, then and now. When I imagine these things, the spirits come.

My relationship with my mother is shaped through images and the imagination of things. When I visit her room in the nursing home with its empty drawers and closets, these images are accompanied by the ones I carry within myself. Her closets at home were packed with dresses and shoes. Even in her present condition, her mind taken by Alzheimer's, she is still a physically beautiful woman. She took such pride in her appearance, her nice things, her carefully selected clothes, the furnishings of her room.

Her children place photographs of their children on the bedside tables, the windowsill, and the dresser in the nursing home. She doesn't recognize anybody or anything, but there is a feeling of spirits in those pictures. Every image has a distinct spirit. Our most sacred altars are typically these unconscious displays of artifacts arranged in homes or rooms away from home. The pictures in my mother's room surround her with the family's aura and her distinct place in this world. I remember when she hung my paintings prominently in every part of her house. She especially treasured the early ones from childhood. When she got a second home in Florida, I spent my first vacation there making art for the walls. Our direct contacts with each other were accompanied by many rich and lasting interactions through things.

When she could no longer speak or identify anyone, the visits to the nursing home were gruesome. It felt like she was already dead and my presence there was irrelevant. An idea from *The Tibetan Book of the Dead* transformed my attitude. I read that after death, a person's soul needs the help of others, and especially loved ones, in its journey. Maybe familiar objects can help too. When I shifted my thoughts from memories of what my mother used to be, and how painful it was to see her this way because she was such a proud and competent woman, and began to accept the presence of her soul in its current state, I felt a sense of purpose. Her soul, still present in her body and her room, or already off on its journey, needed company and support.

If we cannot be present with our loved ones in body, we leave them with artifacts that convey a presence of spirit. The thing functions as a counterpart to the actual person. There is a feeling in my mother's room, expressed by the photographs, that everyone is with her. She is surrounded by their spirits.

Domestic spirits ....

The saviour is either the insignificant thing itself or arises
out of it.   —C. G. Jung

Earth angels flourish in our most familiar habitats, through the presence of things whose spirits have been warmed by continued use and contact—the coffee cup I use each morning, a favorite pillow, the computer keyboard, my desk clock, the chair next to the fire, the picture of my mother. Anyone familiar with the way a painting or sculpture quickens the soul of a viewer is probably ready to abandon the idea of "inanimate" objects. But I would like to take this receptivity a step further, or a step closer to home, by demonstrating the way domestic artifacts and activities stir the soul.

If we are apt to take our partners and intimate human companions for granted, we are even more likely to move through anesthetized routines within our physical environments, missing their communications. The familiar spirits are the ones we are less likely to see. Our most basic tendencies can be reimagined as expressions of soul—the way we arrange things, or don't arrange things, in refrigerators, shelves, drawers, closets, counters. Every home is packed with unconscious ritual acts—heating water in the morning, dusting the table, mowing the lawn, feeding the cat, reading before bed.

Even people who deny the presence of angels and describe beliefs in spirits as old superstitions nevertheless carry on archaic spiritual practices unintentionally. In looking for spirits, pay more attention to what people do than what they say. Spirit is a quality of an action, something that emerges spontaneously and unwatched, as distinguished from thoughts of what we think we are doing. Walk into any home and you are likely to see conscious and unconscious shrines invoking spiritual animation.

New and unfamiliar environments heighten powers of observation and receptivity to environmental expression. When I enter another person's house, I feel an influx of spirits from the furniture, pictures, lighting, views out windows, smells. When we expect company we go around the house getting everything ready—tidying tables and floors, lighting the fireplace, preparing drinks and food, opening a window for fresh air. We unwittingly surround ourselves with the plurality of angels and solicit their graces, not just when we are having guests but in the basic activities of daily living—placing flowers on a table, folding an attractive blanket on the bed, trying to keep some clean and open space on a kitchen counter, or appreciating soul in the dirty clutter.

Because angels tend toward safe and intimate places, they thrive in homes. In religious households we see sacred artifacts consciously arranged in personal altars or places of honor. But without any intention of setting up a sanctuary, most of us cover refrigerators with children's art, photos of friends, postcards, and other objects that carry and evoke intimate connections to our souls. The tops of televisions, radiators and dressers, shelves and windowsills, are filled with personal memorabilia that hold special significance. We have all kinds of things going on within these designated places that acknowledge the spirits of a house. Even the most formal houses with their ancestral portraits and polished cherry tables blanketed with family photographs are constructed to evoke an atmosphere of spirits. And we cannot overlook the use of familiar and cherished music to elevate our mood. These distinct and thoroughly personal spirits of a household call forth a sense of the sacred that is distinct from conventional notions of spirituality.

When he was dying in a New York hospital room, the poet Charles Olson asked for the following things from his Gloucester home: a map of the Atlantic seafloor, a photograph of himself on the back steps of his house, an Indian blanket, two oranges, a Russian spoon, wrapping paper, and a crystal ball. According to Olson's biographer Tom Clark, "The poet was deliberately surrounding himself with personal sacred objects, setting up a force field of magical aura-action."[1] Every person's domestic temple contains artifacts that carry a history of relations and express the thoroughly personal and particular nature of the soul's rituals. As with the things Olson requested, our most sacred objects are often common things endowed with meaning through past experience. Spirits live in the things we remember and want to have close to us.

The things that we save are likely to convey the presence of the earth angel. When I reflect on the function of saving, I think of salvation, saving souls, saviors, preservation, and rescue. I wonder whether the objects that we keep do this for us: the thing saved is the savior of the one who saves.

Spiritual disciplines always encourage letting things go. As with any piece of good advice, there is a flip side. In this case it is saving things, the tantra of keeping, holding on to something, the eroticism of abundant energy and fullness, which can of course turn quickly into the pathologies of excess. The most intense pleasure lies in holding the edge between extremes.

I remember as a child thinking about what contemporary artifacts I should keep because someday they would be valuable. I loved my grandparents' radios, the polished metal toasters, and especially the cars from the early 1950s that I wanted to store away for forty or fifty years. I sensed their aesthetic lasting power as relics of an era. My mother never let me buy comic books, so I missed that opportunity as a collector. And, like everybody else, I threw away the shoe boxes full of baseball cards—Ted Williams, Willie Mays, Ernie Banks, and Roger Maris. These things become valuable because some people were attached to them and did the keeping, or they were left in attics or other untouched spaces. Actively used spaces have little room for collecting.

Saving easily turns to hoarding where there is no savoring or active enjoyment. I try to maintain a relationship of some kind with all of the things in my house and my workplaces, for their sake as well as mine. I remember an old lady who lived alone in Salem in an apartment next to mine. All of her rooms were filled with piles of newspapers she had saved. I found myself imagining the spirits of her relationship to them. They were everywhere and unavoidable, unlike things stored in an attic or an unused garage.

The old lady who saves newspapers might not be too different from people who write down their dreams every morning but never read them again, artists who paint pictures only to store them away, and people who save dollars under the mattress and never do anything with them. There is something about the company they bring, the sense of abundance, the filling of a space. We Northern people are hoarders by nature, stockpiling stores for winter. I buy books that I never get around to reading, but I savor the feeling that so many of them are on the shelves ready for me if I need them.

Wherever we do something unconsciously, ritualistically, personally, and imaginatively to sanctify an environment, there, usually, is where the spirits live with the greatest vitality: the woman who places a picture of her family on the bedside table of her hotel room, the man who places an acorn next to a photograph, the child who says good night every day to the same objects, the lighting of a candle at night for dinner. We think we have left religion and spirituality, but many of us have simply brought the spirits closer to home.

My wife is always moving things around in our house and trying new ways of arranging furniture and helping objects "find the right place." When I see a familiar object in a new location, it renews my sense of the object as well as the space where it stands. The whole process is energizing, and it animates the house with new spirits. I experience especially strong feelings when someone moves an object without my awareness and I enter the space where it used to be. This simple experience reveals the energetic forces that operate within our supposedly inanimate environments. These changes in a space show how the loss of a familiar object is characterized by an openness of space that corresponds on a more subtle level to feelings of loss that come when an animal or person is no longer present. The experiences confirm the life that exists in objects and how they actively influence their surroundings.

When we are attuned to our environment, we can make changes as a form of soul medicine and revive the folk remedy of transforming external appearances in order to stimulate corresponding effects on inner spirits. I feel a surprisingly big emotional transformation after cleaning and waxing the car or reorganizing my desk. But many people are just the opposite—they feel lost and abandoned without the company of clutter, confirming the highly individuated ways of angels.

Little habits reveal the way we relate to the spirits of things. I like to keep my money neatly arranged in my wallet with the bills grouped according to denominations, whereas my wife stuffs hers indiscriminately into her purse or jacket. My sense of psychic order and cohesion is finely attuned to the conditions of my pockets. My orientation to the world is strongly influenced by the condition of my body and the things with which I live. My personal space is not so much the object of my attention as it is the creator of my being.

When things are out of place in my home or on my person, I feel a tension. Even within the clutter of my desk, everything has its place. There is order in what appears to be chaos.

The discipline of appreciating domestic spirits is a poetic reverie. There is an element of "home improvement" involved, but it is not a literal method of fixing things. The repair work has more to do with the renewal of imagination. If we revive the spirits of our most ordinary acts, imagination's stream will spread to other things with corresponding effects.

I walk through my daughters' rooms in a glum mood, and I look at two stuffed animals sitting together on a miniature chair and my spirits are immediately lifted. I laugh at my saturnine state. At that moment I see how the earth angel is a spark of passion conveyed by things in our environments and these spirits revive the soul.

But even the most apparently stationary objects in our homes reflect the process of change. Every time I meet a familiar thing, our relationship is different. We are shaped by the feelings of the day, the things to be done, and the events sweeping us into their vortex. The visage of the moment uses everything passing through the environment to manifest its forever changing appearance in exactly the same place.

When I look into my daughters' rooms and become immersed in the imagination of the spaces, I don't feel that I am regressing back to my personal childhood. The things in the rooms carry the imagination of childhood within themselves. The rooms are psychic fields full of expressions that resonate with the field of the childhood memories I carry. When I go into these rooms I am involved in the immediate, fresh, and distinctly unique qualities of their presence.

The small children's rooms bring nostalgia for the rooms of my son and oldest daughter before the teenage cyclones hit. Actually there are fascinating spirits in the chaos of things thrown everywhere, the defiance of adult control in the last years of childhood. There is a vital imagination in the piles of clothing refusing to go into dresser drawers, and a child sleeping until noon amid this disarray. We adults close the doors on these spirits, move them to distant parts of the house, and prefer the museumlike atmosphere of the little girls' rooms, where we still have a hand in the careful arrangements. We want to go back to the environments and artifacts of the early years where adults and children played together. These were the meeting places of pure imagination between generations, a time

of mutual influences and affections, before the adolescents pushed
off, and away.

Home is the place where I have my most personal relationships,
where I feel comfortable and open, my most essential place, but
this intimacy has shadows of habit and unconscious actions attached
to it. So I try out different ways of walking through my house and
different places to sit and reflect. Routines have an important place
in soulful living, but they also call out for counterrhythms, small
acts, and variations that contribute to a deeper resonance of what
once seemed insignificant. Each simple change of perspective carries a new life and each day is a journey offering unseen vistas. So
rather than wait until a person, place, or time is gone in order to
feel nostalgia, I long for what I have; I dream with the things around
me; and I desire the life that already exists within my house.

Shrine-making ....

SHRINE. A place hallowed by venerated objects and their associations. A sanctuary. A container of sacred things.

A friend who is spending a period in her life traveling between
other people's houses tells me that she carries a picture of her father
with her, letters from loved ones, a selection of CDs, and a small
souvenir peace symbol of the Woodstock festival twenty-five years
ago. She says, "I take these things with me when I travel, and they
make me think of the past and the person to whom they are connected."

When I travel, I don't intentionally carry things that connect me
to others. I don't even carry pictures of my children. I travel as
lightly as possible and I am probably guarding against my forgetful-
ness and fear of leaving something precious behind me. But there is
always some little thing that indirectly joins me to my life at home.
I usually bring two or three books that I put on a table in my room,
together with a pad of paper, a pencil, and a pen. Before long I have
a collection of notes, dreams, and other reflections written down in
my handwriting, my most unwatched and expressive marks on
paper. These are my familiars. They subtly establish my presence
in the room.

One of my colleagues is constantly on the road. As soon as he
arrives in a hotel room, he finds a place to construct his altar of
personal artifacts carefully placed on a cloth—a stone, a tarot deck,
a candle, a cup, incense, and a flower or some other thing from
nature. I am so accustomed to these arrangements in his room that
if they were gone, I would feel as if a part of his being were missing.

His presence is more than a physical condition, or even a spiritual body. It is a constellation or field of things. The same principle applies to what we wear, in keeping with the old saying, "The clothes make the man." Persons cannot be considered in complete isolation from their "things."

The man I just described is an "artist type." I have many other male friends who establish their presence by hanging up their suits together with an entourage of ties. Their personal things are kept in closets and drawers, out of sight, as contrasted to the tarot shrine with its flames and smells in the most prominent place in the room.

Closets are loaded with spirits. We will never forget Imelda Marcos's shoes. I remember snickering with contempt at the madness of keeping so many hundreds of them. But in retrospect, I see that the soul thrives through these object obsessions. I am sure a lot of the men who mocked Imelda have as many ties in their closets, carefully stacked sweaters, or shelves specially made to store and display their collections of baseball caps. An unfriendly camera can easily distort how the soul latches on to particular object identifications for gathering and display. I know a man who loves small sculptural figures of frogs. He collects them when he travels, and his friends and family send them as presents. Without planning, the frog becomes his familiar spirit. It offers a theme and personal direction to his collecting.

The things that surround us, or their absence, constitute our beings. I have close friends who are nuns, and I am touched by how they arrive to visit our house with very light bags, in contrast to the person who comes for a short stay with a carload of things that take over the guest room.

I have a feeling that the way clothes are kept designates a person's relationship with the world as much as the vestments themselves. But the revelation of personal character traits in the way things are organized, or not organized, is not my concern. Psychology has been so caught up in these diagnostic differentiations of people that it has missed the ritual significance of archetypal acts and how *they* shape the person. These deeds that we do every day, unawares, cultivate soul in our environments.

Today, closets are a major focus in the homes of people who can afford them. Large, walk-in closets, rooms in their own right, have become ritual places. The way everything has its place within a closet says something about the soul's need to carefully store intimate things.

We give special consideration to the arrangement of personal artifacts in bathrooms and on dresser tops. When visiting another person's house, I tend to get my strongest sense of shrine-making in these spaces. If I came from an aboriginal community and did not know the contents or functions of things in the cosmetic containers, jewelry displays, grooming tools, shaving equipment, and other items laid out in personal rooms, I might think they were shrines and collections of talismans. We use these tools of transformation to influence events in the future and endow ourselves with good fortune, and the presence of benevolent and protecting spirits.

When I was living in Connemara, I noticed how village people stored their clothing, towels, and linens on shelves constructed around the hot-water heater. The damp climate generates this way of keeping things and the simple pleasures it brings. The villagers do not arrange these closets as shrines or sanctuaries; they are purely practical places. But, as I have said, angels are a way of looking at the world, a way of seeing the spirits in ordinary living. And these spirits are often most alive in the unconscious, informal things we do, in our domestic actions and rites, outside the realm of conscious spirituality.

Can an operational definition of shrine-making be established that links together the spectrum of actions I am describing?

A shrine is a place that contains sacred or special objects to which we proffer attention and give value. These things carry memories and bear a significance that connects us to other people or experiences in the past or future. If we have more than one shrine in our house or room, each has attributes that distinguishes it from others. They are carefully maintained and focused places which bind us to the particulars of their beings and sometimes to things beyond themselves. The shrine is a living thing that generates feelings. It acts upon us, transforms, soothes, and gives pleasure, solace, or guidance. It is a place where spirits visit, congregate, and regenerate.

For many years the woodpile has been one of the most meticulously kept sections of my property. A large, dry pile generates feelings of abundance. I can count on the wood for warmth and the aesthetics of fire during the winter. The spirits of the woodpile are connected to the rites of Hestia and the keeping of the hearth in the center of the house and soul.

When I cut and stack wood, it is more than a household chore. The process has a practical dimension, but there are so many other spirits involved—the smells and textures of the wood, the primal work, the aesthetics of stacking and viewing the finished arrangement, knowing that this pleasing configuration is one of the most functional aspects of the household, the secure feeling that there will be plenty of wood when people gather in winter. I have similar affections for the compost bin. When I was living in two houses, I found it difficult to throw good compost into a disposal. So even the rites of garbage have qualities of shrine-making attached.

I am probably unconsciously enacting the Hellenic pantheon in my daily life. The Greeks saw a god in every condition, and it was the responsibility of humans to cultivate these deities in their gardening, cooking, cleaning, repairing, eating and drinking, entertaining, coming and going. A person communes with Hestia at the hearth, Janus at the threshold, Dionysus in the ivy, and Saturnine moods by keeping a dark and shady spot in the garden.

The deities are engaged through places and things that manifest their qualities. Putting this another way, we can say that a mood or spirit is engaged through the presence of physical substances that correspond to it. The same is true of people, who are distinguished and shaped by their personal trappings and accoutrements. These effects are familiar spirits and perhaps more essential to identity than the abstract entity we call the self. When someone mentions Babe Ruth, I see him together with his uniform, old-fashioned cap, the Yankee logo, and a baseball bat. Billie Jean King appears with her eyeglasses, tennis whites, and racket. The moment I mention glasses, Roy Orbison and Buddy Holly appear in my mind's eye. Georgia O'Keeffe is inseparable from the New Mexico artifacts of her art—adobe, cattle skulls, and open space. Well-known cultural icons are accompanied by fairly constant objects in their public images, but their personal relations are no doubt characterized by the spirits of private things.

An intimate relationship with a person is accompanied by equally intimate images of things. Objects as well as people bond us to others. When I reflect upon someone in my life, I envision the things that participate in our relationship and establish connections between us. Sometimes the objects are kept secretly like private treasures in a locket, or they might be openly displayed to communicate affections.

Two of my daughter's best friends are identical twins, and it is virtually impossible to tell them apart. For their eighth birthday, their mother bought two completely different necklaces, which became signs for distinguishing one child from the other inside the family and with close friends. My daughter says, "Whenever I think of the twins, I see their necklaces and not necessarily their faces."

The making of shrines builds upon these intimacies of object associations. The person's spirit appears through the presence of particular artifacts. I keep a relationship or a memory alive by giving a place in my daily life to the things that hold it.

Many shrines appear without planning and without any direct connections to other experiences. I might hold on to objects just because I like them. A thing appears on top of a bureau or office shelf and grows on me. By not taking it away, I keep it enshrined as an object of my attention. The shrine might refer to nothing beyond itself. The objects themselves become the intimates of the person who contemplates them.

I don't go about making home shrines or object displays intentionally. The process just happens as a quality of daily life. The shrines make themselves without plans but with a purpose that corresponds to the unwatched movements of soul in an environment.

Most people do this in their homes. My friend says, "You should see what I've got going on top of my TV. I keep a little blue figure of Ganesha (Shiva's elephant-headed son who is the Lord of Obstacles) that I made myself, and he has attracted a variety of companions to join him: tiny figures of nuns and a monk that I got in Spain, a white horse, a miniature baby cradled in a red high-heeled shoe from a Barbie doll. I found the shoe in an all-night coffee shop in Bombay at three in the morning."

The young child's dresser top is covered with artifacts that generate auras and designate the space as inhabited by a particular soul in the company of its constellation of objects. The parent cleaning the room observes that there are things on the dresser that appear to be junk: a pink plastic ring from a gum machine, a bright green comb from a party grab bag, a spider taken home as a prize from Chuck E. Cheese's, a red pipe cleaner, and a penny. But what appears to be bureau clutter might have been carefully constructed with emotional significance for the child, carrying the spirits of special events.

When my wife was sixteen she played the lead role in her high school play, and someone gave her a bouquet of flowers. She kept one of the roses until it dried, and when the petals fell off, she put them in a box, which she has carried with her ever since. Now that the emotional connections to the play have faded, the object is important because it has been with her for so long.

My oldest daughter is a "keeper." She holds on to every letter she receives, and whenever she wears a piece of jewelry she thinks of the person who gave it to her. When she misses people, she'll put on something they gave her. Every object in the apparent clutter on her dresser has a personal meaning. She says. "I can't throw anything out. If someone gives me a shirt that I never wear, I still keep it in my drawer because every time I look through my shirts, I see it and remember the person who gave it to me and the moment. When I was packing for college, I found things that I hadn't seen since I was nine, and they reopened a part of my memory. I love photographs and have them all over my room, because they make me feel that the people are with me. I hate it when people try to clean my room, because what they think is clutter is organized in my mind."

I remember the last home of my grandfather. After my grandmother died, he moved from their house into a tiny apartment. He gave away his furniture and large belongings, but kept all of the small things that carried memories. Every shelf and window sill was covered with objects. There were a few religious artifacts, but their sacredness was equaled by that of the other things in the room. Both the crucifix and the porcelain hounds he collected lived with him as special companions.

In my childhood home there were formal religious artifacts in the living room, halls, and bedrooms—pictures of the Madonna and Child, an Infant of Prague dressed in silken robes, and the omnipresent crosses—but my strongest sense of a living shrine was the family room, its walls covered with varsity letters, my sister's All-American certificates, one of my first paintings, photographs of the children and my parents, weddings, and grandchildren playing at the beach. Once something made it to the wall, it was there for good. There was a bulletin board at the other end of the room where newspaper clippings, notes, and other ephemera were pinned. It is these informal, instinctual things that really display the family soul, and they are rarely constructed with a high degree of intent. Things find their way to these casual walls. The shrine begins with an effort to hang a few things together, and over time they are joined by others, until there is a sense of overflowing fullness and abundance.

When my sister moved into the house with her family, I cringed when I thought of the family room walls being changed, but like every other "living shrine" it must come and go with the spirits of the people who keep it. I couldn't expect my sister to maintain a museum of the past in the heart of her house. Her family had to cover the walls with their spirits, establish their presence, and make the house into an intimate place of the soul.

As I anticipated, the family room was one of the first places to be transformed by the new family. A selection of things from the past were kept to honor my family traditions, but they were joined by pictures of my brother-in-law's family. These felt odd at first in such a familiar place, but it didn't take long to adjust to the presence of new spirits. The external act of placing the new photos needed to be done to ritually enact the shift. The lives of the two families and the new generation were joined on the wall, and considerable space is open now for the imagery that will emerge from their lives.

In a recent conversation, Vincent Ferrini emphasized the total space of his home as a sanctum. I said, "Vincent, you've got artworks, found objects, and things people give you arranged throughout your house. Your whole house is a shrine."

"Yeah," he replied. "I live here. I cultivate the angels through my dedication to the life in the things in this house. Everything in my house has a specific relationship to a person and a place and it is still going on. It's alive. All of these things are images of my specific experiences with people. The thing and the person are very close."

Vincent's statement corresponds to Henry Corbin's notion of every thought having an angel. Although Vincent sees "every pore" of his house as an abode for angels, many people tend to concentrate their psychic energy on particular places within it. Areas are designated in terms of personal feelings of relative sacrality. Historical epochs tend to do the same thing. The Greek Revival era made a temple of the portico and celebrated the place where the front of the house met the street. The house opened to the outside world of a human community and enshrined passages from personal and public spaces. The back of the house was plain and utilitarian. Today we are more apt to focus on accommodating our cars, and the sanctuary is behind the house where it opens to nature, and it keeps the public at bay.

Inside our houses, contemporary shrine-making in bathrooms has become a universal rite. Real estate brokers will attest that several well-constructed baths positively influence the appeal of a house. If we think archetypally about the functions of dressing, grooming, bodily transformation, and water rites, then it is no wonder the bathroom has gained in significance as a valued space. Technology has brought rushing water and pools into our houses, where we mix the Nordic sauna with tropical flowers and sunlight.

A friend who just bought a new house described how her first priority was the reconstruction of the bathrooms. "I'm obsessed with them," she said. Another friend describes how she takes herbal baths by candlelight with special oils and makes her most personal arrangements of objects in her bathroom. It is truly a sacred place.

Nineteenth-century claw-footed tubs, adorned with gold leaf, are enjoying a revival as people desire more imagination and less utilitarianism in these spaces. An Oriental rug is now more apt to lie next to a tub of this kind than a utilitarian mat, and potted plants bring the spirits of nature into what was once the most austere room in the house. Another woman hangs her mother's ornate living-room chandelier directly over her tub. In keeping with the traditions of sanctuaries, the atmospheric qualities of light are as essential to today's baths as bright illumination. Since indoor bathrooms and toilets are a relatively recent addition to the life of the common person, it is no wonder that they are undergoing rapid changes as ritual places for cultivating the soul. Houses now incorporate water rites that were once restricted to palaces and public shrines. As the rituals of water move into the house, the soul changes with them, and privately enacts what was once a more communal experience.

I personally admire the marble sinks, well-maintained brass fixtures, and preserved porcelain that I see in old homes. When I interact with these objects, I feel the spirits of quality, care, permanence, and the sustained appeal of classical design that still functions as well as, and often better than, the newest technologies. An old bathroom may stimulate these spirits more than antique furniture, because of the way it keeps its luster while being constantly used.

I realize that these thoughts and feelings are generated by the spaces when I enter them. I do not carry them inside of myself. The bath is a chamber within the temple of the house that is clearly distinguished from other rooms. It is an intimate space where doors close for daily acts of cleansing, anointment, sensory stimulation, and the performance of other private rites. As these functions are performed over time in a culture, the space begins to take on the spirits of the rites. The value of the room corresponds to the significance of its function in ministering to the soul. As with kitchens, bathrooms are experiencing an escalation of cultural value because of the way the rites of the soul have been increasingly focused on them. The temple has moved into the sanctums of ordinary life. The holy places of religion are not necessarily being abandoned, but they are not the exclusive containers of today's sacred rites. Without planning, rituals are being enacted throughout our living spaces. The soul is correcting a schizoid vision of sacred versus profane phenomena while subtly ushering us into an appreciation of the essential things in our lives.

Each house tends to have its idiosyncratic shrines. I just visited a home where the tool room is arranged like a museum. Everything was displayed with the care and reverence accorded to valuable works of art. When I was younger, I had a friend who treasured his stereo and his vinyl records. Large, expensive speakers stood prominently in the rooms, and it was understood that he was the only one who touched the records. Like a priest at an altar, he had his ritual ways of cleaning them before and after they were played, and he went into trance with the music.

The refrigerator has always been one of the most enshrined places in my house. Like many other families, we cover it with children's art, photos of friends, invitations to events, newspaper clippings, and ornamental magnets. A friend describes how in her mother's home, the items *inside* the refrigerator had significance. "My mother never felt comfortable if there wasn't a container of milk in the refrigerator. If I was going out, I'd always ask her, 'Do you need milk?' It's not just that the milk was required for my parents' morning habit of coffee drinking; more than that, the presence of the red and white carton on the shelf, knowing it was there, made them feel secure, cared for, *fed.*"

The most prominent shrine in our house is a hall covered with family pictures, in keeping with the tradition established in my parents' family room. Just about every available inch of wall space is used. Most homes have these ritual places that emerge from a family's history. In fact, photos have become primary artifacts in domestic shrines throughout the world. They have an uncanny way of catching and preserving the history of the soul's formation, the fleeting instants caught by the camera as well as the carefully planned rituals of a family. They carry memories and hold details that would otherwise be lost, and unpretentiously carry on archetypal functions associated with shrines.

These unintentional shrines are manifestations of what I call unwatched rites of the soul, which are often more potent and alive than institutional worship or calculated icon-making.

The word *ritual* has actually taken on a popular meaning that suggests a conventional act without a vital purpose. We "go through the rituals" without deep feeling. Thomas Moore considers the origins of the world in the Greek *rheo*, "to flow, run, rush, or stream," and he says that "the point in ritual is to give up intention"; this helps us see the world with imagination.[2] When we are in the ritual zone, contents move through us fluidly, and the most haunting images are the ones that arrive unexpectedly, when we are in the flow, immersed in what has been called a "stream of consciousness." For the ordinary person who doesn't sit down to write or go out to the studio to paint, the stream is the flow of things through the everyday transfers of mail, gifts, events, and things saved. Objects emerge from this welling of life, and the ones that touch our souls are kept and somehow arranged in our living spaces.

The most soulful acts always happen instinctively, daimonically, as if they come from an intelligence other than ourselves. In the case of the unintentional accumulations of a household shrine, I am not so much impressed by the magnificence of a single gesture as I am struck by the accumulated life that appears without planning or any effort that I can remember. The totality of the configuration is impressive. It is a single presence composed of so many separate actions and spirits. Whenever I look at one of these accumulated displays in someone's home, the individual objects always seems perfectly located, but they probably found their way to the shelf or sideboard with very little thinking on the part of the person who placed them. The collection of things makes a composition that feels right and holds the numerous movements within it, as though the soul of the shrine knows what it wants and uses human operatives to build it. Everything comes together in a feeling of collaboration. All the parts, no matter how different, connect and gather together like the strange combinations of dreams, where things congregate of their own accord with people acting as agents.

I ask my nineteen-year-old-son if he ever makes little altars or shrines in his room, and he laughingly says, "Of course, not."

I ask, "Do you ever gather things in a drawer or on your bureau?"

He replies, "Everybody does that. You take things that you like and put them together."

This makes me wonder to what extent I do this myself. A collection of things has been forming for many years in my office. There's a photo I took of James Hillman tap dancing at his sixtieth birthday party, and next to that is a photo of my friend Vincent Ferrini. I realize that the two of them are mentors of soul life, but I didn't put them up there with that thought in mind. I have other mentors, but these two men are my connections to the poetic tradition, and I see this now only by reflecting on the unplanned placement of their pictures on my office cabinet. The objects carry this message to me.

The other objects on the cabinet are participants in the same field of connections. The small fire engine is a toy I bought in Europe for my son, and I always kept it on my desk when he was young, ready for him to use. I don't think he played with it very often, so it became my link to the spirits of childhood and his person. The papier-mâché bust was made by an old man who came every day to the art therapy studio I ran in a mental hospital in the early 1970s. The carved wooden rhino is a present that a woman in the hospital gave me. The silver bowl is one of many I won as a child in father-son golf tournaments, and the silver tray is a prize from a recent event. Bringing home silver is a link to my father and sport. The champagne glass is one of two left by a friend. There is an old brass menorah behind it that I brought back from a Tel Aviv market, and on the far left is artwork one of my graduate students gave me.

The student's artwork is very close in spirit to the nostalgic connections I am describing. She took a doily her grandmother made and pinned a silver piece from her charm bracelet to it, together with other things that carried memories. I have been given many artworks over the years, but this one is particularly valuable because of its personal qualities. It feels like a living thing, a relic that I have to keep, a shrine within a shrine. The art object appeals to me visually and sentimentally, but I also like the woman who gave it to me. There is a dual dimension to its aura, and I can easily imagine a situation where I would not display a masterpiece because it carries bad vibes.

From time to time, I fiddle with the things on the cabinet to keep all of the objects in full view. I want their company and the grace they exude every time I look at them. They are reminders of the visions guiding my work, guardian spirits keeping me on track, like a Saint Christopher medal, icons that will not let me forget the soulful basis of my vocation. I especially like the way they gather in a cluster, generating the feelings of fullness that come when so many spirits interact with one another. The things are defined by their "close" relations with other things. They are to my office and work place, what a statue of Saint Francis is to a garden, helping the soul open to all of the spirits as they arrive.

Catherine the Great of Russia described how the things in her winter palace soothed her soul. "I walk up the marble staircase and then into room after room of things I love and delight in." Most of us don't have anything like Catherine's two-mile walk through the interiors of our homes, but we similarly pass from one thing to another, looking and imbibing their spirits. We also arrange things so they can affect us as we pass—something outside our doors to designate the rite of passage, objects that catch our eyes as we walk across a few feet of linoleum or carpet, things that keep the spirits of our children or parents in the house even though they are not physically present. And in our dreams we experience the passage from room to room just as Catherine did in her palace. If we don't have these places in daily life, desires for them are fulfilled in sleep.

As I reflect on how things gather in the places inhabited by people, Sigmund Freud comes to mind. The image of him that I find most intriguing is the collection of artifacts he kept in his office. The qualities of his personal environment, and the shrines that he made, reveal that he was ultimately engaged in cultivating the life of the soul. This observation makes me realize how much places and things speak to me and form my life.

Garages, machine shops, laboratories, clinics, banks, and bureaucratic places never appealed to me. As a young person I'd walk into an artist's studio or a writer's library, and say to myself, "I want to do that." The space acts on me, and I enter its imagination. I don't have to see people at work. The presence of their things is more evocative and influential. I can easily imagine the person in action, and maybe the absence of the artists and writers enables me to interact more freely with their things.

When I was beginning my work as a graduate school dean, the way my mentor kept his desk was an important influence on how I worked every day. There was never a conversation about the desk, even though it was so different from anything I had seen before in an office. It quietly worked on me.

The "desk" wasn't really a desk. It was an antique table that functioned as a desk. It was open and light, a real piece of furniture that had soul, and did not shield him from people. It didn't dominate the room the way desks usually do with all of their things, packed drawers, metal, and imitation wood grain right in the middle of everything. His desk participated naturally as a graceful figure in the life of the room.

There were few things on his desk, a personal object or two, and only the papers with which he was working at that moment. Other papers and files were stored out of sight. When I was a dean, I kept his desk as a guiding image and practiced a discipline that kept paper moving. I tried to touch it as little as possible and send it on its way, as contrasted to accumulating unfocused piles of documents.

In addition to my mentor's manners with paper, his office always felt like a living room or den, with a fireplace, comfortable furniture, and his trademark wooden shutters on the windows. There was a pervasive feeling of culture, reflection, and ease. There was considerable movement from building to building in those years of the graduate school, and he left a trail of shuttered windows after him. When I met with him, this way of arranging the room and its objects reinforced the instinctual focus that he brought to things. His object environment had a direct influence on the work of the community and the shaping of our culture. I observed how my office and those of the other deans in the school resembled his. They were oriented to people and not paper. We didn't disparage paper or demonize it, but it had to be kept in check because organizations have a way of getting addicted to something that is not primary to their missions. These secondary things have a way of devouring everything around them. Go into offices and you will see paper everywhere, even in this electronic era. The aboriginal visitor will wonder what god or spirit is being worshiped or propitiated through this substance.

I do not want to belittle consciously religious places and acts, but when I think of shrines, my mind perversely spreads beyond intentional and standard forms like Madonna grottoes in the garden, little home altars to a person's guru with the teacher's photo prominantly displayed, the dashboard statues of Jesus that were commonplace in the '50s, and the public shrines of religions, nations, and communities, which are closely related to everything I am describing. My intent is to expand our sense of the phenomenon, and the shrine-making instinct in people, so I am more apt to emphasize places that we do not normally approach in this way.

After a lecture I gave in Galway about the sacramental qualities of creative expression, a man said, "Here in Ireland we have clear separations between sacraments and daily life, and we don't mix them." I realized how these distinctions restrict the creative spirit's place in daily life.

The more particular and demure the shrine is, the more of an impact it has on me. Sporting clubs of all kinds make shrines with trophies, photographs, and other artifacts to honor the spirits of the game and the particular history and existence of the place. Schools, camps, retreat centers, and every other kind of organization with a history similarly display shrines expressing the continuity of the enterprise. Whenever I walk into these places I am intrigued with the way these arrangements of artifacts carry the cultural history of the group—specific people, dates, events, and accomplishments are displayed as markers of the community's presence. I am drawn to old photographs of teams, board members, club presidents, headmasters, and honored members of the organization.

My daughter spent a summer working at an Appalachian Mountain Club camp in Maine where there is a tradition of "crews" of young people working closely together. In the cabin where four or five crew members stay, the wooden walls are covered with memorabilia and graffiti from previous years. My daughter's group marked its presence early in the summer by making entries on the walls. The posting of their year, names, and personal qualities bonded them to the tradition of the camp. The walls of the cabins were shrines to the exuberant spirits of adolescents and gave young people away from home a sense of a new family, community, and continuity.

"Local shrines" tend to carry intimate spirits. A young boy in our community was killed a year ago when he was struck by a car. It happened on a causeway over the water, and within days after the accident, friends left a cross and wreaths on a pole near the spot where he was hit. When cars pass, many toot their horns. From that act grew a chain of reactions, all focused around the keeping of a memory. Now the place and its artifacts hold the sentiments of a community.

The Elvis Presley home shrines that are springing up today are fascinating because of the way they cross conventional boundaries between the sacred and profane. Their worldliness is appealing, and they show how unpredictable the collective psyche's spiritual attachments can be. Elvis shrines are expressions of the eternal longing for the lost soul, a lost era that he represents, the remembering that death inspires. His image and music arouse my nostalgia. I shared this experience with an entire generation. Elvis is a connection between our individual and collective souls.

I am intrigued by shrines made to honor universal figures, if they are made in a personal and idiosyncratic way. If a shrine to the Madonna combines standard artifacts with highly personal items, it is more likely to attract me. There is not such a distance between God, the saints, and the household. These shrines bring the most personal parts of life into direct contact with archetypal figures. They speak to me of how the maker of the shrine imagines the presence of the divine in the simple acts of daily life.

Home altars constructed by Sicilian and Portuguese women here in the city of Gloucester, Massachusetts, convey this sense of individuation. I feel the creator's hand on the work. Images of Jesus and the Madonna are arranged with photographs of deceased relatives and objects associated with them. These personalized displays express a connectedness to actual people and the earth, that I miss in shrines composed only of mass-produced artifacts. The shrines grow directly from the object life of the family, the house, and a particular region, while simultaneously carrying the archetypal qualities of the home altar.

My spirits are moved by subtle and indirect aspects of shrines, where the lines between sacred and ordinary things are not so clearly drawn. The conventional shrine makes clear distinctions between divine and common things, whereas I see a person's house as the holiest of temples. My more than thirty visits to the "Holy Land," which I adore and respect together with all of its religious traditions, has confirmed this instinctual sense. I cannot say that the Holy Sepulchre is any more sacred to me than my living room or the chambers of Gloucester City Hall, all of which carry memories of past lives and the divinity that moves without gradations in all things. I am in awe of ordinary things viewed from uncommon perspectives. The inability to split the sacred from the profane is the basis of my vision of the earth angel and domestic shrines.

Christopher Cook is an artist who also worked as a museum director. For a year in the early 1970s he connected his interests by running Boston's Institute of Contemporary Art as an artwork, and then creating an exhibition displaying the artifacts of that experience. His desk was enshrined together with pencils, memos, correspondence, and a host of documentary artifacts including photos and videotapes.

For me, his most touching creation was an exhibition called "Fishing for Art." As with the split between administration and art-making, our literal mind sees fishing and art as two completely different things. In Christopher's exhibition they were joined together. He re-created in a gallery room a space in his home where all of his fishing paraphernalia are kept. He added other things like paintings related to fishing with beautifully lit arrangements of flies and lures. This environment illuminated how splits in our lives are created by inherited attitudes. They can be eliminated by declaring a new perspective like Christopher's demonstration of how art does not have to be separated from fishing, office work, or any other activity in life.

"Fishing for Art" intentionally reproduced a space that took shape over the course of a person's life through an accumulation of actions. It showed me how we create our most significant works *together with* our environments. Cities and cultures grow in a similar way.

My sense of creation counters the iconoclasm that pervades conventional notions of religion and art. The sacred image is everywhere, and not just in those places and things that have been anointed by institutional culture. As an artist I know that the creative spirit acts through me. I can't restrict its sphere. It is as present for me in a shrine of fishing paraphernalia as it is on an altar.

When I paint, the process can be likened to a ritual of icon-making. My studio is a *temenos* set aside *exclusively* for creation. It has no other purpose. This singularity of function makes me realize how we are less likely to see the sacred as a subtle presence in something whose purpose is more practical, like the arrangement on a dresser top. The idea of the earth angel helps me to see the spiritual qualities of every material thing. The studio is a sanctuary, and the objects that emerge from it are like talismans or charms that spread the creative spirit into other places.

When I speak of my painting as a shrine, I want to evoke its existence as a gathering of spirits. The way we present paintings and the words we use to describe objects will significantly affect the way we see them. I recall Mark Rothko reflecting on the spiritual qualities of his color field paintings and saying, "They're not pictures."

I use sacred words to accentuate the spiritual qualities of images and things. My language expands rather than limits the movements of soul. If I want to restore the icons of the commonplace, I have to take liberties with language. When I use the word *shrine*, I consider the essential meaning—a place hallowed by the presence of sacred things—and I look at the complete spectrum of life from this perspective. The idea of the shrine has no limits. It spreads everywhere to everything I see through it. The ongoing act of shrine-making is an expression of an archetypal, or divine, purpose that is as important as the particular shrine.

The physical qualities of images are gatherings of energies and spirits, fields of forces. For me the painting is like an icon, which I define as a sacred image. Sanctity is a quality of the thing itself, not a result of its reference to something else. I don't worship the image as a deity, but its spiritual qualities help me appreciate the presence of the divine in everything. I don't see particular objects as more sacred than others, but I realize that, as in our relationships to people, we are closer to some than to others.

My emphasis on spreading the creative spirit into all aspects of life has delivered me to a form of "soul work" in which I lead group studios for people who desire what I am describing. We live for two to five days in a retreat setting where the entire atmosphere becomes a *temenos*. People see how the spirits arrive when the community commits itself to them.

We make paintings and other plastic art works and respond to them through silent meditations, poetic reflection, and imaginative dialogue. Performance art has become one of the most important elements of our studios, perhaps because of the way it carries the archetypes of group ritual. When the body and the physical space are the modes of expression, even the most secular types are immersed in sacred feelings and a ritual presence. If I place an object on a stage designated as a performance space, it becomes a participant in the event. It appears from our experimentation that the creation of a sacred space, and holding it as a sanctuary, is the act that empowers any person or thing that enters it. Power is focus. The enshrined object appears to receive its power from the venerated place while simultaneously contributing to its sacred aura.

For a recent performance, three women hung their paintings and arranged artifacts on the stage before the event. The audience was asked to go into the theater and sit before the performance began. Usually I ask the audience to pause and reflect in silence before the performance in order to shift the mood away from the din of conversation. But in this instance, they were immediately silenced by the presence of the images on the stage. The first phase of the performance was carried completely by the enshrined things.

Objects are sometimes more expressive than bodies in creating the ambiance of a theatrical environment and the way it acts upon people. When the performers enter, they also let themselves be carried by the spirits of the environment. They might carefully plan what they are going to wear and what they will have with them on the stage, but once the event begins, they become agents of the spirits of the moment, which always move them in unexpected ways.

If the designation of performance space in our group studios so clearly establishes a sense of sanctity, then it seems that a similar making of special places in our houses will help to establish the presence of the sacred. My wife's friend Sandy arranges things in her house into aesthetic "displays." She teaches young children and introduces similar activities in her classroom. Sandy is a religious woman, but she does not connect her "arrangements" with sacred disciplines as I do. As with many other people, religion is for her a sphere of its own, whereas I insist on joining the two spheres.

According to my definition, Sandy is an inveterate shrine-maker. She has her perspective on this activity and I have my interpretations, but as Martin Heidegger says, "The concept of the phenomenon is understood from the beginning as that which shows itself in itself."[3] The thing manifests itself to both Sandy and me, and we have our different conversations with it.

There is a sideboard between her kitchen and a sitting room that she has covered with objects that have personal connections. The "arrangement" is not at all functional or utilitarian—a feature that fits my criteria for shrines. Things are on display in order to be seen on a daily basis, as contrasted to practical things, which are put away out of sight.

I ask Sandy to describe what she does on her sideboard.

She replies, "I put stuff on it that I like, things I enjoy looking at, that I find interesting. I like cobalt blue, so I collect blue glass objects. They catch the light and I watch how it passes through them. I have an old tile that someone found in the attic in my display. If someone sends a card that I like, I keep it. I have a gallery of photographs of children that I like, friends' children and not just my own. Their pictures are visually pleasing and they connect me to the families. I walk by, look, and say to myself, 'Oh, aren't they wonderful. I haven't seen them for a while. I should call.' There's a pair of antique, translucent candle sticks there too. I saw them in a store and mentioned how I liked them to a friend, and she bought them for me. I arrange all of these things in a place where I can look at them together."

I ask, "How does the display take shape?"

"I start our with a few choice objects," she says, "and in the natural way of things, clutter takes over. It is not intentional. New things arrive. I saw a photograph taken of my sideboard five years ago, and there were only two objects on it. The first thing was a brass menorah with a picture of a prayer shawl and a passage from the New Testament attached to it."

"It is interesting," I say, "How the display, *which isn't a shrine*, actually begins with sacred objects and grows from them. This first object joins religious traditions. There is a finely attuned purpose within the apparent random accumulation."

"I do need carefully and aesthetically arranged places," Sandy said.

"We are influenced by their qualities," I reply.

"I have a friend who is a jeweler and makes meticulous displays of her work, but her house is all clutter with things thrown everywhere."

"The chaos arranges her psyche as well as the order does," I say. "She may need them both. She probably prefers chaos, since she has it all over her private space. My daughter, whose room is never neatly arranged, says that her way of keeping things feels more personal, and she has a sense of complex order in what appears chaotic to me. I have a cousin whose house has things piled everywhere on top of everything else. His place really has an impact on me because I tend toward the neat end of the spectrum. His environment is so foreign that it hits me like an art exhibit when I walk in. It confronts me with my spatial bias."

"That's how I feel in my friend's house," Sandy says. "The environment makes me think about how we are different. She doesn't need order at home the way I do. I can't live and work in a space unless it stimulates me and offers areas of harmony at the same time. As a teacher I create an environment that is conducive to experiencing different energies. I make displays at school too. I set up a table according to a theme and arrange artifacts that relate to it. It is important for me to have things on different levels. If someone puts a pocketbook, a snack, or a clipboard with fire rules on one of the tables, not realizing that they shouldn't, it drives me nuts. I don't say anything, but I discreetly remove the things and put them somewhere else. They don't belong, and I hate to see the display interrupted. It is put together with a purpose. If the children fiddle with it and rearrange things, that's fine. They might also bring things from home to add. But when something intrudes, it's different."

"The integrity of the place is not being kept," I say.

"As we talk," Sandy says, "I am beginning to see how much I do this in my life and how much it means to me. I never thought about it before. I have displays in my room at home. My bureau is arranged in a way that pleases me, with medicines and bobby pins interspersed with photographs. I need visual feasts throughout my house."

"Is there a purely sensual aspect to household shrines," I say, "or is it an archaic pattern of humans needing the company of things? It could be both of these things and more."

"This is why houses have mantels," Sandy replies. "Even people who don't display things as I do have objects arranged on the mantel. There is a space in every home for this."

"And there is the style of Japanese minimalism," I say, "where the absence of things is a statement. The space is open and unattached. But when things do enter the room, like the objects used in a tea ceremony, they are endowed with attention by the space. The room might be empty of things, but it is full of energy ready to be focused. I don't want to suggest that one way of arranging a space is better than another. There are just so many different ways, and each contains spirits corresponding to its structure."

Sandy says, "I have to make places of beauty in my home and work environments. They can be serene or energetic. When I rest my eyes on a table, I don't want to see a pile of medical bills."

"Beauty is itself a spirit," I reply.

"I need it in my life," Sandy says, "so I create places that give it to me."

Sandy's pattern of making arrangements is carefully focused on designated spaces, whereas I am not so deliberate in my creations. I don't make clear distinctions between sacred and profane spaces, and I try to appreciate the spirits in every place. If someone were to ask me where I make shrines in my house or workplace, I would have difficulty identifying areas because I think of my whole environment as a sanctuary with many different aspects.

I asked my daughter Kelsey whether she has places that are more sacred than others in our house.

"My room," she replied. "My things are all concentrated in one place."

This makes me realize that children can't keep their things everywhere. If they start to make things in living rooms and kitchens, parents like me will ask them to move the stuff into their rooms. This suggests that shrine-making has something to do with places that we can control and that will keep our things safe.

I ask Kelsey, "Are some areas more sacred than others in your room?"

"My dresser top," she says. "I also have a little wicker stand where I keep all my letters and little doodads that people have given me. Everything from mail to porcelain pigs, to copies of my high school literary magazine, and a button I got at a fair when I was eight."

"Do you have areas that aren't special?" I ask.

"My desk. I have to keep it empty so I can do my work. I never put anything on my nightstand."

"So sacredness has to do with places where you keep things?"

"Yes, because the places with the most memories mean the most to me."

"You definitely have special places."

"I don't do it consciously. Somehow, I always group things together. My mother gave me a beaded bracelet on Easter, and when I went to put it away in my room, I automatically placed it in one of three drawers in a box on my dresser top with other beaded jewelry that people have given me. Another drawer has jewelry that I bought myself, and the third drawer is for necklaces that my friends made me. I never intentionally arranged the drawers in this way. Even within this little box, some areas are more sacred than others."

"Do you make these arrangements when you travel?" I ask.

"When I am in a hotel room, the first thing I do is unpack. Some people wait, but I move right in. I put my shoes in the closet, books on a table; I set the place up like home. I always designate one area of the room—a dresser top or a bedside table—for important things. It starts out with just a brush and some jewelry, but by the time I leave, it has postcards, museum ticket stubs, rolls of film, presents for people, maps. All of these things help me feel connected to a space that was initially a room where thousands of people have slept. But for the days that I am there, I transform it with little things that make it feel more personal. I sleep better when I am familiar with the things around me."

"Familiar spirits?" I ask.

"That's exactly it. When I am at a good friend's house, I feel personally connected to the space because I know all of the things she has collected and why they are important to her. This physically affects me when I am in her room. I feel completely comfortable and relaxed. But if I go into her sister's room, I don't lie down on her bed or flip through her picture albums or look inside all of the little boxes on her dresser. I might sit on a chair and look around, because I feel like I am intruding on her space. It's the same thing with sleeping. I am not as comfortable without familiar things. I've watched people going into our house for the first time; they tend to be hesitant, quite, and they linger at the door. It's a combination of things—they're unfamiliar with the space and we're intimate with it."

"Things and places really do give off vibes?"

"Definitely," Kelsey says. "Things convey feelings and not just memories. When I am surrounded by familiar things, I am more secure and relaxed. I have never thought about this before, never noticed how I arrange my things so specifically. I knew that certain things were meaningful to me, but I never realized how religiously I group them together."

I had a conversation with my friend Truman Nelson, a historical novelist, in which he spoke about the sanctity of place and how he experiences his home as a sanctuary. He described how the house felt like his body with its distinct circulatory motions from the kitchen (stomach), to the library (head), to the bedroom (sleep and dreams), and the sitting room (entertainment).

He said, "I take risks all the time in my life, but my house encloses my vulnerabilities like a protective skin. I can pull in, like a turtle in his shell. I have to maintain vulnerability in order to be sensitive and to create from it without feeling threatened. This sense of sanctuary is the meaning of place for me. The intactness of a place and its character have to be preserved in the same way as one's body and consciousness."

I asked, "Do you have a central place?"

"Yes," he answered, "the library. It has the continuum of my interests. The titles are a landscape. When I sit here and look at the sermons of Theodore Parker, I have reverberations to him. I see the same thing when I see the books on the Transcendentalists. I set

my books up chronologically. My intellectual life has its beginning
in the English Revolution of 1640, in the left-hand corner, and pro-
ceeds from left to right to the American Revolution, the Transcendentalists, the antislavery movement, and onward to date. When I
sit in my chair, a casual glance runs the whole gamut and gives me
a sense of continuity, like the cave paintings. I need my points of
reference.

"But my sense of place cannot be restricted to a single space. I
need more than one room to have a complete sense of place. There
must be a full landscape and larger sense of coherence. The Yankee
town is supposed to ripple out into the meadows and not a ring of
shopping centers."

"The soul," I said, "corresponds to its landscape."

"The dissolution of a coherent sense of place makes for schizo-
phrenia. There is a landscape of the mind that has to be fed by the
actual landscape."

We absorb the spirits of the places we inhabit, and our souls do
correspond to the things we perceive. But political attempts to
make a correct world in the image of a particular moral vision have
a poor track record, because the needs of individual souls are so
varied. Greater sensitivity to the essential needs of the soul in all of
their complexity and differences is a more productive course. If we
become more aware of the subtle spirits guiding our lives, a more
deliberate remaking of the world may not be necessary, because we
will see how it makes itself in spite of our intentions. Every moment, the world invites us to create with it in shaping life.

The process of making sanctuaries where we preserve and enshrine vital experiences, as illustrated by Truman's, Kelsey's, and
Sandy's statements, is an archaic pattern of cultivating soul. Their
reflections show how we instinctively enshrine our personal environments and mark our presence and sentiments. The world forms
itself in the same way on a larger scale.

Personal shrines help us to remember and feel personally connected to our environments, but they also function as companions, earth angels. In our psychological era, it is fascinating how this creative realm of the soul's expression has escaped notice. We've been so focused on ourselves and relationships with others that we've overlooked a huge part of our being, which is our intimate interactions with things. The angels themselves have been restricted to human appearances.

We consider objects to be inanimate and soulless, decry materialism as immoral, while the soul's fascination with things persists and continues to shape the world. As our vision of the sacred moves away from exclusive focus on saving individual souls, and toward the realization that we are inseparable from the material environment, the presence of earth angels, the spirits in all things, will reappear. I emphasize the idea of renewal because our ancestors understood these truths. The soul has been lost for a while, and this is in keeping with its nature, which requires momentary separation to feed the desire for a return and more complete cooperation.

The soul always *saves itself* and preserves its vitality. No matter what we think about the presence of spirits in things, a belief that does not accord with the doctrines of scientific rationalism, the rituals of shrine-making endure in virtually every home. The life of the soul survives in spite of our intentions.

Things to do ....

• Sit in any part of your house and contemplate the expression of the room, the furniture, the artifacts, the walls, ceilings, doorways, windows, and floors. Watch how they interact with one another.

• Move something to a different place in the room and notice the difference in the space.

• Select an object and meditate on its expression for three to five minutes. What does it say to you about itself within the language of its form and substance?

• Shift now to an object next to it and repeat the exercise. Do you see how radically different the expressions are in a space that we never saw as containing such diverse personalities? As we become more aware of these details, we are attuned to the larger ecologies of environments.

• Look at the things in your rooms as if you were an avid bird-watcher. Find new species. Use a zoom lens to get up close while you are still distant. Locate things you never saw before. How do these new discoveries affect your feelings for the space?

• Take a walk around your home, inside or outside. Try not to plan anything. Don't select objects for observation. Let them impress themselves on you. Pay close attention to the details of your perceptions and cherish how things relate to you.

I went out into my garden and contemplated a flowering clematis vine climbing a lattice I built. I never before took the time to go beyond the first impression of the vine. I looked into the spaces between flowers, leaves, and stems, at the shadows, feeling the sense of depth that comes when I stop looking at surfaces, and when I peer into the space as the object of my reflection. I went around looking at other plants and shrubs in this way, gazing into their spaces. I was amazed at what I saw for the first time in the most familiar things.

• Find a simple domestic object—a drinking glass, a shoe, a spoon, anything that catches your attention. Carefully study its colors, its form, and the way light touches it. Imagine yourself painting it. Observe how the object is influenced by its surroundings. Shift your focus to whatever ground is holding your object—floor, rug, table.

How does the object introduce itself to you?

Imagine a different kind of person reflecting on the object. How does it introduce itself to that person?

Imagine the object in a foreign country or a different historical epoch. How does it introduce itself?

Imagine the object interacting with a group of wild artists. Let it say outrageous things about itself.

Now contemplate the object interacting with a conservative group of people.

Did the object have a spirit or personality that remained constant in all of these situations, or was its spirit shaped by each engagement? Did your perception of the physical qualities of the object change in relation to the spirits of the different situations?

• Continue meditating on the object, and begin to look at it as an entity without any function. Don't even think about its physical composition. Reflect upon it as a pure presence.

How does its spirit change?

How do your feelings change when you look in this way?

Can you imagine the spirit of the object existing without the actual physical thing?

• Sit in your grandfather's chair and imagine it holding his body. How did he feel when he sat in it?

Does it reverberate with echoes of his voice?

Wear or hold your grandmother's necklace and reflect upon its past life around her neck. Does it remember conversations, the rhythms of her breath, the smell of her perfume, the music as she danced, the warmth of the candles on the piano as she played?

• Get out your albums and old family photos, and look at these images as icons. Imagine the soul as a photosensitive material that holds the reflections of light and receives imprints from the auras of things. Select a series of photos that you take for granted, and sit with them as though they are the most sacred things in your life.

• Take a long walk around your house, apartment, or room. Look at your things and the environment as though you were visiting a museum or temple. Are some places more sacred than others?

• If there are places of relative sacrality in your home, spend some time at one of the sacred locations. Is it arranged like an altar? Are artifacts on display, or are they secreted away in enclosures?

• Photographs are today's most universal materials in making home altars. Observe how photos are displayed in your house, and reflect on the placement of certain images. Why are they suited for their places? How do they affect these environments and you when you look at them? Are your photographs always of people? Do you have pictures of places and things that you love? If you don't have any pictures of places and things, consider making a little altar displaying photos of them, and see how this affects your feelings for your environment.

• Go to one of the most unholy spots. Why do you see it this way?

Try to reverse your attitude toward the place and endow it with great sanctity. What spirits does it convey to you?

Imagine the place imagining you. How does it feel about you? Does it appreciate the changes in your way of relating to it?

• Feel your needs for different things in your environment: your reliance on the car, the refrigerator, the washing machine, your shoes, your toothbrush, your cup, the floor of your room, the bed, the windows. Reflect on the specifics of what each of these things does for you each day.

• Is there a place in your house, or your community, that bothers you? Go to that place and let it present itself to you. Look at it as pure form, color, light, shadow, as an aesthetic composition of elements. Realize that alteration of any kind will eliminate the particular spirit of the place. Let go of your dislike and contemplate what its structure does to you.

• Can you recall your parents' workplaces when you were very young? How far back can you go? What objects do you remember? What do you remember your parents wearing? What did they do with you in their workplaces?

• Do you remember your parents' bed and the spreads covering it? What did they have on the walls, the windows, and the floors? Did you have a favorite object in their room? Were there areas in the room that attracted you more than others? Did you go into their room often when you were alone?

• Imagine yourself moving from your house. What things do you want to carry personally rather than give to the movers? What objects, other than utilitarian things, do you unpack first when you settle into the new home?

• Listen to rhythms in your environment. This morning at breakfast, I unconsciously began tapping my hands and feet in time with the gyrations of the washing machine. My wife and four-year-old daughter joined in and made me aware of what we were doing. Vocal improvisations were added and we had a jam session following the beats of the different wash cycles. Clocks and dishwashers are other rhythm sources inviting us to join their expression.

• Make artworks in boxes in which you display small things connected to a person or place that you love. Designate different shelves of a bookcase for your beloved persons or places, and gather things that hold their spirits. You might only have to set aside a place in your house for displaying personal things, and the process of gathering will take over from there. I make little collections of things in the areas where I work, or on my bedside table—a postcard from a friend with a stimulating picture, special letters, small objects, a child's drawing. Set up relatively permanent displays, or gather things in temporary arrangements, or make some combination of the two. As you reflect on the objects, they will suggest possibilities for placement. What matters most is the quality of attention you bring to them, and your openness to an ongoing interaction.

3

The
Creative
Spirit

Angels fly out from everything .....

The whole world was transformed for me—became a living heavenly thing, of heavenly joys and sorrows. —Edith Sitwell

We have grown accustomed to thinking that it is people who project life onto things through their perceptions. Not only the world of objects but nature has suffered from the belief that only humans have souls. When we see everything as living and collaborating in the process of creation, the making of life becomes a complex participatory ecology and not just a single person's movement.

Although the way a person looks at something will influence its expressiveness and personal significance, objects are expressive in and of themselves. When I contemplate a burning log, I do not see its condition as expressive of my feelings. The vitality of logs, paintings, houses, and environments exist independently of human perceptions. They display their natures and project their spirits out to people. As Homer said in the *Odyssey,* "the soul flies out of things."

Objects convey energy, spiritual forces, and medicine to viewers who are able to open themselves to the life conveyed. The world is full of potential remedies if we can learn to access their resources.

If we shift our sense of the angel toward the way in which an object displays its soul, and away from exclusive identification of them as ghostly specters, then the active involvement of the viewer is essential to the communion. Popular notions of the relationship between people and angels have the spiritual figures arriving without any dependence on human participation. The human being is perceived as a passive recipient of the visitation. It is no wonder angels and spirits defined in this way are infrequent visitors. Those of us who have never been visited by a winged figure can see angels everywhere. The world is constantly displaying spiritual qualities through its physical being. In order to see them, we have to look more attentively and imaginatively.

When I was a graduate student, Rudolf Arnheim helped me to see how "expression is embedded" in formal structures. Everything has something to say, a spirit to convey. He demonstrates that "what strikes the eye transmits a life-giving energy."[1] It is not we who impart life to created objects and artistic images; rather, the artwork displays its own life through forms, colors, and textures. Arnheim's emphasis on how objects express themselves is the inspiration for my sense of the earth angel. His studies of physical things correspond completely with James Hillman's belief that we connect to the soul of psychic images through their "sense data."[2]

Although the expressive quality of an object is not exclusively determined by what a person brings to it, the liveliness of a picture or sculpture is affected by the person's ability to see and to respond to its expression. Arnheim describes how ancient theorists, including Plato, imagined vision as an interaction of fires streaming from the eyes and "counterfires emanating from the object to be perceived." The intensity and sharpness of the fire in our eyes will affect the degree to which we see.

In his studies of art and visual perception Arnheim talks about a "vector" as "a force sent out like an arrow from a center of energy in a particular direction." When the environment is free of restrictions, vectors stream in all directions "like rays emanating from a source of light."[3] Arnheim's studies of the physicis of vectors correspond completely to my sense of how objects and immaterial images transmit psychic energy. Poetic, sacred, and scientific inquiries do not have to be separated. As the poet Charles Olson said, "Image, therefore, is vector."[4] Images and things convey expression.

Not being familiar with the physics of vectors, I looked up the word and discovered that it suggests a force or influence, with the

Latin word *vector* meaning "carrier." My old teacher returned through my rereading of his books to clarify my sense of the earth angel as a carrier of the creative spirit. The idea of the angel gives a poetic and sacred sense to the messages and expressions constantly being transmitted in the physical world.

Conventional psychology still tends to locate feelings and other psychic phenomena exclusively "within" the person. Attention is given to what is inside the person and the literal "fixing" of the body's chemistry, whereas the indigenous healer is more concerned with adjusting the physical field in which the person lives. Shifting attention to how we are formed by external things, places, and events, moves psychology into the physical world. Artists, naturalists, historians, and even advertisers have been there for years, but psychology is reluctant to give up the notion that psychic life is a human possession.

Ideas about energies emanating from things are tied to very old traditions. Ancient philosophies of correspondences teach that reflection on the outer world reveals what lies within us. Action taken in one sphere will have an influence on what happens in another. Arcane predecessors of contemporary ecological ideas, holistic beliefs, and morphogenetic theories conceived of everything in the world as an expression of mutual relations. Remedies for people were contained in water, earth, and the stars, and healers perfected skills of interpreting these phenomena and accessing their medicines. In the early sixteenth century, Paracelsus, the Swiss physician and philosopher, said, "The physician should proceed from external things, not from man . . . from the external he sees the internal."

New Age ideas about healing auras are also survivals of archaic patterns. Angels are like auras that emanate from objects. They are impressions, distinguishing qualities, and the expressive gestalt of the whole configuration. The English word *aura* is derived from the Latin for breeze. In this sense auras are the "airs" that emerge from people, places, and things. The emphasis is on movement, the stirring of the soul as it experiences things passing through it.

An aura is a distinct presence, but it is by definition an "invisible breath" that emanates from a thing. This poetic sense of auras is getting lost in the contemporary emphasis on literally seeing colored lights around people and objects, which misses the expressions of the things themselves. My sense of the earth angel begins with what everyone can see. We then focus on the qualities it expresses, its radiance, all of which are available to anybody who wants to experience the thing's more complete and subtle presence. The aura is exactly what is presented to the senses. It will emanate out to anyone who is able to look carefully at the thing's appearance, from which it is generated.

Everything is a potential source of expression, and physics will confirm that whatever exists in an environment effects the atmosphere in different ways. Therefore, if I reflect on the qualities of a substance, what I see will stimulate a corresponding inner condition. When I meditate on a garden, I begin to access the different spiritual qualities conveyed by each plant and the environment as a whole. Every detail of my perception is a source of expression offering its particular gifts.

Isn't this what we are doing all of the time in decorating our home environments? We choose paintings, objects, and colors because of the feelings they generate, the memories they evoke, and the assuaging or stimulating characteristics of their expression. The way objects relate to one another is another important consideration in constructing an environment. Some people desire harmony, uniformity, and subtlety. Others want diversity, contrast, and boldness. There is also an aura generated by the total space and the way the different expressions of objects interact with one another together with persons in the area.

The same thing applies to meditational gardens. Careful attention is given to how the plants relate to one another, producing an overall effect or environment which is more than the sum of the parts. The gardener considers the different life cycles of the plants in order to sustain the color and vitality of the garden. Some gardens are carefully regimented in order to instill feelings of order and harmony, whereas the cottage variety offers a potpourri of spontaneous blooms in which the plants are given more freedom to establish interactive patterns.

So who or what initiates expression when I reflect on an object or a plant? Let's return to the question as to whether or not what I see is an extension of myself or an autonomous expression that influences me when I perceive it. Do gestures and energies fly out from things, as suggested by Homer?

During the first century BC, the Roman poet and philosopher Lucretius claimed that objects express themselves by throwing off "images" through the air. He described how the canvas awnings surrounding a theater radiate color from their surfaces. Everything in an environment has some impact on the energetic field.

Lucretius was trying to correct the superstitions of his time by articulating the doctrines of Epicureanism in a poetic text, *The Nature of the Universe*. Everything is just as it appears to the senses, and if our perceptions become more discriminating and creative, we will see more. Indulgence was not the objective of the Epicurean tradition. They advocated an education of the senses, greater sensitivity, and aesthetic appreciation. Vitality was perceived as the "conjunction" of mind and body. Saint Augustine, with an Epicurean echo, said that the soul "perceives by means of the bodily senses."[5]

My feeling for the angel is closely allied with that of Lucretius. Spirits, as he said, "ceaselessly stream out of objects and slide off their surfaces." He described the invisible "films" that these objects generate as "images." He anticipated modern physics in describing how light particles interact with objects, which "send off a great many images" from their surfaces. Everything is interactive in a cosmos of movement. Images are, as Lucretius said, "flying about everywhere, extremely fine in texture and individually invisible."[6] A more discriminating perception of physical things furthers the flight of the invisible images described by Lucretius. He presented imagination as the interaction between these moving images, which results in yet another image: for example, a man and a horse shaped into a centaur.[7] He would no doubt attribute our contemporary visions of angels to a similar amalgam of bird and human. Lucretius thus suggests that centaurs are images of the imagination. We can assume that he would say the same about their angelic relatives.

How and where the angel is located is a matter of personal preference, style, and culture. Some people are more apt to feel angels as forces in their bodies or the vibrations of sound or movement in space, all of which can be configured as spirits who take shape through the unique qualities of their relationships to individuals. The angel, like the Hellenic daimon, is a stream or current of energy that moves inside the person like feelings. It is all a matter of approach. Our biological and aesthetic sensitivities have more of an impact on shaping the figures of the angelic realm than we may realize.

Once we have recognized all of the subjective factors of culture, taste, empathy, and creativity, we are still faced with the way *a thing expresses itself to us and how we connect to it.* Every perception, inner and outer, has a dynamic vitality within itself which interacts with the sensitivities of the person experiencing it, the Platonic communion of fires. The daimonic element is the quality of an emotion that we experience as other than ourselves. In the words of Lucretius, it is the spirit that "streams out" from a thing. Through the imagination of angels we personify the expressions of the world and deepen our dialogue with them. Maybe the trees, animals, rocks, winds and waters are doing the same thing with us.

Positive proof is foreign to the experience of angels. Insisting that "it was really there" actually denies the reality of the imaginal realm and limits its ongoing creations. Fixation on the external "reality" of a particular appearance is actually an expression of distrust, an obsession with one figure that blocks further engagements, since we have left the field of imagination. Does it really matter whether or not we prove the existence of spirits? It will not further our engagement with them. I am sure that the angels do not want to lose the mystery that is the basis of their being. They smile at the crazy efforts to "prove" them according to an "external reality," which may itself be an expression of an all-encompassing imagination. The conservation of angels creates sanctuaries where imagination can flourish and send its medicine back into the world.

The ability to experience angels is not a special gift or psychic power, and there are many ways of approaching them.

For some people it is impossible to "see" an angel, since they can only be imagined and experienced within the cryptic recesses of the soul. They are accessible only through meditation, reverie, and the images of our psychic interiors. Thus, by their very nature, they remain invisible to "direct" sensory perception. They are seen only through the subtle faculty of imagination. Purists think that these interior or imaginal figures, which have a long and objective tradition within the world's psyche, have nothing to do with the perception of objects. I see no reason for a strict dichotomy. The invisible spirits and the things of the world need one another. They are necessary partners. Perception and imagination collaborate in every creative act.

Others experience angels as tangible qualities that are experienced as spirits: the enthusiasm of a person, the gentleness of an animal, the graceful slope of a hill, the sounds of a brook, the massiveness of a rock, the moisture of moss, the forcefulness of a breeze, the consistency of tides, the perfect stroke, the record leap. Machines, buildings, furniture, and art objects also have characteristics that can be imagined as angels. This way of looking at life is aesthetic and not opposed to science. Angels simply offer another way of imagining the material world.

Within the different world traditions of angelology, thoughts are themselves considered to be angels. Meister Eckhart (*Sermons*) said, "That is all an angel is: an idea of God." Mary Baker Eddy (*Science and Health with Key to the Scriptures*) wrote that angels are "God's passing thoughts to man." Ideas are angels who guide our lives and offer poetic relief.

My four-year-old daughter said to me, "I know how angels are made."

"How?" I asked.

She said, "After someone dies, they become an angel."

I replied, "Yes. I agree with you, but I also feel the spirits of living people and things."

The angelic way of looking at the world says that we humans are not here alone. Every environment teems with life beyond the reasoning mind and its discoveries. But I do not literally see angels, and to the best of my knowledge I have no supernatural powers, other than the resources of an ordinary imagination.

Poets and artists have helped to keep the angels alive in our Western culture during a time when imagination has been degraded as "unreal fantasy." Angels have also flourished in folklore: faeries of fields, woodlands, and gardens; spirits of sky and sea; intelligences of the heavens; and the persistence of superstitions. They are always present and accessible, but we have been looking in other directions and missing their gifts. The belief that our senses offer only partial images of much larger realities has contributed to the obfuscation of angels presenting themselves through the qualities of physical life available to everyone but seen by few. We are so busy thinking about what lies behind the world that we can't see what is before us.

Why not imagine that everything is physically displayed but not always seen? Nothing is being withheld. The belief that the depths of life are hidden is the projection of a human perspective which is not in keeping with the generous self-expression of the world, calling out for more imaginative interpretations.

Angels are personal figures, and their appearances are as varied as the imaginations from which they emerge. These diversities enrich the angelic ecology. For one person the angel is an invisible guardian, for another it is a deceased loved one, a recurring dream image, a treasured object. They can be persons, things, or inner images with which a person establishes an intimate relationship. The connection to the angelic figure can be sustained over time, or it may be a momentary glimpse within a meditation.

The reflective gaze, attentive ear, and sensitive body invoke the angels who exist whenever there is a psychic interplay between a person and something else. Some say that involvements with angels are self-centered, but this judgment misses the autonomy of psychic figures. They are offspring of our imaginations with ways of their own, and perhaps imagination is itself a child of the angels. The psychic life is a mysterious interplay of influences in which the angel appears to those who take time for them in dream review, meditations, creative activity, or prayer. When I read a poem, I engage its imagination with mine. I do the same thing when looking at a painting, listening to music, attending a play, taking a walk through a city, or feeling the imagination of water as I swim.

Some will say that my association of angels with imagination disparages them and denies their existence. I believe that angels exist within the splendid and mysterious "reality" of the imagination. We don't have to sit around lamenting how Gabriel, Michael, and Raphael never visit us. There is also a reality of divine mystery, inaccessible to reason or any other human expression, and I honor this realm and its invisible spirits. But I can actively engage the angels of the earth. Anyone can practice the meditative discipline and entertain the images, or angels, that fly out from things we contemplate. I am "stuck" in my creative work when I sit around waiting for something to appear according to a preconception. Creation, like the movements of angels, is dynamic and full of surprises that alter the way I look at things. The world presents a new face with each instant.

The skeptic may doubt whether there is truly an angel in everything. What about loathsome substances?

Ecologists will tell us that everything has its place in the total interplay. Human misuse of substances is the problem. The materials are not at fault. Saint Augustine said to God in the intimate speech of his *Confessions*, all things "are from You." Augustine goes on to say many times, "I saw Your invisible things understood by the things which are made."[8]

I wonder what Augustine would say about Styrofoam? How would he imagine its spiritual being?

Would he affirm that all things in their natural state are good, born perfectly, but capable of being corrupted? Or would he embrace the Styrofoam, feeling some compassion for it, sensing the angel in its substance that longs to return to its native condition? Perhaps if we tune in to the essential being of the material, it will tell us what to do with it. Imagine if manufacturers had meditative dialogues with products about their places in the ecosystem! Or maybe the Styrofoam, guided by the spirit of the saint, will assault my virtuous inclinations and ask me to accept its perversity and the complexity of the spirits inhabiting all things and revealing themselves through the most "lowly of heart."

Echoing Augustine, the spirit of the Styrofoam says, "O Good God, what is it with people that makes them celebrate when a soul is lost and abused and then saved? What is about the soul that takes more pleasure in recovery than continuous possession of its bounty? Why can't they see the angels in the most ordinary things, the debased as well as the exalted forms?"

A one-sided orientation to the heights misses the offerings of the lower regions, the angel of the Styrofoam. Today we are apt to think of angels as winged, benevolent, fair-haired Caucasians wearing pastel robes and playing a stringed instrument. Our mental picture is typically a composite of a Botticelli woman adopting Victorian manners. She flies in an artistocratic environment of gold leaf and richly colored linen. No wonder D. H. Lawrence could not tolerate "this angel business." I hear him howling against the betrayal of darkness.

The spirits are in everything dark and light. The wicked and nasty angels are as vital to the soul's life as the sweet and proper ones. Morality is for me a lively interplay between angels and demons. Their conflicts and interactions are the inner drama of conscience.

But this is a time when well-meaning people are trying to rid society of anything offensive, and it is no wonder the pure and gentle angels are dominating popular culture. Fairy tales and nursery rhymes are being rewritten into gentler and more acceptable versions—"three kind mice" are replacing the blind ones. Will Oedipus be the next to go?

I cannot imagine a rich life of the soul without embracing all things, and ultimately loving our demons as ourselves. I invite Janus to stand at the gate of my reflections, where he looks in opposite directions. Janus, the god of beginnings and endings, also embodies the good and bad sides of the same thing, the necessary interplay.

I savor the angels of a wondrous autumn day by the sea, visions of my children living in an ideal world, rituals of a kind community, or replays of the shot I once hit to win the match. In my life these beauties are accompanied by the spirits of mistakes, discomforts, and confusions, the absolute blooper of a ball I launched with all eyes on me and while I dreamed of heroically hitting it out of sight. Can I live with these humbling moments and still love the pursuit? Will I ever discover the blissful comedy of errors, the serenity of acceptance? I laugh at others but why not myself? Whatever challenges my idealized self-image, and my control over events, carries the angel of humility.

The soul perversely demands bad feelings as well as good ones. It is not just the nice and aerial spirits that we crave at night, but the sensual, disturbing, and complicated scenarios that resonate with our interior, with soul's desire for potent images. We trick ourselves into thinking they can be conquered and don't see how negative obsessions increase the power of their objects. Such is the way of polarization. Through disturbances the soul teaches acceptance of the necessary tension of creation.

The world of things good and bad is constantly shaping us, no matter how far away we retreat and how staunchly we defend against its entries. The Hellenic sense of the daimon, the cultural forebear to our Western angels, had room for both dark and light forces and viewed their conflict as beneficial to the unending exercise of virtuous living.

In Greek antiquity the daimon was many things, but it is essentially experienced as a divine force that enters against our will, taking us by surprise and stunning the habitual mind. Jung liked to emphasize how we are "seized" by arrivals of the numinous. He defined God as whatever crossed his "willful path, violently and recklessly" and changed the nature of his life.

Do you see how differently we can approach the intruders in our dreams and the disturbances of our lives? The essential purpose of the habitual mind is the repression of anything contrary to its agenda. We want the nice apparitions, and guard against uninvited and unruly guests. In the Greek imagination, respected by Nietzsche and later by depth psychologists, the Gods appeared through disease, illness, and tragedy as well as good fortune. There are angels in these things too.

It is healthy to welcome all of the energies of life into our imagination of angels. In this way nothing is denied its place within the larger ecology. Rather than negate these forces, we learn to interact with them and transform the powers they carry. Demonizing unpleasant feelings keeps them at bay, but repression only increases their energy and makes them into monsters. It is the disturbing figures that often have the most to offer because they challenge habitual ways of living that tend to bury whatever does not fit the prevailing schemes. If we entertain the troubling images, we discover that they may be trying to show us where we hurt. I have found that the demons or negative angels have been the most instructive forces in my life. They protect and guide through their irritations and conflicts, which really get my attention and show where I am stuck, preoccupied, or reluctant to take the next step into life.

In psychology, Jung restored the ancient sense of the dream as an angel that frequently upsets the conscious mind with alarming and distasteful experiences. He said, "The particular fact that the dream is the divine voice and messenger and yet an unending source of trouble, does not disturb the primitive mind."[9] Instead of trying to conquer and control vexations, why don't we accept them as stimulants for new creations?

Angels sometimes appear against a person's will, like intruders in dreams who may be helping dreamers look at things they avoid. They also arrive in the form of anxieties. A woman who was preparing to be married dreamt that a group of men broke into her mother's house. She fled though a "safe" in the wall and met her fiancé, who was waiting outside the house. Men intrude and the woman flees the safety of her childhood home; or staying at home is no longer safe, and she is forced out by the intrusive male energy; or the tight passage through the shamanic doorway into a new life is accompanied by conflict and fear.

The man who is in the process of selling his family business dreams of outrageous complications—roofs falling apart, toilets backing up into offices, and torturous buyers who inflict him with hardships. He responds to the dream by feeling that the spirits of the family business within his soul want attention. It is not simply a matter of buying and selling. He can't just walk away from the familiar haunts and life-supporting rituals of the family without complications. When we are making major changes in our lives, and do not consciously perform rituals of passage, our dreams carry on the primal rites of the soul.

Accepting the demons and paying attention to them transforms our relationship to them. When one of my daughters was three, she was afraid to go to sleep in her bedroom, where the shadows of three huge oak trees frightened her. We went outside to the trees, and I spoke to her about how they were there to watch over her. "They're angels who live outside your window. Strong ones who will protect you every night when you sleep." We touched the trunks and kissed the bark good night. Afterward, as part of her evening ritual, we looked out to the angel trees and thanked them for watching over the sleeping child.

Years later I discovered that my older daughter, who slept in the same room as a child, thought there were witches in the same trees outside her window. Like the early New Englanders who cut down the forests, she felt there were demons in the woods. She was terrified of them, but never spoke to me about her fears. Children, like adults, may need help in transforming the figures of their imagination in accordance with the principle that these "persons" do not come to do us harm. My older daughter later went on to write marvelous stories about witches, so this particular "holding" of fears within the psyche ultimately made a contribution to her creative life.

With my my younger daughter, the fear that was lodged "between" her and the trees was reframed into another way of looking at the relationship. We didn't belittle the fear as "imaginary" or try to rationally explain the fear by saying, "It's only a tree and trees don't hurt people." Instead we entered the imagination of the situation and created another story, another way of stating the relationship between child and tree.

The spirits of things are not always saccharine. Many of us have probably kicked the tires of our cars and uttered savory expletives when the machine refuses to start. As soon as the thing does not submit to our will, it becomes a "being" in its own right, something to whom we address aggression or a plea for cooperation. Whenever "a thing" acts, or does not act, in ways contrary to a person's will, it is immediately animated. We howl and plead, "Why are you doing this to me?" I take the car for granted until it fails me, and then I become absorbed by its being. People who scoff at the idea of talking to trees and stones have no trouble speaking passionately at a mechanical device with a mind of its own.

It has been a long time since I have said a Hail Mary, maybe thirty years, but when my computer set off a bomb suggesting that I might lose ten hours of inspired work, I said the prayer from my childhood. What else could I do? I didn't get down on my knees, but I did pray to forces outside my control. The prayer didn't overtly change anything, but it did feel good to say it. This is probably the way healing charms operate. They do not act directly on external processes, but they alter the energetic field of the person, and this ultimately affects the environment.

The computer experience shows how objects can act in ways contrary to our will. The machine is not expressing malevolence toward us. The attribution of evil intent is an expression of the person's frustration. As in any other relationship, the interaction between a person and a thing involves a subtle dance of control, a mutual give and take.

Problems inevitably stem from making the assumption that the thing with which I relate is completely subject to my control. Our relationships to things will improve, and become more productive, when they are pervaded by a spirit of collaboration and mutual care.

"Every instant in a new cloak" ....

There is nothing permanent about earth angels. They are
rediscovered in each instant.

I tend to think about angels in vignettes, brief sketches or epi-
sodes, moments of daimonic possession. These spontaneous forms
correspond to my sense of the angel. When I try to evoke angelic
spirits through a more systematic discourse, I am left with just
words and dense thoughts, abandoned by spirits who have scurried
off to the next spontaneous thought. The plurality of the sketches,
the way they visit us one after the other, corresponds to the historic
imagination of angelic hosts. In order to evoke the angel, I have to
use a style and form that correspond to its nature. No wonder angels
have always been so closely identified with poetry and imaginative
expressions.

The creative movements of soul are closer to a lively social gathering than the logic of developmental stages. Like dreams, creative
connections hop and abruptly jump from one thing to another,
drawing diverse and previously separate phenomena into a new creative purpose that eludes analysis according to a linear sequence of
causes. The earth angels are apt to move like a stream of relaxed
conversation that makes surprising and fresh connections between
things and draws everyone into a spontaneous field of creation.

In his studies of Islamic religion, Henry Corbin approaches
angels through a belief in One God which not only accepts but requires the pluralism of the world's spiritual phenomena. Native
American spirituality similarly posits the existence of a single Creator while embracing a complex world of spirits in every animal,

place, and thing. The *one* and the *many* do not contradict each other because the Great Spirit or Creator is inclusive of all the world's spirits. Conflicts between singularity and pluralism are expressions of the human mind, whereas in the psychic realm, paradox is welcomed as the essence of a spontaneity from which all changes emerge.

In Corbin's studies of medieval Sufism, I have found the most precise correspondence with my personal sense of the angel. Sufi mystics believed that "each sensible thing has a created Spirit by which its Form is constituted," and the spirit of the thing is in turn constituted by the Holy Spirit. Corbin writes, "It is the Holy Spirit, whose perfection is individualized in each object of the senses or of the intellect."[10] Rather than polarizing sacred and profane life, the Sufi vision imagines the spirit in each thing as contributing to God's being. The multiplicities of spirits do not oppose the unity of the divine presence which transcends the contradictions of a reasoning mind.

For the Sufi, prayer is an ongoing interpretation, a *ta'wīl*, of the "divine Face" presented by each thing, and the angel's connection to the physical form is analogous to the relationship between words and their meanings. Where others may see only a physical substance, the mystic perceives a real spiritual body that is the soul or essence of the thing.

Creative imagination becomes the instrument of prayer. Actual dreams and objects of the physical world are essential to the divine presence because without them there is "nothing to interpret." Therefore, the angel and physical thing depend upon one another. Their partnership is the basis of the mystic's creative prayer, which requires an *intimate dialogue* "between two beings." Interpretation of the physical world becomes a meditation through which the essential Being of Creativity manifests itself.

Because the Divine is unlimited and incapable of being fixed, God is imagined as the incessant flow of creation, "manifested at *every instant* in a new cloak."[11] Corbin and the Sufi mystics experience One God whose being is expressed through a necessary "diversity and plurality" of epiphanies. These meditations take us back to archaic beliefs in an animated world without threatening direct relationships with a personal God and its Holy Spirit.

Corbin illustrates how images are shaped in the intermediate world of imagination where "immaterial beings take on their 'apparitional bodies' and where material things are dematerialized to become 'subtile bodies.' " Images are manifestations of God "corresponding to the innermost being of the mystic, who experiences himself as a microcosm of the Divine Being; a limited Form, like every other form . . . but a Form which . . . emanates an aura, a 'field' which is always open to 'recurrent creations.' "[12]

The visions of artists and creative people are essentially theophanic. There is always a sense of angels when we hear descriptions of how poems, paintings, and music emanate from the soul in the flying sparks of the creative spirit. The artist is the agent or "active" instrument through which the soul expresses itself and realizes its purpose. This is why the creative arts are always wedded to religion and spirituality. The freer the artist's spirit, the more it expresses the divine energy. Controversial artists, the ones that many people love to despise and censor, are ironically closest to the sacramental nature of the creative experience. They challenge boundaries and forge new realities by following the instincts of creation.

Creative spirits cannot tolerate fixed forms, and they understand how interpretation is a transformative "movement" that never stops. The artist's sensibility is especially offended by interpretations that do not see themselves as creations. When authoritarian types make absolute declarations about the nature of things, the artist instinctually rebels, because fixed ideas interrupt the stream of creations. Just like the angels of imagination, artists are themselves living in a creative realm where spirit takes on physical forms and material things become "subtile bodies." The artist is deeply involved in both the spiritual and material worlds, and the friction between the two is often the angel of their reciprocal transformations.

Eastern indigenous cultures also see every physical thing as having a spiritual counterpart. In Japan there is the ghost of the teapot. Tibetan folk beliefs engaged local spirits, or "earth-owners," inhabiting particular places, things, and natural elements as well as "house gods," ancestral gods, and the person's good and bad familiar spirits.

The tremendous contemporary interest in angels contributes to the historic pluralism of notions as to what an angel is. If we look across cultures, ideas about the natures of angels multiply and their names change to spirits, ghosts, demons, bodhisattvas, jinns, devas, and devis, and so on. The endless scope of interpretations is a reflection of the angel's imaginal body. No matter how definitively a religion tries to classify and control the realm of angels, the individual imagination insists on its intimate relationship with spirits.

A critic might say, "You are talking about primitive animism and not angels. The pagan mind sees spirits in everything. Angels are God's messengers."

I reply, "Actually the idea of messenger fits my sense of a spirit in every thing. The angelic messenger corresponds to the way objects express themselves to us. They communicate and transmit spirit. I assume that your sense of God's messengers is restricted to scriptural angels like Gabriel and Michael. I embrace these angels of religious tradition, and I don't think they contradict the spiritual life conveyed by the urn filled with red and white geraniums on my porch. These are also God's messengers for those who meditate on their spiritual nature."

The function of "messenger" is only one of the aspects of angels. Even in the restricted realm of Western culture's anthropomorphic spirits, angels also function as guardians, guides, protectors, companions, and helpers. The English word *angel* is derived from the Greek *angelos,* based on the Hebrew *mal'akh,* which means messenger. It is clear, then, that *angel* is only one of many possible names for the spiritual counterparts of things. I like the word because I have a history with it going back to the earliest spiritual feelings of my childhood. Angels are personal and intimate spirits.

A second critic, in the spirit of the Protestant enlightenment, says, "All of this talk about angels is poetic fancy. Angels are nothing but figures in your imagination."

I reply, "I agree with you completely. Angels are figures of the poetic imagination, which the mystics see as the mind of God. They experience every image, idea, and feeling as an angel. Imagination is the faculty that opens us to the creative spirit and its particular manifestations."

There are no limits to the forms imagination's angels may take. The experience of the creative spirit is a never-ending interpretation in which history, culture, place, personal inclinations, and the specific context of each engagement interact with one another within a movement that ancient China called the Tao, the total spontaneity and creation of all things.

"Ah, ah," says the second critic, "now you show yourself as a pagan Taoist poet trying to expropriate our monotheistic tradition of angels who serve the one true God."

"Perhaps," I reply. "Your need to label me and classify what I say may express how the angels work through you, but my way is different. The creative spirit has many names, many forms, and as soon as I experience one, another will appear. I am comfortable living in the moving stream."

This exchange makes it clear why I have difficulty with authoritarian doctrines. I really do not oppose what they present, since I experience it as yet another cloak that the angel wears. If I reject them, I become caught by negations that thrive on restricting the forms of the creative spirit.

Maybe Lao Tzu would like to answer the critic who rejects Taoist poetics. He says, "I ride the wind where all things are one. I lose me."

Everything makes its contribution to the sustained interplay of spirit, every blade of grass, every feeling. It is a mystical and poetic vision of creation through which persons experience themselves and their ideas as manifestations of divinity. As Corbin said, we are all limited forms, but each "emanates an aura" or angel that stimulates others and the enduring recurrence of creation. It is an ecology of spirits, of small things, participating in an intelligence that thrives on every contribution, the complete spectrum of actors in the unending play of divinity.

Anyone who has been seriously involved in self-inquiry knows that confession, or self-revelation, involves the telling of stories about oneself. This is especially true if we attempt to describe past experiences. I once read about a person who wrote twenty-five different autobiographies, each one distinctly different from the other. The themes, feelings, and environments of the particular moment will elicit different contents.

Even when I am telling what is apparently the "same" story, it will be influenced and changed by different people and surroundings. The retelling corresponds to the dynamic flux that is our nature. If people seem totally consistent, that is because they are probably living their lives according to rigid and mechanistic visions of the world that do not open to the constant movements and influences of an environment. This fixity tends to characterize many severe forms of emotional disturbance where the person is rigidly defended against environmental influence and cooperation. The creative person, by contrast, is in an ongoing process of transformative interaction with the environment.

This kinetic basis of reality is the reason why creative artists and mystics focus on the importance of "instants." They live in the moment, because they realize how ephemeral the creative process is. Opportunities come and go in a flash.

Presence ....

*If I am present to the thing before me, it takes me to myself
and our reciprocal being.*

My sense of the earth angel is inseparable from the creative spirit, which is for me a partnership with the world, and not something that comes solely from within a person.

I read a passage from Hermann Hesse's *Die Märchen* (Tales) that I first thought related to my theme of earth angels, but now I see that it is the antithesis. He says, "All things are open gates through which the soul can enter the inner world when it is ready," and he goes on to talk about giving up the "pretty illusions on this side" in order to experience the "reality of the inner."

Imaginative responses to artistic expressions are blocked by the ingrained assumption that truth and meaning are locked "inside" matter, or kept "within" the soul, which is itself solely imagined as an interior realm. I don't want to deny the existence of the inner life, but this perspective overlooks the magnificent vistas of earth angels and the depth existing on the surfaces of things. Gnosis is outside too. It is conveyed by things and events, carried in casual conversations, and readily available to anyone who truly listens, looks, and feels its presence.

We imagine knowledge as lying buried in the crypt of the psyche rather than living in the open, in our facial and bodily expressions. We fear disclosing secrets but don't realize that we reveal our soul with each gesture. These attitudes have shaped our experience of angels, whom we imagine as residing in some other realm, rather than in the constant displays of the world seen through appreciative and imaginative eyes.

The things of the world are regarded as masking the truths that live behind them. Great poems and influential psychological theories have been based on this assumption, which nevertheless disparages the angelic nature of immediate things. Each expression is a revelation if we are capable of opening to it. The masks are themselves spirits. Disclosure is a point of view that pays attention to what is *not* being presented. It imagines the psyche as a locket, whereas I see it as a flower. Humans may lock up their experiences, but nature does not. A life lived within the perspective of private crypts misses the constant expression of gestures, surfaces, and the marvelous depth of nuance in the most ordinary contacts between people and things.

Creation emerges through a disciplined and full immersion in a particular thing. This is the only way into the zone of creative vitality. If I am preoccupied with something other than what I am doing, I stop the flight of spirits. Creative blocks come from being somewhere other than where I am. They take the forms of impossible perfections and expectations that interfere with being present with whatever is moving through me at a particular moment. If I am "stuck," I cannot move with the currents of the immediate situation.

The earth angel is a state of presence, an attunement to changing instants, a love for the specific thing that is happening, and a heightened sense of how a stone in a stream or an object in a room presents itself. Martin Heidegger might describe this process as a "presencing" of the inherent qualities of things, which we cannot see unless we relax our expression and absorb theirs.

The psychology of creativity and our methods of schooling have placed all of their emphasis on what goes on inside "creative types." My experience shows that the creative spirit is not likely to respond to a willful discipline that wants to make things happen. It is more apt to flourish through a person's skillful engagement of unplanned arrivals. The creative act is always attentive to the gestures and cues of situations that draw people into their orbits. When I am in the creative zone, I let the inspirations act through me, and they make me more aware of my own being. I become an agent of soul's will, keenly attuned to ephemeral opportunities.

Creation is a partnership between the person and daimonic forces, but we tend to think about creativity as a purely individual gift and miss the basis of creation in reciprocity and collective effort. The creative act calls out for mutual relations, and skilled creators know how to interact with the spirits moving through an environment and those of the materials they use.

People struggling with creation often say, "I can't get into it," or "I don't have it today." In my experience, these conditions stem from a lack of committed presence in the immediate situation.

I know a Kiowa healer who describes how he always works with the artifacts native to the place where he is. If he is in Massachusetts, he does not use the same tools he employs in Oklahoma. He selects substances from the local natural environment and familiar objects from the home of the person he is treating, because the creative and helping spirits are always local. Transformation of a condition occurs through the spirits of its environment as the Great Spirit cooperates with them. If we want to change a neighborhood, an office, a relationship, a painting, a manuscript, or a garden, we have to engage the deities inhabiting the particular situation.

Creative spirits do not fly in from Tulsa to do the work of the soul in Cambridge. Similarly, we can't chase the spirits around the world, hoping to find something on a New Mexico reservation that we cannot see in Vermont. The creative spirits are embedded in the local material world, ready to be released by a consciousness that opens to their presence and desires to interact with their native expressions. If we can become present in a place, we will be able to access its spirits. Marsilio Ficino, who felt that each material environment had its particular relationship with the firmament, said that we must first "warm" the physical substance though our attentions, and ultimately it will release its daimonic forces.[13]

My sense of creation involves the introduction of an outside agency or stimulus for change, which establishes a working relationship with the spirits living in the immediate situation. The material, or context, carries the spiritual potential for its own transformation. The creator is an instrument for the release of forces brewing in a locale. Visionaries sense what a situation needs to complete itself, and they become agents for the realization of this purpose.

The way human agents facilitate creation can be likened to moving with a dance partner. The skilled pair give and take energy from each other. There is a feeling that they are carried effortlessly by the dance enveloping both people. Dominance of one over the other interrupts the flow and brings self-consciousness, a loss of spontaneity, and awkwardness.

I find that thinking too much about what I want to do before I do it always interferes with the creative spirit. I might be possessed by an idea, an image, or a desire to work, but the formation of the creation always takes place through the act of making it. Ideas come through talking, moving, or writing. Images in paint are similarly created through the process of making a painting. If I want to receive the spirits of creation, I act with discipline and commitment, but without excessive effort and willful planning. I locate myself in an environment where the angels act through me. I enter the life of the book, the painting, the dance, or the workplace and dedicate my being to its emergence. The creative spirit lives in motion, and it appears most wondrously through unplanned gestures.

It helps to imagine that places, groups of people, and materials carry the creative spirits I want to access. "Going into myself" does not seem to work as well. I move with the environment, which is not always a benign partner. Robert Frost described how the material world can apply pressures on the creator. It can be a tormentor as well as a gentle guide, but ultimately it is the push of the external world that moves the creator, who responds.

I tell my painting and writing students that in order to create, they must begin to paint and write. If they work at the discipline, the creative spirits will appear through the medium. Discoveries in writing have as much to do with running a pen across a page, with the rhythms of fingers touching a keyboard, as they do with the mind thinking. I encourage painting from the lower body and shoulders, to get the inspiration all the way up from the feet and through the hands to the canvas. When we imagine artistic imagery moving only from the brain down the arm and into the fingers, we get stuck in our heads, which are not the exclusive centers of creation. The whole body must be present in the act of creating.

Ideas emerge through what I call a total presence with the artwork. If I am immersed in its soulscape, forms, characters, and new directions present themselves.

Time is necessary if the creation living in the project is going to freely manifest itself through me. The emanations are osmotic, gradually absorbing and diffusing themselves through me, through the materials, via insights, influences, and glimpses that somehow find their place within the all-encompassing receptivity of the project. Creation has its sudden breakthroughs and startling visions, but my experience is closer to an incremental movement of things finding their place within a process. Ultimately, the overall purpose completes its own form, somehow carried in the genes of situations.

The skilled creator is present with instants, witnessing others and themselves as they act, openly acknowledging distractions while keeping a faith in the wisdom of the process that carries them where they need to go. Creation moves. It is current (adjective) and a current (noun)—the creative act that flows now. Dreams are our most useful guides to the currents of the psychic landscape and its ways of transformation. They move constantly, one image immediately following another. The act of creation involves a meditative immersion in a thing, a feeling, a situation, a gesture, a sound, a rhythm. I enter the world of the image, and offspring are made from our interaction. The earth angel is the current, the impermanent Buddha-flow, Heidegger's presencing,[14] the time now moving and always passing into another.

Offense, disturbance, and shock are often the means through which I immerse myself in a situation or feeling. Presence is not an exclusively positive condition. If images, things, and environments are carriers of expression, then they must carry anxieties as well as uplifting spirits. *Objectus,* the Latin root of the word *object* is something that "throws" itself at us. In addition to our objects of love and desire, anxieties are also embedded in objects that impinge upon us, shattering our environmental controls. Broken appliances, leaking roofs, computer Kalis who devour writings and thoughts, frozen pipes, higher taxes, lost keys, family problems, complaints at work, and other discomforting objects throw themselves upon us with great velocity and completely absorb our energies.

The thing that most forcefully challenges my control dramatically pulls me into its being. Rather than fight the overwhelming vortex, I can access the energy of its negative flow, which has activated every fiber of my emotional being. A woman dreamt that *her bike tire had been slashed in a park. She went into a men's clothing store to get it fixed, and a repairman rubbed her belly intrusively and then started sticking his hands down her pants. She was outraged, indignant at being molested.* In working with this dream she began with the feeling of molestation, but as she immersed herself in the environment of the dream, the feeling began to shift. She slipped out of the victim role and saw the man as the aggression she needed to break through her repression of pelvic energy and sexuality. He was her repairman. The demon was re-visioned as bringing a message of transformation. She went into the men's store to get her tire repaired and to ride her bike again, to reactivate the motion of her lower body. The dream pulled her into creative energy.

The creative imagination routinely endows objects with malevolence—the dream truck that chases a man across the country, the garden rake waiting for a misplaced foot so it can knock the person on the head, the jinxed mirror that brings bad luck to anyone who looks into it. When a particular object is associated with a bad experience, it carries the memory of that event. The wicked spirits haunt the thing or place. Over twenty years ago when I was in conflict with a woman, I built a stone wall on my property, and a particular stone was somehow touched by the conflict and became identified with it. Whenever I saw that stone in later years, long after I had forgotten the problem with the woman, the feelings immediately returned. The stone became an extension of memory.

Folk medicine and superstitions give objects a primary role in transferring spirits. If the stone in my wall is capable of absorbing bad feelings without any intent on my part, then it seems that physical substances can be used purposefully to throw off an unwanted presence. In folk culture someone who wants to unload a malady passes it on to a stone or some other thing, which is buried or thrown into the sea. The remedies are sometimes cruel and self-centered, like the practice of transferring the problem onto an object that is left in a public place. The next person to pick up the thing is believed to carry away the affliction. The use of benevolent talismans no doubt grew from the negative, which is always the most potent way of getting attention.

Earlier peoples who experienced soul in inorganic as well as organic life were acutely attuned to the way objects transmit forces. Talismans and charms permeated every aspect of their daily lives. Even if we don't believe in the magical powers of things to alter situations, we can look at these practices as an extension of a worldview in which physical things have spirits that affect people. Careful attention is given to touching or wearing the amulet in the right way. The things of the world are rarely taken for granted.

Are we really better off in our rationalistic world? The perspective of reason is complemented by an earth full of spirits. Maybe we need a generous dose of superstition to help us realize that if we treat things badly, they might harm us.

Compare a poetic ecology of spirits to the anesthetized or purely functional ways we touch and look at things today. Magic is not just an art of controlling events. It is a way or reenchanting the world through attention to beauty. Compare the vitality, craft, aesthetic appeal, and complete individuation of the objects made by an animistic culture to things produced by today's manufacturers. Things and their atmospheres are alive in the animistic world and spread their vitality to everyone who comes into contact with them.

I do not mean to say that mass-produced objects and other ready-mades lack soul. Each thing generated from an assembly line has its unique being. Even monstrosities can become treasured relics, like the Edsels and finned Chevrolets from the late 1950s. Perhaps the plastic potted plants of the 1990s will be enshrined in the future. Construction by hand is not a prerequisite for the presence of soul in a thing. I have seen many paintings and handmade objects that convey less aesthetic appeal that artifacts of industrial culture.

I return to the idea that looking through the eyes of the angel will determine the soulfulness of an object or place. Today, as I see people keeping effigies of serpents and birds in their homes, wearing them on their persons, or painting them in their art, I look for what these expressions say about the needs of the soul. I see them as signs that we are once again making sacred atmospheres in our homes, looking soulfully at the things of this world, establishing intimate relations with nonhuman beings, and creating together with them. Rather than threatening orthodox religions, the celebration of totems and spirit animals heightens the presence of divine life in everything.

The use of talismans in personal prayer and healing does not have to be a literal invocation of magical properties living within the thing. The revival of interest in sacred objects, charms, and healing places is a return to ancient ways of treating problems of the soul through imaginative expression.

The expressions of things are shaping our thoughts, actions, and futures. They speak for themselves in spite of our best intentions. The way I say something may have more impact than what I think I am saying. The structures of thought are fairly limited, and they tend to repeat themselves through history, whereas the subtleties of expressive style and form are far more varied. The earth angels and demons live in these nuances and infinite varieties of presentation.

The atmosphere of a place is an ambiance or distinct quality that I have likened to the earth angel. It is a presence that refuses to be explained but strongly manifests itself to the person who opens to its spirit. Every situation has an atmosphere or structural gestalt that can only be known through an attunement to its frequency. Otherwise, it passes unnoticed. The reality of a painting is grasped through its material nature, the dance through its movement and visual configurations. The earth angel is a contemplation of the pure presence of a thing, its distinct and nontransferable qualities, its unique nature, what Buddhism calls its suchness, or the phenomenologists call its essential being—the different states of fullness I feel when entering a flower shop, bookstore, service station, or the village hall last night as forty children and a group of adults were rehearsing this summer's production of *Oliver*.

Every place, and every thing, carries a spirit unique to its being. Does the form of the thing I make convey the effect I hope to achieve? For example, I just read through an issue of an art therapy journal that looked more like a mechanical engineering periodical than a publication inspiring artistic expression. Do my tone of voice and facial expression say something other than what I think I am saying? Do I have any idea at all what the physical characteristics of my person and my environment are expressing?

Rather than focusing on just the literal contents of what I say, it is fascinating to ponder what the atmosphere of my presence says to others. How do I shape the environment of conversation and the vibes generated from it? Has the essential message got anything to do with what I think I am saying? Imagine the differences in style between my reflections on the soul and those of Gangsta rapper Jeru the Damaja?

It is possible that these considerations may only further stage fright and an inhibiting self-consciousness by giving me too many things to think about, but on the other hand they might be just what I need to get out of myself and my preoccupations and let me see that it is the environment that carries the primary forces of expression. How can I cooperate better with it and enter into a creative ecology with the energies it carries? Every atmosphere expresses itself and unconsciously affects us and our emotions. Too often we try to impose our agendas on places and things, and it just doesn't work.

By emphasizing how the physical qualities of places have such a significant impact on people, I realize how often environments generate unattractive auras and disturbing forces. An example from my art therapy work comes to mind. My practice requires me to immediately establish cooperative working relations with environments that have not been designed for the making of art in groups. I have constructed many hundreds of nomadic studios throughout my twenty-five years of art therapy practice. I feel like a Bedouin traveler who keeps putting up and taking down his tent and I have never worked in what could be called an ideal space.

I once conducted a one-day studio workshop at a conference in a hotel in Washington, D.C. A large workplace was needed, so we were put in an open underground area, separated from a massive dining room by curtains. There were heating and air-conditioning ducts above us, and just as we began to talk, they started to rumble. A half-hour into the studio the fire alarm rang, and two hours later, as I was working deeply with one of the participants and her art, dining room workers noisily began to set the tables for lunch. I was flustered by all of these distractions because I was the person responsible for the space, but that day taught me a major lesson. My anxiety was not shared by the participants. They were completely engrossed in the work.

Although I prefer to work in the best space possible, I find that the vitality of a studio has more to do with the quality of creative *presence* that is generated than the perfection of rooms. Distractions and imperfections may even perversely feed the creative spirit because they are not unlike our often disheveled psyches. There may be a wondrous medicine released by filling an unattractive space with soul's expressions. We "medicine" the disquieted places and this spatial transformation has a corresponding effect on us.

It is strange how showing an aesthetic interest in unattractive situations has an especially potent ability to activate the presence of the creative spirit. I have learned that if I don't want to be somewhere, this condition will show through everything I do.

The process of being present in places that I don't like, and cooperating with them, has taught me about the discipline of desire. My likes and dislikes are usually just an inner dialogue, along with my sometimes neurotic complaining about life. If I am in a situation, there I am. We are bound to each other at that moment. It has me, so why try being somewhere else? The experience in the Washington hotel really delivered this message. I was partnered with a space that I would never have chosen.

I have learned the hard way how painful it is to go somewhere reluctantly, do a lackluster job, and then sit afterward with the feelings of poor performance. These past agonies keep saying to me, "You had better be present when you arrive, and ready to work with whatever is presented." I rarely choose the place and people with whom I work, and this is constantly teaching me how creation is a reciprocal interplay between whatever forces happen to be present in an environment at a particular time.

As with the Washington situation, I sometimes feel over-whelmed or panicked, and I have learned that the only way to trans-form a problem is through an acceptance of the immediate conditions, which allows them to transform themselves. It is an on-going discipline of the soul, which ultimately helps me to relax, accept the limits of a place, and simply do the best I can.

I say to myself, "This is the most important moment in your life"—whether I am running with the dog, putting things into the compost pile, sweeping the floor, or giving a college commencement address. It applies to every conceivable situation.

But it is not all up to me. I am not describing willpower. Being present allows me, the actor, to access the forces being transmitted by the situation. My desire to be there helps me open to *them* and our necessary cooperation. There is an aspect of Eros in this, an exchange of affections, a reciprocal process. As I give to the situa-tion, it infuses me with its spirits.

Maybe it is fascinating for people to make art in the under-ground of a hotel for a day. The place no doubt transmits more unusual spirits than a conventional studio. If my ultimate goal is the sanctification of the ordinary and expanding the boundaries of the creative spirit, then the hotel basement is an appropriate setting for my work. We artists can be the least imaginative people when it comes to expectations about the locus of the creative process. We are so concerned with the control of our idealized environments that we don't see that every place offers its unique spirits to the cooperative interplay of creation. The unusual places are more likely to lead artistic expression into new areas of discovery.

The Washington studio presented me with an environment in which everything happened in a way that was contrary to my vision of how things should be. I became preoccupied with how the space was acting against my intentions. The forces in the environment were knocking me off balance, off center, because I was focused on creating a familiar environment in a place where this was not possible. I wanted something that I carried within myself, and the external context had different ideas. I see what the Buddha is suggesting when he encourages the cessation of desire in order to be present. I feel this way when my work goes well: my whole psyche is attuned to accepting whatever gets thrown at me, because that is the unchangeable nature of that particular engagement. I can accept that the process carries me and everyone else. The discipline is one of presence rather than control. But I would love to talk with the Buddha about desire, about how it might be re-visioned as a discipline of being passionately present wherever I go.

When it comes to the practice of presence, I have the most trouble with faculty meetings. Someone said to me once, "University politics are so intense because there is nothing at stake."

Maybe because I am hopelessly negative toward faculty meetings, I can shift away from my technique of making the meeting the most important thing in "my" life at that moment and instead concentrate on its significance for the people with whom I am involved, for the institution, or even for the room in which we are gathered. If I can get outside my egocentric perspective and focus on the consequence of the event for others, there is a liberation of feelings. I am no longer held captive by the negative attitude. If I have trouble feeling compassion for the people with whom I am involved, the organization, or even the space, then I can focus on a particular thing in the room—a piece of furniture, a coffee cup—and imagine the two of us being in the situation together. Sympathy for the condition of the other, whoever or whatever it may be, transforms the most hardened feelings. How can I create together with this context? How can it take me into unexplored areas of my soul's life? What will happen if I try working with it rather than against it?

I sense that this is the way to practice the presence of love—by seeing the other as the focus of my attention. I am not suggesting that we lose ourselves in the other, in the meeting, the institution, the cause, and forget about our own needs. Nor am I just trying to escape from the personal position from which I inevitably act. All of life's dances are a reciprocal interplay. In creating we need responsive partners attuned to the engagement.

There are many places where we do not want to be present. But right now I am concentrating on those conditions that we cannot avoid, the essential structures of our lives where we are not fully present, or the memories of difficult things that we repress. If something is living in me, I try to become present to its expression, its needs, because it is a vital and unavoidable figure in the ecology of my environment. These difficult situations reveal how the discipline is not so much a matter of "me" being present. It is a matter of me being able to recognize the presence of the immediate condition in which I am situated. As I focus of its presence, I have a revitalized sense of my being. The emphasis is on sensitivity to the otherness in a situation—the presence of soul in the coffee cups on the conference table, the different displays of bodily expressions in chairs, the spontaneous choreography of the event, the configurations of papers on tables, the light coming through the window and the way it touches things and the space holding them, the subtle auras of conversations, the energies passing among people and my visualizations of their invisible movements. I distance myself from feelings and judgments about what people say, and view talk, in and for itself, as soul's expression.

In difficulties with relationships and problematic situations, like my anxiety in the Washington hotel, acceptance is the necessary condition for transformation. If I can go so far as to love the difficult place, then I am really in a position to ride with its energy.

The old religions have so much to teach us about love and the inevitable tedium of existence. Brother Lawrence (1611–1691), a French Carmelite monk who wrote a classic work, *The Practice of the Presence of God*, said, "My most usual method is this simple attention, and such a general passionate regard to God . . . when I apply myself to prayer I feel like my spirit and all my soul lift itself up without any care or effort of mine."

At the age of fifty-five, after living his life as a soldier and footman in a noble family, Brother Lawrence became a cook in a monastery and grew more intimate with God through the performance of ordinary tasks than through traditional prayers and spiritual exercises. His spiritual discipline becomes an appreciation of the sacred presence of every thing. Brother Lawrence described how he felt the presence of God "in the noise and clutter of my kitchen, while several persons are at the same time calling for different things."[15] He embraced everything in life as holy. He felt that our afflictions of the body are "sent to cure those of the soul." When suffering overwhelms us, resistance and hatred may only increase the bitterness, whereas Lawrence talks about how "love sweetens pains."

Creation's magic comes from turning the tables on misfortune. The world is transformed when we envision every possible condition as a potential partner. We create in cooperation with whatever we are dealt. As Ahab mutters in *Moby Dick*, "Here some one thrusts these cards into these old hands of mine; swears that I must play them, and no others."[16]

But what if I just don't want to be in a place? The feeling cannot be avoided. I have learned that if I accept my reluctance to participate, and surrender to the fact that I am there without making a big deal about my negative attitude, the process will always take me into another state of being. Within a relatively short time I become present and engaged. I learned from my early work with group therapy how my bad feelings at the beginning of a group were always transformed by the end of the session if I stepped fully into the psychic streams. The energy of the moment worked on me if I was able to let go of what I brought into the session. Once we "get into it," whatever the activity is, it takes us. The practice of presence is learning how to shift attitudes, like a shaman's discipline of walking between worlds, always moving from one to another. I see in my work how rigid feelings not only keep us isolated from the medicines of presence, but they are exhausting. Resistance is always the doorway to a place where we can empty all of this baggage.

It is hard to rid ourselves of hardened attitudes before entering unpleasant situations. My shortcomings in meetings, my impatience with uncontrollable interruptions like those presented by the session in Washington, have taught me how the discipline of presence is based on entering places with a receptive attitude. If everything is laid out in advance, there is no room for creative movement, for the depths that carry us. Surprises and unexpected things cannot enter. I learn over and over again how to go where the spirits of a situation direct me at the particular moment.

This orientation to following the lead of the creative spirit rather than directing it, has many applications to life.

A newspaper reporter interested in art therapy asks me, "What do you do with a person suffering from cancer?"

I reply, "I treat this person just like any one else in my studio. Your question is framed from within the medical model, which first diagnoses the problem and then prescribes a treatment. I don't do this, but maybe the soul does in my studios, because the cancer, and the soul afflicted by it have a better sense of what they need than I do. I try to create a space in which the soul can minister to itself. But I do help to make the person comfortable, present, and open in the environment, and I do my best to fill it with lively spirits. Art's medicine comes to us *daimonically*, often when we least expect it, and frequently against our wills."

Since the life of the soul affects the body, art does have something to offer the treatment of cancer or any other physical ailment. As Socrates said to Charmides, never treat the body without first engaging the soul. We begin by creating a climate in which the soul is present, and then give it the freedom to act according to its instinctive intelligence.

People who travel on pilgrimages report how the insights of the journey are always far afield of expectations. Things come upon the pilgrim in surprising ways. But there is a universal requirement: a person desiring transformation must get out onto the road and into new environments. The encrusted ways of habit have to be broken, and this alters a person's chemistry. In taking a hike to a favorite natural environment, walking on a city street, visiting a friend, or going to church, we cultivate a salubrious force that finds its way to us in different ways. We place ourselves in an environment with a desire to receive what it has to offer, which is rarely subject to our control.

As keeper of the studio, my primary function is to kindle the soul of the place, to maintain its vitality and its ability to engage people in different ways. Going into a studio can be likened to visiting an oracle, a temple, or the healing place of Asklepios, where the person simply sleeps in order to dream and receive whatever contents the nocturnal messages deliver. We go in with an openness to the spirits of the place and how they will affect us. Different environments and substances will generate remedies unique to their natures.

When I teach, I try to initiate movement and then step back as it takes us along. I have learned that if I get too involved with what I am thinking, or with what I think the situation needs, I will miss the actual contents of the moment revealing itself. There is a self-control in following the other person, the conversation, and the more general movements of the place. It is a paradoxical art of controlling and not controlling at the same time.

Like midwives, we assist the soul in delivering its contents, and constantly making itself anew. It is the soul's nature to keep moving and to be out of reach as it paradoxically passes through us. I like the metaphor of the midwife because she serves the arrivals of others.

But the process also involves engaging things once they arrive. I follow archetypal psychology's simple dictum, "Stick to the image."

Nothing has helped me more. That line is the guiding angel of my work. The images emanating from our souls have a deep purposefulness and sensitive sense of direction. Following the lead of images and situations is not to be dismissed as directionless. It is like a prayer of presence. I try to stay in contact with the thing before me, the place where I am. It will show me what it needs and where we need to go, if I can concentrate on its being, and trust it.

Creating with the world ....

All objects and happenings in the universe are for
thinking with.   —Elizabeth Sewell

Creating is a participation mystique of many things. Yet we still think of creation as something that comes almost exclusively from within the artist. In my experience it is the other way around. The fertile creator is the one who is sensitive to the expressions and suggestive spirits of environments, things, gestures, relationships, and events. The idea that the creative spirit is within us may be the most restrictive notion of all, because it discourages bold and inquisitive relations with the material world.

The contemplation of any physical thing becomes an opening to creation. Children are ingenious at this. Watch them in the sand, in the water, playing on a spacious lawn. They move with materials, in contrast to self-conscious adults who can't let go of their inhibiting restraints in order to follow the lead of paints, clay, or wooden blocks. We adults put too much emphasis on control, and we don't know how to let the materials move the mover. Virtually any five-year-old can paint with spontaneity and imagination, whereas there are few adults capable of freely accessing these expressions. Children can teach us how to look at a thing with delight in its being and our reciprocal presence, never asking, "What does it say about the person who made it?" The child looks through the eyes of the angel.

If we look through something other than ourselves, the object of our contemplation becomes a partner, an earth angel, that helps access the free flow of the creative spirit. When I enter the stream of creation, I discover how it connects things to one another in new ways.

I can look at life from the perspective of an avocado, its round curves, sensuous contents, thin skin, and hard core.

I can engage any object and mine its veins into soul—a poem I wrote or one written by another person, a favorite series of photographs, a letter I received, a piece of music, a collection that has been kept for many years.

As with the avocado, I can work with the first thing that comes across my path and which has no apparent relationship to my psyche. The clock on the wall might be more helpful than my most precious object, because there are few preconceptions, and the object of contemplation reaches out to make fresh connections to my life.

The earth angel lives in the simultaneous presence of the image, its thingness, and the way it relates to other experiences, things we have done before and those yet to occur. Like a dream, it is a "gathering" that is wondrously present in itself, while relating to what has been, and will be. The quality that I describe as the earth angel exists in these links between things. One thing grows out of the energy of another, and the creator is the go-between. Nothing springs into the world as a ready-made, complete entity. Dreams are probably made in a similar way. Memories, feelings, places, and the distinct architecture of the individual soul gather into assemblies and psychic events that I call soulscapes.

As with dreams, the gathering takes place outside the scope of consciousness, and we seldom see the subtle and intimate connections to our lives. We filter the abundance of stimuli offered by the external world according to the instinctual gathering of the soulscape, and these acts are rarely intentional. The soulscape constructs itself, and like any organism, pathological or healthy, it takes in what feeds its being. The scenes are kinetic and always presenting themselves with a fresh face.

Sometimes the gathering requires a corresponding material effort, affecting the soul through the body. It demands more than a casual conversation with an avocado or a clock on the wall.

Not too long ago I was depressed about a lack of direction and desire in my life. I went out in my yard and dug out several tons of a small hill and built a large stone retaining wall. A back hoe could have dug up the area in a few hours, but I had to get my body involved. The mail carrier smiled and said to my wife, "He's a man possessed."

During and after the job I aesthetically contemplated the construction from every possible direction. Friends insisted that a professional must have built the wall, so there is some connection between artistic quality and therapeutic gratification. Somewhere in my genes there must be a Celtic builder of stone walls wanting to get back to work. I had fantasies of a new career.

My children tuned in to my fixation and teased me whenever we approached the granite opus. They said, "Would you look at that wall! Isn't it amazing!" In time "the wall" became one of the most animated and exalted figures in our household. It was full of medicine and spirits.

Let's stick to my image of the stone wall. My attachment to it was unusual. My children noticed this. I treasured the image of the wall inside my soul as well as the actual wall along our driveway. There was a vital and imaginative interaction between the two, an aesthetic entrancement. I contemplated it from every possible angle on the ground and from each of the three stories of the house. Each window gave a distinctly different view.

It has been three years since I built the wall. We have sold the house and moved to another, yet that image lives on with a distinct vitality.

Someone says, "It's just a stone wall. Big deal. You're obsessive."

I do have an obsession with the wall. As I reflect now, I realize that last winter on a cold January day, I went out and took photographs of the stone walls and granite formations that surround the new house where I live. Our home is situated in a rich glacial area, marked by configurations of granite, natural and manmade. Just outside my studio there is a mini-Stonehenge-like configuration. I left the beloved wall at the old house, but the new place is even more dramatically placed in relation to rock spirits.

If we look deeply into ourselves, we will see how the soul constellates itself in material images that gather together varied strands of our psychic lives. To realize is to materialize and to bring imagination full circle to the generation of its spirits from physical things. My experience with stone walls offers an example of how this works. I can do the same thing with sand, houses, cars, ginger ale, a turnip, or a yellow No. 2 pencil.

Looking at life according to my relationship to stone requires that I re-vision the world through the imagination of a material substance. Because it is distinctly other than me, the perspective of stone demands a new and creative response. Gaston Bachelard felt that there are phantoms corresponding to physical substances and that their power depends upon the extent to which "they are faithful to their matter."[17] This vision is close to Henry Corbin's use of the active imagination to perceive the earth and all of its things in the presence of their respective angels. Bachelard's dual interests in poetry and the philosophy of science led him to a "psychoanalysis of the elements" which contemplates how the subjective qualities of matter manifest our souls.

The imagination of stone is an intriguing way to contemplate earth angels because there is probably nothing more basic, material, apparently lifeless, and contrary to the conventional idea of an angel as a transparent being of reverie and flight. I would like to show how the imagination can fly in the company of dense stone. Although the making of new lives and visions is an eternal and precious function of imagination, I am more interested here in how it functions as the faculty for appreciating the unseen spirits attached to common things.

Ordinary, heavy stone will test the belief that angels fly out from everything in the physical world. Few of us have difficulty associating reverie with a waterfall, a gentle stream, moving clouds, campfires, candles, a flower garden, an expansive vista, or a majestic stony seascape, perhaps because we are more eager to incorporate the spirits attached to their beings. Common stone is less likely to move people into reverie. Stones located in gardens or in pools of water and streams are commonly associated with pleasant imaginings because they take on the qualities of their environments, which soften and embellish the pure substance.

When I look at life in relation to stone, there is a sense of partnership and mutual influence, an exchange of spirits that is the basis of my understanding of earth angels. Stone functions as a leitmotiv in my imagination and it opens to the larger spectrum of the psychic field. The stone becomes a shaman's doorway, a passage that draws us into other chambers of memory and imagination. One inspiration leads to another.

I journey into the imagination of stone, letting myself go with the spirits it carries. The same thing happens when I meditate on a painting, person, or place. The structure of the image carries expressions that stimulate me when I open to their imagination. They both contain and inspire imagining. It is an intimate and safe relationship where partners hold one another and concretize the spirit. The things of the external world are made into soulscapes through what Allan Gussow describes as "the process of experiencing deeply . . . A place is a piece of the whole environment that has been claimed by feelings."[18]

Herman Melville begins *Moby Dick* with a reverie on water. He described how "water-gazers" are forever led to rivers, oceans, and lakes that function as partners in meditation. We all see "the same image" in the water, what Melville described as "the image of the ungraspable phantom of life; and this is the key to it all." Melville explored the sea, which corresponds to the perpetual movement and spaciousness of the imagination, while its deep waters hold the mysteries of the soul. The same vastness and depth of space can be imagined in any substance or object which yields an endless stream of possibilities through imaginal reverie.

Gaston Bachelard felt that the material imagination is based on the experience of giving a "dual existence" to matter.[19] The thing is simultaneously a rock together with an endless series of poetic counterparts, or spirits, that spring from it.

The object opens me to the imagination. We experience the psychological interiority of a substance through reverie because, as Bachelard said, a person "does not arouse dreams by describing." If I dream with a simple rock, it becomes my angelic partner. It joins me to the powers of material things and their spirits.

Ordinary people might be more involved with stone spirits than we realize. But these relationships are not part of our regular discourse, perhaps because the truly deep and symbolic mainstreams flow through us in silence, below the utterances of prosaic speech.

I read recently in the *Gloucester Daily Times* that a million dollars had been raised by the city to repair the Lane's Cove breakwater constructed from blocks of granite chiseled in the early 1840s. Because the five- to eight-ton blocks of stone have not been able to withstand the force of storm tides over the past hundred and fifty years, there is a plan to protect the outside of the breakwater with reinforced concrete. The people of Lanesville were alarmed that the shape and granite face of the historic breakwater would be altered. The following passage from the paper makes me realize that my affections for stone may be more universal than idiosyncratic: "Lanesville people were reassured that as original blocks of stone were removed to work the reinforced concrete in place, the stones would be replaced exactly as they were. It seems that most villagers are familiar with each stone in the breakwater and they don't want them out of place when it is completed."[20]

The granite configurations of the Lanesville breakwater are symbols of the community where quarries and maritime industries flourished in the nineteenth century. The stones carry memories of the past for the entire village and the individual people whose lives were formed in proximity to them. And the structure continues as a living force, an aesthetic environment, a breaking point between the sea and the village.

Each of us can take an archetypal substance like stone and reflect on our lives through images of it. I see the gray stones of the Gothic buildings on my college campus. Education is remembered as a time of stone enclosures, formidable edifices, and a pervasive hardness. The process was not soft and flexible. It was a cool and stony discipline, a hardening. I never thought about schooling in this way before. Stone does offer a new and elemental perspective.

I recall the smooth and large rocks in the first "serious" painting I made as a child. It is a serene water scene with a man rowing. I remember the rock cliff near my childhood home, the rocky face of the old man of the mountain when my grandparents took me to New Hampshire for the first time, sitting on curbs with other boys waiting for a ride, old cobblestones showing through holes in the asphalt of a Salem street, the rocks that hurt my feet when I went into the ocean as a child in the years before synthetic beach shoes, the rock on the beach next to our house where my mother liked to lie in the sun (we called it "mother's rock"), climbing over the rugged granite that edged the neck of land where we lived separating Beverly and Salem harbors, tidepools in the rocks, my rock garden, the jasper stones I collected with my children in Maine, the warm aura of white Jerusalem stone that puts me into a spell when I am there, the wet gray stone of Galway and the National University of Ireland where I visited for a semester, the freely made walls of stone that I saw everywhere in the west of Ireland.

In the west of Ireland I carried on a sustained meditation on the rocky environment. The soul of Connemara is inseparable from the stone, and the walls express human interaction with the land. The omnipresence of their irregular shapes and invariable gray and coarse rock are for me the most distinct expressions of the region.

I emulate the spirits of this free and natural movement, and for weeks I tried to draw stone walls while looking at them along the borders of fields and roads. Each stone made its unique contribution to configurations that moved through the landscape. I went back and forth between contemplating the shapes and placements of individual stones and how they fell into line with the overall pattern of rocks.

I traveled into the Connemara hills and bogs every day on an old bicycle with drawing materials packed inside my coat. I spent months admiring the walls and experiencing them from every conceivable perspective, just as I did with the wall I made at home.

When I consciously tried to draw the stones on my expeditions, my pictures were stiff and contrived. At some point it occurred to me that I could draw the walls with the same spontaneous gestures and energies that constitute their natures and the way they were built. I stopped looking directly at the walls and remembered them through my feelings. When I tried to "describe" the walls through my pictures, there was no life, no angelic counterpart. Things lose their soul if depicted too literally.

In any creation there is a meeting between the participants where they give of themselves to a new life. When we look directly at an object through the eyes of the soul, we bring our own spirits and those of the atmosphere to a gathering that I describe as a soulscape. When an object is depicted without this interplay of influences, seen and unseen, it is no wonder that it does not give a sense of soulful enthusiasm that corresponds to our perception of the wall.

The aesthetic contemplation of any object is full of spirits and subtle expressions emanating from the physical structure. The most direct observations of things involve the experiencing of qualities that cannot be literally described. If I am inspired by a wall, I echo its being and express myself in a way that corresponds to its construction. I resonate with the wall, and my expression is a transformation that carries traces of our respective beings. It is not an exact imitation.

The shift in my drawings of the walls came when I expressed their qualities through the medium of imaginative expression and my stored feelings about them. My lifelong impressions of stone were able to flow into the drawings. Immediate observations of the Connemara walls were mixed with personal experiences of making stone walls and other rock configurations in Massachusetts, from childhood through the present.

A soulful expression of stone is not an exact duplication or literal depiction. It requires the distortions and exaggerations that come from our deeply felt communion with the thing and its spirits. In this sense we create together with material things. We imagine with them, and with our memories. When I am deeply engrossed in imaginative work, it feels like a black hole that draws every strand of related life experience and knowledge into its being. I cannot enter the deep zone of imagination if I am too involved in daily business and projects. If the unplanned interconnections and daimonic discoveries of imagination are to appear, I have to give myself up to the process, essentially sacrificing myself to their intentions. I let go of my attachments and dream with the creative work. The deeper I go, the more it deconstructs my habitual life, and I either fly with the angels of exultation or struggle with the demons of a dense nothingness. Yet even in this state of abandon, the process of imagining is always connected to the initiatives of things and my cooperation with them. As Bachelard says, "Each contemplated object, each evocative name we murmur is the point of departure of a dream. . . ."[21]

In creative expression we travel from things and with them, but I have to hold the original stimulus loosely, giving it room to transform itself through the journey we take together. As a sailor once said to me, "Keep a soft hand on the tiller." Rigid control keeps the angels of imagination at bay.

Pictures and other creations are worlds unto themselves that are only related to the things that inspired them. As soon as I realized that I could never replicate the walls in a picture, I had a new appreciation of their expression and qualities. I saw them more completely through my inability to re-create them.

When I stopped trying to depict the walls, I came closer to their spirits. I imagined them with quick and impulsive strokes of my pen. There was a correspondence between my movement and the gestures made by the shapes of the stones. Rather than representing the walls, I painted as a child does, and "made them up."

As I became like them, everything changed. Instead of "reproducing" the objects of imagination and the things of the world, I tried to immerse myself in their spirits—to paint in a way that corresponded to the infinite variations of contact between the irregularly shaped stones. When I realized that I could draw "like the stones," it was liberating to continuously "make up" new forms rather than construct stiff and self-conscious replications. As I internalized the randomness of the rock's formations, everything came together and I couldn't stop making them. In addition to emulating the formation of the individual rocks, there also had to be a sense of how they related to one another in an overall pattern of the landscape, so I moved as they do along meandering roads and flowing hills. Accessing these expressive qualities of things can be likened to painting like a dream rather than academically depicting the contents of a dream. As I imbibe the spirits of the landscape, their structures are the basis of my imagining.

This is the way earth angels act through me. I meditate on the tangible expressions of the physical world, receive the influx of their spirits, and become more like them. They are my partners and guides. Creating is a cooperation with the expressions of the world. The vitality of my creation is influenced by the extent to which I open and respond to them.

I recall the pleasure I felt making the Connemara stone walls long after I left Ireland. It was only after leaving the country that I really got the sense of the walls' improvisational configurations. This is in keeping with the adage that drawing a thing from memory is more apt to be soulfully expressive than a direct rendering. Distance from the literal thing enables it to be reconstituted in imagination, where its actual characteristics merge with our personal impressions. The communion is freer because the restraints of the literal presence are gone. It is when I feel strongly attached to something that I am most apt to forget the way creative expression works. I fall in love with the image I see in the world and try to keep it intact in my drawing or poem, not realizing the impossibility of the effort.

I let the walls go in order to rediscover them again in my art. The physical structures of the muse have to join with the style of my gestures, and the distinct spirits of my expressions, to make a new experience of Connemara stone walls.

Drawings, photographs, and other meditations respond to the expression of the material world which acts upon me. When I look at an actual wall, I try to aesthetically inhale its atmosphere and the qualities of the material substance continue to influence my thoughts and feelings through memory. The spirit of the thing seems to clearly shape my experience. The world is constantly making me.

Reality is a collaboration between inner psychic experience and the outer physical world. Perceptual experience is the intermediary. Yet there are many people who believe that human consciousness makes things expressive. John Kensett (1816–1872), an American painter affiliated with the Hudson River school, made the following statement:

> *Things* are nothing but what the *mind* constitutes them, nothing, but by an infusion with them of the intellectual principle of our nature [it is] thus this humble habitation becomes a shrine of continued worship—which otherwise would be passed by unregarded and without a thought and thus the most indifferent, and of itself unvalued thing—be it but the fragment of a rock, a broken weapon, a tattered raiment, a decayed branch, or a simple leaf,—receiving a spiritual touch, is rendered an object of intense interest, a relic, priceless as memory.[22]

I am in complete sympathy with Kensett's apotheosis of simple things that usually go unnoticed. I also accept the important role of the mind in appreciating and giving spirit to things. But his statement also reveals the one-sided attitude that it is only the mind that conveys spirit. Ensoulment, or inspiriting, is for me a reciprocal process between the person and the thing perceived. They influence one another with their attentions.

The material substances of the world shape inner life. It strikes me that the insistence that "*things* are nothing but what the *mind* constitutes them" is an inversion of the real source of soul in our lives. Objects and places construct our aesthetic beings and the contents of our imaginations. As Ralph Waldo Emerson said, "Things are in the saddle and ride mankind." I am but a humble witness to the display of their expressions. How can a person "make" the expression of a natural place that affects thousands, or millions, of people in much the same way?

Even now as I remember the stone walls of Connemara, I am drawn into *their* spaces, led along *their* paths, immersed in the abundance of *their* stones and open spaces. I am filled with the imagination they carry within themselves and offer to me as their witness.

I anticipate what lies around the bend in the road. I imagine what it is like to drive a car on these narrow and unpaved Irish passageways that wind extensively through the atmosphere. I am filled with airs of spaciousness and solitude. I can hear the wind. Like the cows and bushes, I stay close to the stone walls for protection. I imagine myself walking down the road and kicking one of the stones. The road beckons. I want to see more stone wall configurations. I wish I was there riding a mountain bike through the rugged landscape.

The serpentine patterns of the stone walls make me realize that the best environmental art works I have ever seen are spread across the Connemara hills. There are so many stones, so many walls covering the mountain. They express a fullness to me, an infinity carried within themselves.

I reflect on these landscapes with the eye of an artist. But I can imagine a farmer looking at a newly constructed wall with feelings of visual delight, just the way I felt after building the stone wall along my driveway. The aesthetic sensibility is in no way restricted to the consciousness of art. I feel great excitement in looking at a freshly painted fence, a newly mowed lawn, the fruit growing in a garden, or a cleanly swept floor. Even when looking at the most functional creations, there are moments when the thing seizes the viewer with an aesthetic appreciation of its pure being, what Emmanuel Kant described as a sense of the thing unto itself.

I remember stone houses that display the skills of working with stone. Where the stone walls of the countryside convey free spirits, the stone buildings in Irish villages express containment, protection, and the focusing of energy on a particular place. The walls of the building appear thick and cool and they make me wonder what is inside them. The houses feel earthbound, stationary, and fixed to their particular places, whereas the country walls give a sense of movement, action, coming and going, a partnership between the land and the heavens. The soul needs both its enclosures and open spaces, the fixed stones of the house and those of the wandering field.

My reflections on Connemara stone walls are an interplay between their structural qualities and the responses they evoke from me. My mind does not constitute them or their characteristics. Their aesthetic appeal is actually due to the inversion of "mind over matter." The walls are made by stones that were probably lying nearby, or exhumed through the cultivation of the land. The existence of the material suggested the structures, in keeping with Sir Herbert Read's notion that image precedes idea.[23] The stones tell us what to do with them.

In the case of these Irish labyrinths, there can be no suggestion that the idea of the partition preceded the existence of the material. As I walked through Connemara fields, it seemed that the walls might have even come into existence as a way of laying aside rocks unearthed by digging and plowing the land.

The walls feel as much like pure matter in its most natural state as any human construction I have seen. They are made by freely piling stones on top of one another, with gravity rather than visual appearances, being the prevailing force in their formation. The fortuitousness of their construction is their most prominent perceptual feature. The method of building allows each stone to keep much of its overall appearance while simultaneously participating in the whole. The unplanned openings created by spaces between the rocks further their stability by allowing the harsh west winds to pass through.

I am especially attracted to the casual expression of the walls. They don't take themselves too seriously and their builders were not overly concerned with exact measurements, straight lines, precise angles, and other qualities of mathematical engineering. The walls give the sense that they go as they please and their relations with property lines and other boundaries are relaxed. What would be considered imperfections in the walls according to a meticulous perspective on construction, accounts for their formal attraction.

This low-tech contracting and minimal humanization of the land suits my sensibility, together with the way a culture and an entire region is defined by such an archaic continuity of form and material. The infrequent stone houses of the countryside are made with a similar simplicity and consistent design that fits right into the overall composition of the landscape. The sparse population, in terms of both people and trees, furthers the prominence of the walls that rove unbridled through the hills and fields.

The walls evoke strong aesthetic feelings and yet this is not the purpose of their construction. They are totally without pretense and self-consciousness, in contrast to the way many contemporary architectural and artistic fabrications situate themselves in environments.

Compare the humble and self-effacing display of the Irish walls to things demanding our attentions and regulating our actions through their structures and placements. Every configuration expresses its nature and carries traces of the consciousness and intent of its maker. The Irish walls suggest an instinctual cooperation between their makers and the earth, whereas so many of our contemporary forms are uneasy, self-conscious, willful, and intent on asserting themselves with absolutely no consideration for their surroundings.

I don't want to extend political correctness to art and architecture by suggesting a "natural law" of environmental construction that discourages the making of strange spaces. From a broader perspective, we need all kinds of constructions, bizarre ones together with pastoral simplicity, and the West of Ireland is the paragon of the latter. It is a preserved sanctuary where commerce has done relatively little to change the landscape because of its barren and rocky constitution. Returning again to the imagination of stones, we can see them as the protectors or even saviors of the archaic soul of the place. Their presence shapes not only my aesthetic reaction, but the history of a region.

Another person will see different things in the walls and perhaps similarities to my comments, but this fecundity of possibilities conveyed by stone configurations, paired with the varied interpretive positions of viewers, is not to be confused with the notion that perceivers create the walls. The creative act is a partnership between persons and the physical expressions of the world.

John Kensett's nineteenth-century statement, "*Things* are nothing but what the *mind* constitutes them," is deeply embedded in our psychologies and attitudes toward the physical world. D. W. Winnicott, a British psychoanalyst, writes: "The individual only communicates with a self-created world and the people in the environment only communicate with the individual insofar as they create him or her."[24]

This view implies that people communicate primarily within themselves, and never as full partners with the things of nature, in a relationship where each participant gives of its unique nature to the other. It seems natural for the person who begins to sink deeply into analysis with Winnicott to feel the unreality of the world. "Experience is a constant trafficking in illusion," because the world is viewed from the perspective of illusion. The entire fabric of this type of analysis is based upon a self-referenced world, detached and foreign. No wonder alienation has been a psychic theme of our twentieth century.

Eros leaves when we no longer make contact with a material and living environment. Consciousness becomes entangled in itself. Participation is a more sensible way of looking at what actually happens in daily life than illusion. Reciprocity between our thoughts and the expressions of the world furthers creation, productivity, and health. We need the earth, its people and things.

Intimate relations require a poetic sensibility and a vivid sense of otherness. Gaston Bachelard felt the soul "suffers from a deficiency of material imagination," and he wished that scientists and philosophers could read the poets in order to deepen their contact with the world. He says, "The object designates us more than we designate it . . . scientific objectivity is possible only after one breaks with the immediate object."[25] The perspective of illusion needs a more physical relationship with the earth.

In my work in helping people relate creatively to their lives, the primary obstacle is the way everything in dreams and artworks is referred back to themselves. The self simply takes up too much space and doesn't leave room for others. I am always trying to help people say to their creations, "For this moment, not me, but you. How can I relate more imaginatively to the new life you carry within yourself, and let it remake my soul?"

We forget how soul lives in the physical world, and that when we lose contact with things, we lose soul. Through creative reflection on the simplest substances, we will remake the world by regenerating its things and ourselves with them. Our fates are joined.

Things to do ....

ART

• The idea that art is a treasured, rarified, and private object does not have to oppose the aesthetic appreciation of common experience. Art is many things and it serves different needs. Find a common object—a stone, a leaf, a piece of natural wood—and keep it in a special place. Add other objects and change the contents from time to time. This ritual reveals how any thing has unique qualities. The objects become treasures through the attention given to them.

• Either cut out a small rectangular opening in a piece of cardboard or imagine that you are looking at the world through a limited frame. The enclosed perspective will further the perception of things in two dimensions, and this will enable you to look at things as though they are the surfaces of a painting. When you look at the trunk of a tree through this frame, you will see the texture of the bark as an artistic composition. The same thing happens when you look at grass, a stone wall, a rock, the grain in a piece of wood, books on a shelf, or the side of a house.

• Look through a larger frame at sections of a table or areas within a room and you will see how the artist makes the composition of a painting. View things like walls in two dimensions and contrast these views to hallways and other spaces that accentuate the third dimension.

These exercises will help you observe the expressive qualities of things that you would not normally see.

• Imagine looking at a thing or a place from a metaperspective which is not tied to a particular position in space, two or three dimensions, a specific time, or any of the restrictions of physical relativity. This transcendence of time and space will connect you to the spiritual qualities of matter, viewed simultaneously from many different vantage points. The thing is more than what meets your eye from a particular perspective.

• Involve the poetic imagination by asking how the objects feel about this attention you are giving them? Did they like it better with you were less involved in their lives, when you stayed out of their space? Are they self-conscious? Do some like it better than others? Or are the objects totally free and generous in their self-expression? Are they happy to be acknowledged, to have their radiations received, to be warmed by your eyes and touch?

• Spend fifteen minutes moving more slowly than you normally do. When you reach for an object, do it slowly and concentrate on the gesture. Experience your most basic body movements as a dance, a dramatic expression of a gesture.

• Get yourself set up with art supplies, close your eyes, and make simple gestures on a piece of paper. Go on to other sheets of paper and express other feelings and movements. Vary the materials you use and notice their different feel. Continue making these gestures with your eyes open. Don't try to control the gesture and make something that you see in your mind. Let the movement manifest itself through you. Concentrate on your feeling and its expression.

Try making these gestures on large and small surfaces. When you work big, use your entire body to make the gesture. Move from your feet, thighs, back, shoulders, and both arms. Don't get overly involved with your fingers and your hands; use them together with other parts of your body. Try to access the same totality of bodily expression even when you make very small pictures.

Meditate on these images. Look at each gesture as an unique spirit. Watch how the different marks interact with one another and the surrounding surface. Imagine these simple gestures as angels and they will become fascinating carriers of expression.

If you want to spend time making art, keep working on a gesture and shape it into an image that grows from the original movement.

THE MUSEUM

• Art objects may need more help than the things in the mall when it comes to experiencing their angelic natures. Spontaneity is cherished in the physical act of shaping an image where we expect sudden seizures and unexpected arrivals, but interpretations of art are believed to follow pedantic rules.

People don't look at a new Volkswagen and say, "What does it mean?" They instinctively know how to meditate on it and imagine its existence. But when it comes to objects of art, we try to read them through Freud or an art critic whose column we read in the paper. We don't have to go to these expert interpreters to understand how we feel about a blue sky, a red silk dress, or a beautifully prepared meal.

Reflect on a painting in your house or in a magazine without any regard for meanings. Try experiencing it in a purely sensual way. Look at it in the same way you approached stone, wood, and other natural substances through your rectangular viewer. If it is a three-dimensional picture of a scene, look at it two-dimensionally, and vice versa.

• Go to a museum and look at a painting that portrays a scene of some kind, preferably one that is freely made like a Rubens, Delacroix, or Chagall. Try looking at it simultaneously on two frequencies, as a representation and as pure form and color. Enjoy the interactive movement of the double dimension that goes from one way of looking to another. When we think about a picture only as subject matter, or as telling a story, we miss the material vitality and the purely physical spirits of paint, formal relations, and color.

This sense of multiple presence is essential to my vision of the earth angel. Paintings cannot be reduced to a singular dimension.

Many things happen at once, and each quality contributes to the vitality of the other. The way figures in a painting generate its visual expression can be likened to Henry Corbin's reference to how earthly things have a double nature as sensible forms and angels. The figures and scenes of a composition—people, fields, animals, streets, rooms—are carriers of forces that are completely other than what I have described as their representational factuality. The angelic expressions of the artwork are not hidden or inside the forms. They are the surfaces and aural qualities that transmit subtle spirits to the viewer.

If you keep looking at "representational" art in this way, you will see the movement in a picture as an elemental force. Expressive pictures of recognizable figures carry themselves as pure structure, as though they are "nonrepresentational." It is the genuine spirits and expressions of the medium that give life to a picture. Figures are a way of getting to these wholly structural expressions because neither of the two qualities can become overbearing. Each of the partners guards against the excesses of the other. When they fully realize their double functions as imaginal characters and expressive material, the dichotomy between representation and abstraction is dissolved.

Enjoy the way a good painting expresses itself simultaneously on two levels, with the imagination of a scene interacting with the purely formal qualities of the composition. Go back and forth between the two, just as if the painting were a stone wall or a tree whose textures you are contemplating.

• Select a "nonrepresentational" painting by Mark Rothko, Helen Frankenthaler, or Jackson Pollack. Look at it the same way you would approach any object from nature from a purely formal basis, up close or from a great distance. Demystify the art object and see it as though it were a configuration in the earth outside your house; and conversely, mystify the earth to experience its expressive qualities. This shifting of perspectives is the basis of the earth angel, which disappears as soon as I am restricted to one way of looking at something.

The term "abstract art" is an oxymoron, because pictures are physical and take us into the essential being of matter. They don't necessarily go "inside" the material word, but rather help us see the textures of its face with more sensitivity. The idea of "abstract art" requires a dualistic worldview. Everything from a natural configuration of stones to an imaginative painting is both a material and spiritual presence. We tend to go through life, looking only at the superficial idea of the thing and never open to the distinct qualities of its expressive and material spirits as experienced through our individual sensibility. This is the way of the earth angels where matter and spirit create together and deepen the imagination of the world.

I have always felt that "abstract expressionist" compositions of sheer painterly movement, color, form, and textures, are carriers of the primal spirits in things. These pictures are the most physical form of painting, expressing essential substance and hard core earth angels, spirits without any pretense of human form.

• If you want to experience the auras of a painting, look at it as a whole without focusing on any one thing. The colors and forms will start to vibrate with one another, and you will become part of the energetic field. My sense of an aura is a distinctive quality, the perceptual "airs" generated by the painting as distinguished from the aureole, a radiant light surrounding a heavenly body, which is heightened by haze.

PHOTOGRAPHY

The photographic image holds a view of the world and distinguishes it from the ephemeras. The photo sits for us, keeping itself constant, as we change. It becomes our witness and simultaneously furthers our ability to appreciate the expressions of physical things.

After a lifetime of viewing photographs, I am still delighted by the magical way they frame a situation and help me see so much more in it. The camera preserves the imagery of instants and reveals the vast expression taking place in the most ordinary environments.

• Cameras can become allies in appreciating the world. They open the soul's eye and its desire for images. Freezing rain has been falling for the past two days, and I feel trapped and depressed until I look out the window through the camera to see the wonders of bushes and trees covered with ice. I go outside and walk through the village, witnessing nature's art that will pass with tomorrow's sun.

• Take a camera into the most ordinary place, or an environment that you find unattractive. Rather than taking pictures of the entire scene, photograph details, closeups, and parts of the environment. Selecting images in this way will draw you into an aesthetic relationship with the place. You will open to its expressive spirits. The pictures will show you the forms, textures, and illuminations that you do not normally see because your eyes and your soul are not usually open to these places.

• Imagine your camera as a field apparatus used to both stalk and unwittingly receive images, as an intermediary that helps us interact with the expressions of the world through snaps shots that hold instants.

Contemplate photographs as images that collect and return soul to the world. Look at them as witnesses to the way every object and environment expresses itself to those who take the time to look with an open and receptive eye.

• Give yourself themes to photograph. Go looking for circles in the environment. Photograph hubcaps, fire hydrant caps, and other circular shapes as though they were mandalas. Look for groups of things, and frame your photos in a way that emphasizes the visual expression of groups—for example, a picket fence cropped so that you see nothing above, below, or to the side of the pickets. Look for pairs of things, threesomes, foursomes, large groups, and so forth. Identify symmetrical designs like leaves and asymmetrical patterns in stone walls and other configurations.

• In addition to your carefully composed images, take pictures at random, with as little planning as possible.

A friend gave my four-year-old daughter a camera with an automatic flash and told her she could take pictures freely in our living room. In addition to the sensation of looking through the camera, the sounds of the machine and the illuminations of the flash were an experience in themselves. When the prints arrived, I was fascinated with the totally spontaneous images of the child's eye. By adult standards her compositions were disjointed, imbalanced, and uncentered, but these observations only made me appreciate them more as unbiased images from the child's eye. She caught whatever appearances interested her without the constraints of adult composition.

Even with the instantaneous magic of photography, we frame the images according to our interests and styles of looking— centered, balanced, close or distant, isolated or crowded, vertical, horizontal, serene, or agitated. The way in which the young child's photos involved minimal interpretive composition immediately revealed the extent to which we adults shape what we see. Her pictures framed only one side of the fireplace and mantel, as contrasted to my centered images, with vertical lines rising and falling far afield of the ninety-degree angles to which I am unconsciously accustomed.

• Consider doing the things I suggest without a camera. Photography is the medium par excellence for reflecting on how things express themselves and how the viewer's perspective determines what is seen. If you are not interested in the actual process of taking pictures, use the principles of photography as a way of viewing and imagining the world. In other words, look at life as a photographer, and watch the illuminations and the display.

Take a walk down a street and be aware of the infinity of potential images. Try to simply focus on whatever engages your attention and do your best to open to its expression.

• In taking photographs of my children, I will often take a roll of film of closeups in order to get one or two pictures that aesthetically catch their essential image and expression at that moment. The successful pictures are always the ones where the face and body are relaxed, open to the camera, and in a mutually supportive position with the surrounding environment.

Explore the subtle changes in the gestures of a face by taking a 24-exposure roll of color film and snapping a fast series of pictures of your child, spouse, or friend. I will sometimes follow this series immediately with a roll of black and white film, which captures a completely different atmosphere of the same situation. The different films express the different ways objects express themselves and the varied sensitivities of the surfaces receiving their expression. Black and white film is a more transformative medium which makes an image farther removed from the actual appearance of the subject. When I take color photos, I like to use slide film because the projected image magnifies like an aesthetic microscope. I often take my fast series of pictures with a 36-exposure roll, and I am forever amazed at the endless possibilities for expression in what appears to be the same situation. I see more subtle variations in closeups of people than I do in pictures taken from a distance where the person becomes an object in an environment. In the closeup, the person's face and upper body expression are the field within which there are endless nuances and gradations.

I like to vary my series of portraits with images exclusively of faces, upper-body images that catch the expressions of hands, and full-body images. In taking many pictures, I see how what appears to be the same position offers endless variations. The camera witnesses the kinetic nature of soul and deepens my appreciation of subtle expression.

• Look at an object or place from a variety of perspectives and notice how slight changes in point of view can change your relationship to something. With each change of viewpoint, the object expresses itself differently. Meditate on how it presents itself from a metaperspective displaying every possible angle at once. Imagine your own body expressing itself in this way. In order to do this meditation, you must imagine the world from the perspective of a thing, something distinctly other than your habitual way of viewing life.

• As a photographer, imagine yourself in a partnership with your subjects. Watch how your emotional involvement in their expressions furthers their cooperation with you. Let them know that you need them to be involved and that you are not there just to skim the surface with a quick take, even though your pictures might be made in the flash of a second. Watch how your respect for the subject and your interest in its expression affects what you see and receive in the photograph.

4
Topsy-Turvy

Inverted perspectives ....

To live in the world but outside of existing conceptions of it.
. . . The thing seen becomes the thing unseen. The opposite
is, or seems to be, impossible.   —Wallace Stevens, *Adagia*

The creative process thrives on the inversion of habitual thoughts. When I reverse a fixed point of view, such as the location of value exclusively in the light and not in the dark, I open to alternative ways of looking, and I see how custom and bias can hinder a more comprehensive interpretation of a particular situation. Practically everything I say about earth angels is an inversion of conventional ideas, especially my focus on the spirits of material things.

I take the term "inverted perspective" from Rudolf Arnheim, who showed how Picasso and other painters inverted the perspective of a painting to heighten expression and visual movement while also offering a more comprehensive display of a situation or thing.[1] For example, a table drawn from a convergent perspective hides the sides, which are shown from an inverted view. Convergence draws the eye and imagination toward distant "vanishing points," while divergence brings the object toward the viewer and shows more of its dimensions.

What we call "realistic" perspective (convergence) bases reality on the point of view of the person who does the looking. Why not invert this notion of realism by considering how the thing displays itself to the person? Heidegger spoke of how "the thing things." In its "thinging" it displays itself and invites us into its sphere. Heidegger eliminates the notion of an inanimate world through his use of language. If things express themselves, then our use of verbs can be expanded to articulate how things manifest existence and action. The grass grasses, greens, blades, and envelops the person who interacts with it. The house houses me when I contemplate its presence. Each thing is ensouled in a particular way, so the various houses I contemplate have their distinctly personal way of housing.

These inversions of perspective will reveal how realism cannot be restricted to an individual or human point of view. "Realistic" perspective actually distorts the perception of things because their totality cannot be grasped from a fixed reference point. Convergent vistas are a vital part of our artistic heritage, and I thoroughly enjoy looking at them and being drawn into the space of the pictures. What I am questioning is the exclusive identification of reality with only one way of looking at the world.

For too long, notions of reality have been restricted to the linear planes of a single person's vision. These straight-line perspectives are flat and inflexible. Everything has to "fall in line" with the prevailing view, which is just one of many possible angles. Education is especially afflicted by the illusions of linear reality. Standardized learning emphasizes falling into line with habitual logic, which has little tolerance for deviation. There is a deeply lodged fear behind any point of view that is so threatened by a loss of control that perverse views are assumed to be negative and unacceptable.

The transformative education is always different from the one you think you're getting. It tends to go contrary to the will, coming upon us paradoxically. Remember John Lennon's line, "Life is what happens to you when you are making plans." Even when we invent something for a particular purpose, the larger impact of the discovery, its unimagined applications to life, come afterward in the most unlikely ways.

It is the passing glances, the half-heard utterances, the memories that linger, only to be unraveled afterward, and the indirect influences that shape the soul's formation in ways we do not see. The spirits of learning are conveyed through receptivity to the subtle influences—the way she listens and then speaks only when she has something that needs to be said; the way he never listens and always speaks; the tone of her speech that conveys empathy and understanding; the way he goes silent and avoids taking the bait in unnecessary argument.

Genius works unexpectedly within us, usually contrary to what we think we are doing. Through the exercise of inversion, we continuously shake things up and look at our lives from different and foreign perspectives. Our habitual attitudes about hidden meanings blind us to the messages on the surfaces of our lives that we cannot see.

The angelic way of looking at things imagines their completeness from a metaperspective that transcends singular views. Imagination enables us to simultaneously entertain multiple perspectives. I look at a stone, appreciating the angle from which I look, but simultaneously I see the stone through the imaginal eye, which perceives from every possible perspective inside and outside the rock. Similarly, I look at a tree, imagining how it appears to another person with different interests, to a bird, a cat, a squirrel, a flying insect, or a bug living inside the bark. If we can reverse our egocentric ways of looking, the tree is appreciated as an active participant in its environment. As Heidegger said, one of its qualities is to "stay," and by staying, it "gathers" in its treely way. People, animals, birds, insects, zephyrs, waters, sunlight, spirits, and imaginings are all collected by the tree.

As a child I was fascinated with how my perception of a room changed when I crawled under the dining room table. The table was a different object when viewed from its underside, where I saw the unfinished wood, screw heads, the name and address of the Boston furniture maker. There was also a transformation of function. It became a protective enclosure, a place of retreat, a sanctuary. People were identified according to their feet and legs. Restrictions like the cramped space and the caution against head bumping fueled creativity because fantasy was being constructed from changing the function of a familiar domestic object. Sitting, standing, or lying on the table similarly altered its expression.

Through imagination and physical exploration I got to know the table in so many different ways. I remember going around it in games, catching glimpses of its many faces and angles and the way they interacted with the different spaces of the room. The table was relatively constant in appearance, but there were differences in wood grain and subtle markings caused by interactions with people over the years. There was a "sacred" cigarette burn that my mother identified with my father's father, one of his last marks on earth. (Actually, my teenage cousin burned the table while smoking after my mother went to bed, and I told her the next morning that my grandfather did it.)

Life is always making uncanny relations between things. Cigarette burns turn into relics and dining room tables become sanctums of a child's play.

These inversions of things are not unique to supposedly creative types. They occur in everybody's life, but they are often suppressed by the pressure to conform. We miss observing and celebrating the deviations that give new shapes and directions to life. It is the odd and unusual things that truly distinguish people and families from one another, yet we fear this individuation and place our emphasis on how we fit in to the universal standard. In my life I see how this inevitably results in a neurotic denial or self-repression of our truly distinguishing characteristics, those things that express our incomparable spirits.

The angelic way of looking at the world or at another person assumes many-sidedness and inversions. It realizes that a single perspective can never hold the complexity of a thing. The metaperspective complements the physical eye with the imaginal looking of the angel. We feel this presence of the creative spirit when in the company of flexible and attentive people who are able to move with us through the broad spectrum of experience. We also feel the restrictions of those who see us only through their fixed perspectives. We become an object, like a figure in a "realistic" painting that must fall into line with the vantage point according to which the composition is constructed.

But I have learned that we cannot expect others to consistently see us through the eyes of the angel. I do this myself in my private meditations and prayers. As I begin to accept my own many-sidedness, and the complexity of everything around me, I realize that I am always beheld by the eyes of angels. Reverie and the meditations of imagination take me into the metavision, which is so much more complete than the singular perspective.

When I expect others to see me in a certain way, I contradict the nature of the creative spirit and its ongoing inversions. In order to relax the controls of the social ego, I have to truly let go of my ego-image and its expectations. I have to let myself become a movable object within the creative visions of others. My being becomes clay fashioned by the forces of their imaginations. When I realize that there is no single and permanent me, I encounter the angelic nature of my being, the spiritual imagery that accompanies my physical body throughout life. I see the same spiritual substance in others. Through imagination "the soul shows itself to earthly things transfigured."[2] The person is perceived in his spiritual or angelic nature. This occurs in the metaperspective of the imagination, which is not restricted by illusionist lines of perception. Only the imagination can look from many sides at once, combining physical substance with spiritual visions. It is the only eye that can see itself as it looks.

This way of looking takes a certain pleasure in distortions and inversions because fixed and unchanging images do not exist in the realm of the creative spirit. The assumption that there is an accurate way to view my person is an extension of a single perspective from which I view myself at a particular time and place. If I let these fixations go, I enjoy the flux of my interactions with the world. Rather than trying to control the nature of "my image," I creatively interact with the changing images others have of me. Paintings teach us how literal "reality" is created through illusion. Imaginal reality is so much closer to the spiritual nature of things.

The inverted perspective on life encourages ongoing changes of position, in keeping with the Latin word *invertere*, which means "to turn inside out or upside down." My desire is the grail; what disturbs me has the most to offer; darkness illuminates; everything is animated. Whatever inverts the hegemony of a doctrine or ego position is good, but once accepted, it too must prepare for immediate inversion, because this is the way the creative spirits move. They keep imagination fluid and reshape whatever they touch.

We can begin to appreciate these principles by becoming aware of something as simple as looking at a painting. Inversions of perspective help us to see more completely. If I want to really grasp the being of the table, from what vantage point should I look? From where I stand right now? By looking from many different angles? By imagining the table looking at me? By combining all of these?

Young children or "naive" artists, intent upon representing the table and not their points of view, will draw the object in a way that shows all four sides. Can you imagine telling the stories of our lives in this way? We are not so different from the table, in that a single point of view can never grasp our many-sidedness.

The church and the museum ....

Unlikely partnerships always have the most to offer the soul.

When I was in the eighth grade of St. Mary's School, religion was displayed with a heavy hand. The building was in a historic setting on Hawthorne Boulevard in Salem, Massachusetts, and the church was the second oldest Catholic edifice in the United States, but for me the spirits never flew freely in that environment. I was one of the most active altar boys in the school, serving at 7:00 AM Mass throughout Lent. Every Friday afternoon during Holy Week, the entire school filed into the church next door for Benediction and the Stations of the Cross. As an altar boy I had the freedom to leave class and prepare for the church rites. Everyone else had to walk in lines to the service. I had been involved with Lenten stations all the way through grammar school. Hundred of students were herded next door to the church for compulsory services, where the sisters kept a careful watch to ensure quiet in the sanctum. The aura generated from the community of children was one of repression and control. I was bored after the first week.

Impulsively on the second Friday, I walked away from the school, sensing that nobody would miss me in the long procession of priests and male servers. I didn't tell my friends of my escape. Sister Gertrude would never imagine an A student, and an ostentatiously religious child, ducking out on the Lenten rites. She was busy keeping an eye on her "bad boys" as they moved from classroom to church.

I was drawn to the Peabody Museum, a short distance away on Essex Street. It was 1960, and Salem residents could enter the museum free. As the priests and altar boys were walking through the same stations that hundreds of years of Catholics passed, I worked my way through the museum, beginning in the maritime section and moving on to the ethnological collections from the East Indies, Polynesia, and the Orient. I was enthralled by the shamanic masks, sacred tools, costumes, and the densely configured environment of objects collected by Salem merchants during the previous century's China trade.

My imagination flourished in the museum, no doubt fueled by the adrenaline of risk and fears of getting caught for skipping the compulsory Lenten service. I had left the school to educate myself, and I sensed the creative spirit guiding me. As a child I felt a destiny, a sacred purpose inside me like an acorn. I knew it had to be something different than the conventional way.

I went to the museum every Friday afternoon of that Lenten season, and to this day I am amazed that my absence was never noticed. It felt as though I was invisible. My senses basked in the stimulation of the old Yankee museum constructed from the history of the place where I lived. I felt a personal association with the display of its artifacts. It was unusual to live in a relatively small and somewhat obscure city with more major historic sites than any other place in the United States. I felt my personal fate identified with the way a very particular locale could interact with the far reaches of the world while being distinctly itself. The Salem of my imagination was a model for the life taking shape in me. The city and its museum are earth angels, still infusing me with endless currents of imagination.

I loved the museum's respect for and fascination with the foreign things that took their place alongside the relics of indigenous Massachusetts culture. Nineteenth-century Salem opened to the world through the sea and flourished. The spirits of the museum expressed reciprocal relations between cultures and things. The Orient interacted with Salem in the displays. There were spirits everywhere emanating from the objects. Each one was distinctly itself and engaging me on its own terms.

The collection was so vast and varied that I could never exhaust its resources. At a later age I discovered that there were large storerooms full of artifacts that were not displayed or even catalogued because of a shortage of staff. Today the museum has expanded with a large new addition of contemporary concrete and glass. But I feel fortunate to have known it in its earlier life when polished and slanting wood floors meandered from room to room where the exhibits never changed but still offered an infinite bounty to my young imagination. The changelessness of the displays through my high school and college years reinforced my private and intimate relationship to the museum.

My visits to the Peabody Museum changed the way I looked at the city. Old houses and streets lived many lives. They were simultaneously in the present and the past. Every day in grammar school I walked by the House of Seven Gables, and the Custom House, where Nathaniel Hawthorne worked, and looked out over Derby Wharf. The spirits of the previous generations were carefully collected in the Peabody Museum, which offered distinctly local and physical reflections of change, continuity, death, preservation. The museum felt like my private temple of the imagination, my treasury of images and soulful things. I traveled back to Federal Salem, rowed in wooden boats with Herman Melville and Queequeg, and threw harpoons from bowsprits. As I looked at the varied and grotesque metal heads and hooks of the harpoons, I imagined myself as a whale, stricken and dying. I bowed and drank tea with Chinese silk traders, canoed and swam with Polynesians, and swung the war clubs in the museum's glass cabinets imagining the killing of a human being.

I was probably using those stolen hours to make up for years of textbook drudgery and blackboard tedium. School taught me how to tolerate the deadening of initiative, spontaneity, expression, sensation, and creative transformation. Fortunately, I did acquire some basic skills, and the restrictions on creative learning solidified my relationship with imagination as an intimate partner and soulmate. As in medicine, irritants and toxins can feed countervitalities. There is no perfect and controlled educational environment. I have spent my life, no doubt fueled by the restrictions of my youth, trying to enhance the life of imagination in schools, but the bad things have their place in a healthy and real ecology. There can be no depth of soul and creation without conflict and dissatisfaction. These conditions do not have to be artificially induced. Life will generously maintain the supply.

I see now that my life work was anticipated in those museum excursions. I walked away from the compulsory lines. I could not tolerate them. I had to individuate my experience. The museum was usually empty. I had it to myself. It was endowed by Salem society in its era of wealth and just existed there, always open and welcoming. I was probably the only schoolboy who went in over and over again. The images inside fed my imagination and anticipated my later connections with the shamans of native cultures, and my deep involvement with Jerusalem, the place from which the name Salem is derived.

Love of God moved from the church and was concentrated on a love of images. For me, the museum artifacts corresponded to "the very Image of itself which the soul carries in its innermost depths."[3] My religious vision was being shaped in a compulsion to leave the standardized rites. Something drew me away and into another sanctum, a house holding the spirits of distant worlds, largely unattended. My love of spirits could not be limited to a single culture. My angel of individuation lead me through private passage rites, a sacred vision quest, which unwittingly laid the foundation of a life's work.

I see now that the earth angels are spirits who guide and shape our lives. I was ushered into a vision that inspired and shaped my life outside the scope of my comprehension. I never made conscious connections between the Peabody Museum visits and the formation of my work. I went off to high school and college, doing all of the things that convention and habitual life instructed me to do, but the soul had a different purpose. It wanted something from me. The difficulties I had with the conventional ways of studying law, studying art, studying psychology, practicing psychotherapy, practicing religion, were all gathering together in a creative complex that constructed a new form. The museum is coming to me again through memory as an angel that holds the many threads of my life. It is a lifelong companion, today more of a psychic image than a physical presence. The material body of the museum has been metamorphosed into a personal angel who reveals the subtle connections between the things and events of my life and the purpose to which they contribute. They shape me, now and then. The Peabody Museum is a temple in my imagination, holding the physical and divine aspects of life, revealing how they create one another and cannot exist alone.

Similarly, my psychic image of the museum is intimately connected to the nearby Catholic church on Hawthorne Boulevard. As with dreams, the different images within my reflections constitute one another and the overall imaginal experience. Both the church and the museum are essential figures within my story, which gathers their differences into a shared purpose. The monstrance and priestly vestments of the Catholic Benediction are connected to the clay and wooden receptacles of the shaman's rites—silk and feathers, gold and dark earth, Gothic arches and simple tents. They are all elements in the *anima mundi*'s celebration of its divine and worldly natures. It is an interplay of spirits, the necessary juxtaposition of church and museum, which expands my imagination of both.

The sacred space is where the soul discovers the image of its particular angelic nature. The church keeps the traditions of the divine. The confined space can be imagined positively as a hermetic container, a vessel that ultimately lets the creative spirit fly away and into the world, sanctifying all that it touches, traveling until it evaporates, and ultimately it returns again to the alchemical enclosure, to be reanimated through what might be the bitter sulphur of discontent within the rigid and unchanging walls, the lack of space, which stokes the inner fires of soulmaking and a remaking of the vision that once again flies out to the world. Winged Hermes is paired with Hestia, the hearth of Mother Church reimagined as a container and generative womb of constant emanations. The personal vision must abandon the lair in order to individuate and make soul anew.

The angelic body of Salem could not possibly love one temple more than another. Two image-loving institutions, the church on the boulevard and the museum on Essex Street, pollinate in my imagination. One cannot give birth without the transfer of soul from the other. The church and the museum are drawn together by a creative spirit manifesting itself through their interactions.

As a child I was sensitive to the call of the angel and the feeling that something wanted to live through me. I walked away from the church, and I was greeted by a host of wondrous images. I thought I was leaving religion, turning my back on it, but I was opening to a larger vision of the creative spirit, focused on the particular things that people make in order to heal themselves and connect themselves to the sacred.

Love thy demons as thyself ....

You is sharks, sartin; but if you gobern de shark in you, why
den you be angel; for all angel is not'ing more dan de shark
well goberned
—Fleece speaking to sharks in *Moby Dick* by Herman Melville

The idea that images are a fulfillment of the soul's desire is a
provocative notion today. We fear that opening to the satisfaction of
an image will place us under its evil control. We demonize images
that offend the reigning moralities of society. We don't trust the
innate Epicureanism of the healthy soul, and we assume that it is a
weak organism easily subject to corruption. We project immense
amounts of evil power onto the image, a dark form of iconology, and
depreciate the innate moral faculties of the soul.

On the right Jesse Helms demonizes artistic imagery that offends his notion of American morality, ironically making Robert
Mapplethorpe a household name, and on the left there is an equally
repressive condemnation of politically incorrect imagery. James
Hillman has defended pornography from attacks from both the right
and the left, and asserts its integrity as an expression of the soul's
imagining.

Erica Jong, who recently published a biography of Henry Miller,
tries to prevent his art from being cast into obscurity by this bipolar
mania of censorship by both liberals and conservatives, which she
sees as a betrayal of the soul and its sometimes "dark imaginings."
Jong says that "cruelty is built into the dance of life" and its aggression cannot be avoided. She describes how we always hate the great
writers "before we learn to love them" because they courageously

irritate us "by being new, by being honest, by baring bone" and by challenging our points of view.[4]

We are growing increasingly concerned about the way violent media images provoke corresponding acts of violence in the world. Life does imitate images of the imagination.

I don't have a simple answer to how we can deal socially with the way images affect behavior. But I know that repression simply intensifies the life of monsters. The individual imagination has rights of expression that must be protected. The moral course has something to do with distinguishing the imaginal experience from the literal act. But there is also a need to consider what is distributed publicly and available to children with the touch of a button. The rights of expression are always paired with the accompanying right to not look at something. The wisdom of the Greek pantheon suggests that the inherent spirits of each thing have their appropriate and particular placement in an environment. The ecology of the gods is disrupted and threatened when any one thing becomes all-pervasive. The moral task becomes a discipline of proper placement and relationship.

What strikes me as most peculiar is how those who rail against "evil" imagery are the ones most completely caught up in this perspective. They are living proof of how the dark spirits become all-encompassing. My instincts tell me that respecting the total spectrum of the soul's appetites is the only way to avoid being captured by one of them. Opposition traps me in an intimate relationship to the thing I abhor.

In the Irish Catholic culture in which I was raised, Saint Michael was an omnipresent icon. My cousin was recently married in the church of my childhood, which I had not visited for over thirty years. I have been thinking about Michael and the devil for some time, and I was stunned to see a huge and dark painting of him poking the serpent over the altar. The image called attention to how my psyche, in its formative years, received this theme.

I have never been comfortable with the image of the archangel's heel crushing the head of the devil and his spear penetrating its body. One angel inflicts wounds on another. In addition to my innate sensitivity to "underdogs," it didn't feel like a moral way to treat an adversary. Lucifer is commonly portrayed as the serpent, an animal once celebrated for its healing qualities but now the embodiment of the demonized "lower" passions and instincts. In the Freudian sense, people project what they consider to be their own undesirable qualities and conflicted feelings onto the serpent. But we cannot keep sensibility repressed for long. These are forced reactions that wound the natural instincts of the soul.

If I step outside my own fixation and take another look at Saint Michael and his suppression of the serpent, I see their interaction as an expression of the soul's universal condition. The religious doctrine identifies with the angel and his spear, and I get stuck in oppositionism by taking the side of Lucifer. One-sided movements cast shadows in the other direction. I demonize Michael because he offends my point of view. If I step outside of the dualism created by singular perspectives, and reflect upon the complete image of Michael and Lucifer, I embrace the archetypal conflict of their interaction. One participant cannot exist without the other, and their antagonism configures one of the soul's conditions. If I can keep them both, I take a step toward a more complete love of the soul.

Sensitivity to serpents and demons is not a satanic embrace of evil forces. As Gandhi advised, the only devils are those that live within the human heart. Every form of life is sacred, and nothing is inherently evil. Caring for debased figures of the physical world and the dark angels of imagination nourishes the soul. Humans, rather than the disparaged animals, serpents, and monsters, are uniquely capable of being possessed by the forces of evil that flourishes when we do not look into the shadows of our souls and the wounds we create.

Soul's morality is a praxis, a doing or drama that allows the complex spectrum of its characters to freely interact with one another within a sensitive person. From psychotherapy we have discovered how treating the soul involves the engagement of some unsavory substances, what Freud called "crooked cures." Soul's moral instrument is an alchemical vessel, a witch's pot in need of regular stirring, where everything cooks, breaks down, and dissolves, making anew, magically. Good cooking requires distinct, strong, and varied ingredients.

In *Dark Eros,* Thomas Moore reflects on the grotesque in the fiction of the Marquis de Sade.[5] All of imagination's figures are accepted as necessary characters in its ecology. The book caught me in my intolerance and fear of being seen as someone who entertains unacceptable images. Inspired by James Hillman's insistence that curing pathology cures away soul, *Dark Eros* changes the course of Freud's sublimation theory and the bourgeoise commandment to make dark urges into good ones. Freud acknowledged the perverse angels, but his medical method tried to fix and rule them: "Where id was, ego shall be." By contrast, the methods of archetypal psychology look with curiosity at what the soul is doing in perverse activity. What need is the soul expressing? Compassion replaces correction. The ethical act becomes one of proper placement and moral differentiation. The cure lies within the heart of the toxin.

The method allows everything to be itself—dark, light or ambiguous—and interact with other things within the moral sanctum of imagination, where we exercise the ability to differentiate one thing from another. Dreams and imaginal reverie do not require the discretion of our public lives. Oversimplified links between imagination's longings and a person's social actions have contributed to the inability to distinguish the imaginal from the literal. Moore describes the fixities of moralism as "a defense against morality, the safeguarding of a single safe idea about one's life and resistance against the subtlety and complexity of that life. . . . To this hard, white moralism the perverted image offers a route into complexity."

It might be hard for some to accept, but even the images of perversion function as angelic messengers and guides into the soul's terrain. Moralism blocks the path of soul's unattractive messengers, whose mission may require offense, pain, and fear as a preparation for change. Deep prayer opens to the darkness as well as the light, the complexities, the devils of details. The saccharine images of angels pervading popular culture unconsciously continue the reign of artificial sweetness over the bitter medicines of soul. I do not want to replace the light with the dark. It is the one-sided repression of one by the other that needs correction.

Nor do I overlook the poetics of bliss, the magnificent beauties created by painters like Claude Monet and Georgia O'Keeffe; but it is the great tragedies that reach most deeply into our souls, where they comfort through their expression of pain and suffering. It is intriguing how those who intentionally set out to heal wounds through the arts try to replace the suffering through an infusion of positive spirits, not realizing that the soul in grief is touched and transformed by an expressive exaltation of its condition. A Verdi requiem is more likely to alleviate my suffering over the loss of a loved one than meditation on a brightly colored painting of water lilies. It is the noble expression of darkness that medicines and moves dark moods. The creative exaggeration of any dark mood is more likely to move it or transform it than attempts to fix or supplant it with another feeling.

The goading and ill-tempered demons are not in themselves bad, but when repressed or forced to act contrary to their nature, they can get out of hand. Acknowledging our less desirable traits keeps us humble and down to earth. Their denial frightens me. Watch out for the one who has cured away all his demons or who is convinced that righteousness is his exclusive birthright. Look at the history of evil in the world, and you will see that this type of person, when endowed with powers, is likely to hurt others. Dangers may lurk in the one-sided invocation of light that we see in the contemporary angel boom. The soulful vision of angels doesn't like heights and excessively bright lights. It welcomes foibles and earthy beings.

I don't want a world without demons and nefarious fantasies. What would comedy and the arts do without their villains? Can you imagine suspense without the bad guys? Rather than looking literally at what religions say about devils and demons, look imaginatively at how essential these figures are to the sacred drama, to our initiation into morality. Lucifer, Iblis, and Ahriman personify the falls without which we could not have resurrections. It is a necessary interplay, truly universal to every individual and social psyche. The Greek pantheon embraced this polymorphous perversity as a metaphoric enactment that helped people see the good and bad within themselves and the world. The Hellenic gods included men and women who were prone to act in both kind and malevolent ways. Their characterizations were not restricted to good guys and bad guys. Ancient culture seemed to understand how the divinity speaks poetically and calls for a corresponding, nonliteral interpretation.

The moral life requires the freedom to err, reflect, and adjust. Our demons are essential allies in this process. They push at boundaries and keep morality in a state of perpetual transformation. The apparent immorality of demons keeps us questioning and searching. They refuse to let the ethical inquiry stagnate into rigidly fixed principles or assumed perfections. Their provocations guarantee complexity and different points of view. The dream demons are the ones who upset the carefully controlled order of my habitual life. They demand a new response, and in this way they are always the most potent agent of change and transformation. In my psychic life it has always been the most bothersome and menacing demon who delivers essential messages, the revolutionary ones I don't want to hear.

Ridicule is the most common tool through which the authoritative position fends off threats to its supremacy. The demons or bad angels are debased in order to advance the righteousness of the good ones. They have been represented with the traits of beasts and serpents, portrayals that draw animals into the degradation.

Ridicule deprives adversaries of dignity. It basically dismisses their positions and excuses us from giving them serious consideration according to their merits. The same things applies to "demonizing" an adversary. We tend to do this subtly through language that depersonalizes the person we oppose. For example, he or she becomes a label rather than a person. The images of language are potent weapons used to enforce points of view. I could give pages of examples of the terms we use to denigrate those who threaten our worldview. We have also depersonalized the pathological conditions of our souls with diagnostic labels and abstract psychological principles that allow us to maintain a professional distance between ourselves and our demons.

Just as Americans discovered that meeting with our Soviet adversaries, getting to know them as people, was the best way to eliminate cultural demonization, the same applies to becoming intimate with our inner adversaries and irritants. Rather than repression, we might consider more compassion and sympathy for their condition—loving our demons as ourselves.

I trust that the demons will respond to love. Just like any other person or culture, they are unlikely to submit to repression that breeds violence and hatred.

Imagine a man nursing his demons like Mother Teresa tending to the suffering. He asks, "What need are you expressing? How can I minister to you?"

The demons might protest the implication that they are needy. They say, "Can't you just receive our messages and see us for what we are, and accept the necessity of our presence? We don't need treatment; you do, and we have come to offer you something. The message is in our constitution, so don't try to change it. Nursing keeps you in control. We have come to minister to you with our bitter and jarring medicines."

But we come on to them like Rambo, heroically suppressing what challenges our sensibilities, literally trying to kill, wipe out, exterminate what does not fit the scheme of control. Our drugs and other treatments attempt to extinguish the soul's demons. We have not yet learned that these chemical treatments endanger the soul's ecology as much as they threaten our fields and waterways.

In addition to striving to eliminate anything that challenges the controlling will, there is another element of repression that expresses a more vulnerable sensibility. Do I want to show this about myself? What will people think of me? It is a cyclic suppression in which the censorship of certain unsavory expressions in our public life makes it feel improper to have these often very natural imaginings inside ourselves. James Hillman describes how even the more progressive strains of culture are caught between the contradictory commandments of psychoanalysis: "Thou shalt not repress; and thou shalt not act out." Imagination becomes the forum for entertaining the paradox.

We continue to oppose those who speak out with menacing positions rather than honoring their contribution to expanding the moral interplay. We need a Civil Liberties Union of the psyche, to protect the rights of all the positions to speak. Henry Miller can be appreciated for having the courage to speak the dark fantasies so many have but do not dare show. Trust the soul and its wisdom, its morality, its process, the full spectrum of its characters, and the surprising discoveries that can only result from a free interaction amongst contradictory positions.

The most brilliantly creative people I know have strong likes and dislikes. There is tremendous energy in these negative feelings, which makes me realize that demons and the *via negativa* are unacknowledged angels of creation. But we continue to view creativity as a completely positive gift that heals and balms the soul. The word *creative* is almost universally associated with the niceties of invention divorced from the torturous and pathological demons that afflict the souls of creators.

Repulsion can be an especially powerful force for creation and change. When I am repelled by something, there is an intense connection and movement, as contrasted to the deadpan of equilibrium. Conflicts define, stir, and regenerate. The process of change is built upon abuses and the transformative forces they release. If I hate what someone is doing, I am deeply involved with it. Extreme positions grasp us one way or the other and proliferate strong spirits.

Angels of the wound ....

For there is nothing either good or bad, but thinking makes
it so.   —William Shakespeare, *Hamlet*, act 2, scene 2

In treating physical injuries, we know that symptoms, however uncomfortable, often function as messengers. They have stories to tell about how we live our lives and how sensitive we are to the body's needs. The pain in my stomach is a messenger who comes to help me look at the way I eat or how I handle stress; a broken ankle and its resultant condition of dependency may force the "in control" person to sit back and accept the assistance of others.

I distinctly remember how my childhood illnesses and accidents changed the pattern of daily life. I was a constantly active little boy, but when suddenly forced to lie down and miss school, I had a different kind of contact with my parents, based not on checking in to ask permission for various adventures but on conversations about my physical state as well as on quiet time together. The wounded condition made it clear that people need each other; it taught me how to ask for help, how to receive and appreciate it. My wounds also taught me how to minister to others when they are injured.

According to folk wisdom, the disease contains its own remedy, and wounds generate agents or angels of their transformation. This also happens when we suffer wounds to the soul. In my work as a therapist, I see that the angels swarm when a person admits vulnerability and acknowledges wounds. The angel of transformation might take the form of another person who offers support and guidance; it might manifest itself as an inner feeling or vision from which we draw sustenance, or an artistic expression that suggests another way of imagining our lives.

The key to this approach is that the person who has suffered the soul wound must admit to the injury. This seems paradoxical, and perhaps even counter to instinct: our tendency is to deny our wounds, to resist the emotional loss and suffering that they bring. However, when a wounded person denies the affliction, it does not diminish; it grows. Unable to reach the person in whom it resides, the demon of the denied pain turns its energy and need for attention onto others. This is how cycles of soul wounds work their way through families and generations of families, through troubled societies, and finally through nations. The neglected wound tends to continuously up the ante, the pressure, and the risk, screaming for attention, until it bursts into consciousness in a way that stuns and humbles the afflicted person and softens the soul for transformation. The creative work of angels is paradoxically dependent upon the conflict-inducing demons who prepare the soul for change and the healing angels.

My most vivid experience of denying a soul wound came when my grandmother died when I was a teenager. We were very close, yet I did not cry. Perhaps the loss was too much for me. At that time in our culture, boys were not supposed to show their feelings. In fact, denial in men and boys was considered the basis of our survival. Yet I remember, after my grandmother's death, sitting for hours, staring out of my bedroom window.

Years later, immersed in a love relationship, I often burst into primal tears when my feelings were touched. Although my expression resembled madness, I felt that I was finally purging what had been held inside since my grandmother's death. This release was only possible within the sanctuary of a love relationship, where I could feel the depths of the loss and the wounding of the soul. In this case, my beloved functioned as the angel of my wound, recognizing the pain and helping me to feel my repressed emotions.

While, as an art therapist, I am accustomed to encouraging others to give expression to images of their wounds, however uncomfortable this process might be, a recent experience reminded me of the importance of such an approach in my own life.

I was scheduled to give a lecture on the idea of angels of the wound and decided to use images of wounds from art history as a way of making my thoughts tangible. Going through the slide collections of various Boston museums, I was stunned to see how frequently the Crucifixion motif appeared and how often the figure of the dying Christ was surrounded by angels who cared for his wounds.

When I began my search, the Crucifixion never occurred to me, nor did I expect to see angels ministering to the wounded Christ or literally attending to an afflicted person. I imagined people on sickbeds, perhaps injured animals or soldiers. I thought that if I showed such pictures, my audience would respond with an angelic sensibility—as in group therapy, when a wounded person expresses pain or fear and others empathize with the condition and offer support. I also observed, in art therapy, that someone who is suffering might begin by expressing the hurt in a picture, but then in subsequent pictures treat and transform the condition. In this way the pictures themselves could function as angels who minister to the wound.

I saw both of these patterns in the Crucifixion pictures I uncovered. I found pictures that formed a sequence, with the dark, isolated, and agonizing images of the suffering Christ followed by images of him surrounded by angels at the moment before death or just after he was taken down from the cross. In addition to the winged figures, who are often portrayed holding cups or goblets that collect the blood running from Christ's wounds, the Crucifixion motif also frequently involves another kind of angel: sympathetic human figures surrounding the cross or the figure of Christ after he is taken down. Christ is always presented in a supine posture, and the attending people have an angelic appearance.

Collecting these Crucifixion images triggered a complex of emotions in me that I did not readily understand. Although the images I uncovered were perfect illustrations of the points I wanted to make about soul wounds and their angels, I was reluctant to show them in my lecture. I was censoring because it felt too provocative, possibly offensive to many. The audience might think I was prose-lytizing and that religious images should be kept out of the public discourse. But I have no difficulty showing images from religions other than the one in which I was raised. This shows how we tend to censor our personal wounds. The more distant conditions are easier to engage with a clinical disinterest. The Crucifixion motif goes to the core of the archetypal wound in Western civilization and my personal life. It was this image, drawn from my Catholic upbringing, that was causing me trouble.

I have always said that the most provocative images are the most useful in stirring the soul, but I was shying away from the crucifix and its embodiment of the cosmic wound. It said too much to me about my repressions. The wound was too close to home. It has taken me two years to work through feelings about the cross, and my experience no doubt affirms that the vexing image is the one that opens unaccessed regions of the soul. Sticking to this image has not been easy. I keep moving toward it and away from it.

I was raised in a Catholic household with a crucifix over every bed. As an adolescent I didn't want a crucified Christ over me at night, so I took it down.

My mother respected my personal things, rarely touched them, and generally stayed away from my room, but the crucifix was an-other story. It seemed only a matter of hours before it was back on the wall. I took it down again, and she put it back up. I tried hiding it in my closet, but somehow she managed to find it and restore it to its former position.

My mother and I never spoke about this. If I were more inclined toward the supernatural, I might say that the cross kept returning itself to the wall. Perhaps it did communicate to her in ways that were beyond my comprehension, for no matter how well I hid it, the crucifix always reappeared.

I made an unspoken truce with my mother and stopped trying to restructure the sacred things in our house. The crucifix stayed out of my closet, but I took it down from the wall at night and put it back up again in the morning. When I moved out of my parents' house, I kept crucifixes out of my homes.

From the telling of this story I see how actively involved I was with the image. Rather than living passively and unconsciously with the crucifix, I had a complicated set of negotiations with it, an indication of how much it affected my soul.

I repeatedly tell my students that what disturbs you the most has the most to offer: that's where the spirit is most vital. Yet I offered this idea to them over and over without consciously making connections to my childhood religious experiences or my own struggles with what were to me the most disturbing aspects of Christianity.

I remembered, too, that I had broken my earlier vow. I did have, in my home, a crucifix I bought in Mexico. The way the object was made tells me something about the nature of what I had been fighting in the earlier image. In the Mexican crucifix, both the cross and the Christ figure were made of straw. It wasn't so literal, and I enjoyed it as an artwork. I liked the shape, the textures, its lightness, and the way Christ and his cross were one: there was not such a horrible dichotomy between the person and the wood and the nails. The Mexican cross lightened up the ponderous image of my childhood. There was too much emphasis on suffering in those images of Christ fixed to the cross that I remembered from adolescence.

I loved the Mexican cross because it was a "particular," an image whose specific and handmade qualities were strong enough to distinguish it from the impersonal and mass-produced symbol. I see that my rebellion probably had to do with the emergence of my artist *imago*. My dislike for the machine-made crucifix over my bed was aesthetic, and this specific dislike of the image corresponded to my feelings about impersonal religious practices. It never occurred to me that my conflict with my mother over the cross embodied the shaping of my personal religious and artistic vision. My difficulties with institutional religion, then and now, are aesthetic.

I wonder if I would have felt the same way about the crucifix if it had been carved by someone I knew, or if the motif displayed more cultural ornamentation, as we see in Celtic or Eastern Orthodox crosses. The universal and cosmic symbolism of the cross is not lost in these more aesthetic presentations, but they are complemented by the earth angels of creative embellishment and imagination, just as the paintings of the crucified Christ show him surrounded by angels.

The particulars of the expression, which I see as angels, make the symbol more subtle and intimate. I felt the historic reality of the crucifixion in the Mexican cross, but it was personalized and spiritualized through the angels of the specific image. The message of the cross was delivered through the particulars of its expression. In the angelic realm, each image as messenger conveys something specific to itself. The angel can be imagined as a figure protecting the individuation of spiritual experience.

My conflict was also related, I'm sure, to how I associated Christ with the repression of sensual life. As an adolescent, I was beginning to enter into an adult sexuality inspired by a mystical imagination of the world. It seemed perverted to have Christ hanging over my bed. It suffocated my reverie. Now I realize how the essence of the Crucifixion, and of Christ's teachings in general, has been obscured by institutional interpretations. I had to go to the cross as an adult and find my own interpretation; only then could I welcome the image of the Crucifixion into my home.

As an adult, I am also able to find meaning in other interpretations of this image of soul-wounding. In the novel *Mr. Noon*, D. H.

Lawrence embraces the image of crucifixion and reframes its meaning. The title character, Gilbert Noon, is traveling on foot through the Austrian countryside, where he comes upon crucifixes carved by villagers and displayed along the side of the road. In the roughly made icons, Gilbert feels the presence of pre-Christian "tree-dark gods." Lawrence writes of his character's encounter with the crucifix, "Gilbert's heart stood still. He knew it was not Christ. It was an older, more fearful god, tree-terrible . . . dark mysticism, a worship of cruelty and pain and torture and death: a dark death worship."[6]

Lawrence felt the survivals of ancient Europe in the Christian crucifix. The image of Christ on the cross has become so conventional that we are no longer moved by the details of the figure, by the soul qualities specific to the particular image. When Gilbert Noon reflects on the varieties of crucified images that he sees, a whole new world of belief and imagination opens up for him. There is a sense that the theme of the cross can be adapted to the suffering of whoever meditates on it aesthetically. "And startlingly frequent in the gloomy valleys and on the steep path-slopes were the Christs, old and young. Some were ancient Christs, of grey-silvery aged wood. Some were new, and terrible: life-sized, realistic, powerful young men, on the cross, in a death agony; white and distorted."[7]

The painters of the Italian Renaissance imagined the Crucifixion in more extraordinary and lavish ways than the simple wooden crosses described by Lawrence. Renaissance painters frequently portrayed the body of Christ with ideal, beautiful proportions, being comforted by equally splendid bodies, all of whom were painted according to the highest standards of academic perfection. This idealization of the human form creates a sense of distance between the emotional horror of the event and its remembrance through art.

Without judging these representations as avoiding the "reality" of the Crucifixion, we can see how they express different aspects of the ways in which we might respond to soul wounds. The Renaissance versions idealize suffering, imbue it with beauty and grandeur. Such an approach can open us to the sacred level of our own suffering, to the gods in our wounds; when we see that God the Son is not spared the agony of earthly pain, our own pain is elevated to the divine realm. On the other hand, the indigenous effigies encountered by Gilbert Noon portray the suffering Christ as a member of the particular, local community. The Christ on those crosses is both himself and not himself, both the Son of God and an extension of every villager, before and after Christ.

In art history, we constantly see how scriptural figures and angels are dressed in the style of the period in which they were made. This suggests how the religious image is something with which people identify. The wounded Christ is an archetypal figure, a living presence in the life of any person or era imagining his suffering and theirs. He brings comfort, love, and healing through the realization that wounds and suffering are both particular and universal. They are pains that we all share in varying degrees and which bond us together.

In the 1970s I worked with the New York City "folk" artist Ralph Fasanella, who made a series of paintings of his father as a crucified figure. The elder Fasanella, who worked as an iceman, was portrayed nailed to the cross with the picks he used every day, his ice tongs clamped to his temples. The son felt compassion for his father's struggles and suffering and used the Crucifixion motif to amplify the pain to a transcendent scale.

Fasanella, D. H. Lawrence, my mother, and I all have our personal stories to tell about the Crucifixion motif. There are others, of course—the pietàs of men dying of AIDS being held in the arms of loved ones, the starving children in countries ravaged by war, grieving families everywhere. The wound is individual and universal, mine and yours. Like all archetypal images, the Crucifixion is lodged in the personal and collective world psyche. With each individual interpretation and revision, we grow simultaneously closer to the power of the image itself and closer to an understanding of how our own souls have taken it in and understood it.

The angels of our soul wounds cannot flourish without individual imagination and freedom of expression. In my art therapy practice, I encourage everyone to see the images they create as angels and to access the specific qualities of their expression. This approach is particularly helpful when the images evoked are archetypal in nature. The more significant a symbol is within a culture, the more it can teach us about the need to individuate. In my case, the image of the Crucifixion comes alive when it is liberated from institutional interpretations and is intimately connected to my life. Reflection on the angels of our soul wounds might, if we are undeterred by such interpretations, lead us directly to the image of the Crucifixion, where the cruelest death is transformed into redemptive love and exaltation.

Images survive when they embody the deep and common veins of every psyche. In order to continue living, the image must be re-imagined and transformed through continuous interpretation. When a meaning is fixed to something, it no longer transmits vitality and new life. The child who reflects upon the cross becomes an angel to its wound through compassionate feeling and personal interpretation: "He didn't do anything wrong; why such a painful death? It's ridiculous the way they killed him. What would the world be like if he didn't die?"

Yet negative feelings toward an image, such as I had toward my mother's crucifix, also need to be welcomed. Examining the full spectrum of my reaction to the crucifix images, both positive and negative, helped me to access a deeper sense of the inversions and transformations that are the basis of the Christian mystery. The goal is not to find an easy, clear explanation—a "cure"—for our reactions to the images that most affect us. The goal is to continue to work with them deeply and imaginatively, in order to uncover what our reaction may be trying to teach us about our souls.

James Hillman says that attempting to cure the symptoms of our wounds "may also cure away soul, get rid of just what is beginning to show, which at first is tortured and crying for help, comfort and love, but which is the soul in neurosis trying to make itself heard." Hillman suggests that "what each symptom needs is time and tender care and attention." Soul wounds cannot be denied, put aside, or easily cured. Rather it is "the prolonged occupation with suffering" that can provide us with "a humiliating, soul-awakening experience."[8]

I was working with a group of ministers who talked about how their churches have difficulty with the imagery of the Crucifixion and prefer the spirit of the Resurrection. So my reluctance to publicly engage images of the Crucifixion does not seem to be unusual; even the Christian churches have trouble opening to it. Although we know that the strongest and most authentic bonds are established by going through difficult experiences with others, most people are reluctant to acknowledge the effects of wounds, and so they tend to impose themselves against our will. As Hillman suggests, they humble us and awaken anaesthetized feelings. We seek out help when afflicted, when wounds and losses forcibly pull us down and into the life of the soul.

Angels of the wound may appear as simple incidents in daily life that revive our spirits: a smile from an unknown person when I am feeling depressed, an uplifting story, a telephone call from a friend. The richest environment for the discovery of angels is actually the world of incidental happenings, pregnant with meaning, that pass through our lives unobserved. Angels rarely appear in the forms we expect, and so expectations blind us to the way they show themselves. It is often the apparently inconsequential action that transforms a situation and medicines the soul with angels. A friend used to tell me about the renewal he felt after filling his car with gas. The full tank gave him a fresh perspective on the world. He felt its fullness within himself.

When we least anticipate help, the angel appears in the most unlikely forms. "Look for the little things," the spiritual teacher says. "They will change your life."

The medicine of angels is a reimagining of the way we view our lives, a revisioning of our chronic conditions, and an emergence of the spirit of renewal which medicines our souls. I see from my reflections that I hid and repressed the wound of the Crucifixion—I did not want it ruling my life—but the wound must be given its place within the life of the soul. We will no doubt all have periods when, for whatever reason, we stoically choose to deny wounds. But we can also trust the healing opportunities that life brings—such as when my search for images for my lecture led me to an examination of my own complex relationship to the crucifix—and rely on those circumstances in which the time is right to open to our wounds and receive angelic medicine.

Things to do ....

• The best way to learn how to transform conflict is to invert very ordinary tensions. If you are bored with the same drive to work every day, try introducing simple variations. Everything displays a spirit of some kind. New people, things, and attitudes bring fresh spirits. Take a different route, even if it adds additional time. Leave early and appreciate the neighborhoods, houses, and roads. Find new places to stop for gas, a hot drink, a newspaper, or a bank transaction. Rather than become a victim of the commute, let the demons of repetition call forth the intimately related angels of variety and the imagination of new things.

• If you suffer from the ills of institutional life, recall the excitement when you began working. Imagine your life without daily contacts with people at work. When I am in these situations, I tell myself that the place is generally fine but that my relationship to it is like the weather with its highs and lows. Whatever I put into my workplace returns to me.

Try going into the despised meeting like a pilgrim traveler, looking at the people there and the familiar room as rarities. Arrive early and sit alone in the space and commune with the environment and prepare your emotions. Take on the role of fascinated observer rather than the more familiar position of bored and annoyed person who is required to attend. Become a stranger in the most habitual surroundings, in the office, or on the road to work.

• If I approach the physical world with imagination, it will reciprocate. The angels of creative interpretation encourage different ways of looking at things. They say, "Try it this way instead." I remember Hegel's words: "All consciousness is an appeal to other consciousness." The more energy I focus in a particular direction, the more force I give to its reversal.

Consider the things that bother you the most. Don't try to force change, but watch what happens when you look at them from new perspectives. It is generally the way we look at things that causes our problems.

I go to the pile of bills on my desk and look at them as an aesthetic arrangement. I imagine my delay in paying them as a tantric withholding of pleasure. The way I feel about bills makes me think of my tax returns and the many hours of work that I will soon be doing with them. I perversely consider that tax work may become enjoyable, and I begin to aesthetically contemplate the rituals I go through each spring. My discomfort leads me to a new way of looking.

• If you hate to shovel snow, cut grass, clean toilets and sinks, wash floors, clean windows, or sweep the garage, approach these activities as artwork. Carefully prepare your tools, imagine the results before you begin, work with desire, and take time to contemplate the results. If the aesthetic perspective doesn't appeal to you, consider the moral benefits of doing these maintenance activities as simple acts of service to the world. If you don't do any of these things, think of what you are missing.

Do you have obligations to your environment? Will the way you attend to your space be reciprocated in the way it cares for you?

• Most of us don't change without the help of irritants that focus attention. The social body functions like the physical one. It tells us what's wrong through tensions and pains. Review the positive changes in your life. Were they motivated by conflicts?

Take some time to reflect upon the images of your greatest adversaries in the past and present. Step outside your habitual positions with them and consider the energy and attention you give to them. Reflect upon their hold on you. Try to look at yourself as someone who simply plays a role in life. What would you do without your oppositions?

• Imagine yourself as a sage of conflict. Look at the different conflicts in your life and in the world from the perspective of necessity. Step outside the natural tendency to take sides and look from the perspective of dynamic interplay. Practice "relativizing" the ego position. What is your history with conflict? With judgment?

The power of inversion requires that I see the one to which I appear to be most opposed as the one with whom I am most involved. Jesse Helms as my guardian angel? It's a stretch, but a very interesting moral discipline.

• Play with turning the tables on your most passionate beliefs. Entertain the other side of the coin. Consider the merits of the things that disturb you. Acknowledge their power over your emotions. Try to imagine them as partners that activate a lively interplay. Suspend your effort to control or dominate them, and appreciate them as necessary to the formation of what you are.

Heraclitus, the ancient sage, said that conflict is beneficial. I agree. Conflicts always define positions for us, but we are likely to get caught in their destructive maelstroms when we rigidly take one side of a dispute. I see this pattern in history, world events, and my personal life. The creative transformation of conflict begins with respecting adversaries and trying to understand their positions, which may carry you to new discoveries.

Reflect on your past and present conflicts. Recall the moments of greatest friction with your parents, spouse, children, co-workers. Step outside your positions on issues, and look at the conflicts as revealing where your relations with others are most vital.

• Where are you most likely to "take the bait" in an argument? What is it that hooks you? Follow the lead of your irritations. What do they say about your needs and interests?

• Look at your conflicts as habits. What is the attraction? What is it about the conflict that you need and do not want to let go?

• Recall moments in your life where the tables were turned against your will. When we expect the greatest joy, we are often faced with tragedy, and vice versa. We are in a process of creation, and most of it is not subject to our control, although every life situation does paradoxically call out for our participation. We are all vital players in a creative intelligence that is much greater than any one of us.

Remember the most difficult losses in your life. Was there something born through them? Does every fall carry a resurrection?

Did you lose things through your greatest successes? Does every resurrection carry a fall?

• I have a friend who is a nun who teaches courses on spirituality by having people tell stories about their spiritual roots. The creative mode of the story honors differences. Tell the stories of your sacred experiences. What are your first childhood memories? What were the holy places of your youth? Were there particular people you associated with sacred things? Why? Tell the stories of your religious conflicts and alienations. You might find that the places where you are most "opposed" to religion are where the sacred is most alive for you, and where it has the greatest potential to renew itself.

• It might be helpful to invert your ideas about angels as a way of expanding relations with them. If you think angels are invisible, imagine them as the physical things around you, and vice versa. Why would angels want to limit themselves to one form? If we think of them exclusively as spiritual "persons," this habitual perception may be their most effective disguise. What do you see as the most unlikely locations for angels? This may be where they are most alive for you.

If you think of angels as special and extraordinary beings or places, see them in the faces of the most ordinary people and the features of common places. Angels, like dreams, take on the current forms of the external world. As a child of the first generation of rock 'n' roll, my angels were often rhythmic and sensual, looking like Little Richard, Tina Turner, and my favorite, James Brown.

Try not to restrict the imagination of angels to a particular form, place, or function. Magical beings cannot be limited in this way. They are truly intermediaries, forever moving from one thing to another. Enjoy this movement.

In emphasizing the angelic qualities of ordinary people and things, I do not want to overlook the significance of fantastic images and experiences. As a child, and to this day, I marvel at the chapters (three and four) in *Moby Dick* where Ishmael shares a room and a bed with Queequeg. In describing his reactions to Queequeg's "peculiarities," Ishmael tells us as much about himself and his culture.

The person or culture that is most foreign and frightening may be the best foil for understanding yourself. Imagine yourself sharing a room with a sensitive foreigner. Which of your traits does that person find most unusual, fascinating, and worrisome?

• If you are interested in this process of inverting conventional notions of demons and angels, give some attention to the animals and serpents that have been cast in devilish guises. Reflect on why people do this. How does it express and influence our interactions with the animal world? With nature and the earth?

• The images of my parents, grandparents, and other loved ones were the strongest spirits of my childhood reverie, and I feared losing them. Why do angels have to be something other than our most intimate and familiar spirits?

Reflect on the images of those you love, now and in the past. Appreciate the way the actual person exists as a spirit within your reverie. Do something to honor this presence—write a poem, send a letter to the person, put a flower or stone next to a photograph, or light a candle. Take a simple walk as a ritual way of being with the person's image, and watch how your sensations will evoke different memories and qualities of the person.

5

Exaltation
before
Things

Any object, intensely regarded, may be a gate of
access to the incorruptible eon of the gods.

—James Joyce, *Ulysses*

Images of the beloved ....

Angels, like the closely related muses, are associated with objects of desire. In love relationships, each person embodies images of the longing in the partner's soul. The physical being of the beloved is spiritualized into an angel that configures the heart's desire. Every relationship has its peculiar chemistry, and it may help to acknowledge the spirits of imperfections as well as the idealized aspects.

It's intriguing to consider making home altars to acknowledge the spirits of negative traits. Honoring these demons might be more productive than trying to fix them or eradicate them. It is in their nature to resist change. Making them tangible accepts their presence, and that is a huge step in their treatment. It also makes me more aware of them. I literally give them a place, a sacred place, an altar. I make them into icons, visibly present reminders. I gather the perversities of my soul with the assistance of these material counterparts functioning as symbols. There is magic in making the unsavory aspects of my soul into an image that I love.

Consider these object-loving steps as an alternative to our self-centered strategies of therapeutic control: identify the condition; give it attention and form; *let it change itself* with the assistance of your consciousness. Artistic methods of exaggeration, enshrinement, and humor work *with* the energy of the pathology.

The principle of inversion, turning the tables, and changing positions, is the fundamental tool of the creative process. The most creative people I know are always reversing the way we look at things, showing the other side of every coin. This process is different from a psychology of opposites, which keeps us in the perspective of dualism. What is most foreign or despised is predictably the other side of my consciousness and far more intimately associated with me than I realize. I am talking about partnership, compassion, and unlikely alliances. Inversion is transformative. It is an emotional jujitsu that shifts energies and stuns us with change. Magic works through transformative and paradoxical effects that baffle the mind. The creative person practices the magic of turning things inside out and upside down—the person you hate is the one with whom you are most emotionally involved. Humor works in the same way by turning things in on themselves.

Making home altars to honor unpalatable ways might help avoid some of the worst domestic arguments that constellate around the denial of character traits that annoy others. When I am irritating people, they can simply point to a figure in my altar that represents the condition possessing me. Rather than responding with the aggression of argument that feeds on itself, they can point, perhaps, to the little statue of a fighter who corresponds to my pugnaciousness, or the earplugs suggesting an inability to listen.

Objects are intermediaries between people. They convey messages without the oppositionism that accompanies interpersonal conflict. The object accepts all sincere expressions without the emotional defenses people construct, and it acts as a reliable companion within the process of reflection. Psychically charged energies are transferred onto objects that take the heat off interpersonal relationships.

From the jujitsu masters we can learn the importance of using all of the forces of an environment. The home altar dedicated to my imperfections recycles their energies back into themselves, and magical changes may be possible. The moralistic insistence on curing the bad with the good feeds a condition of sustained opposition, whereas creation sees how ills contain the spirits of their transformation.

Mystics, artists, and devoutly religious people can show us how to expand the spectrum of love beyond singular fixation onto a partner. Loves might be shared with a partner or they can be private. When two people share a love for children, God, an animal, a place, a house, a boat, a garden, domestic objects, a sport or daily ritual, the feelings focused on these things are reflected back to the relationship. This full spectrum of shared loves creates a magnifying effect, which turns the love relationship into a splendid angel whose being is an incalculable multiplication of interacting aspects. The relationship is in this way imagined as a spiritual being whose nature includes the participation of other spirits. The imagination of love is extended in a way that corresponds to the medieval fantasy of identifying and counting angels who exist in an unmeasurable realm. The seasonal rituals of February 14 remind us how to let the angels of love loose in everyday life.

Deep and healthy relationships are complex ecologies of loves and spirits, good and bad. Exclusive focus on one person or one thing tends to put too much pressure on that particular love object and results in unrealistic expectations. One thing cannot hold the varieties of love and their ongoing changes, the angel's appearance "every instant in a new cloak." A relationship with one person can encourage plural loves within the context of its singular commitment. Deep loves lighten over time as demands lesson. When love is focused exclusively on another person, this restriction makes long-term relationships very difficult. The expectations are impossible. I might marry one person after another and never realize the unworkable fantasies I have about marriage and love. I ask: What do I expect from a partner? Where is the perversion in my image of love? If I know and honor the spirit of these demons, I make a place for them within the temple of my heart's love.

Like creation, love is based on the free interaction of contrary spirits. In addition to their evil and fiendish characteristics, demons are also defined as attendant spirits or a personal genius. The pathology of demon possession is complemented by the person who "works like a demon." The word suggests zeal, immersion, and being inspired by a spiritual force.

Demon derives from the original *daimon*—a divine power, a force, or fate that does not have a particular image. This invisible stirring contrasted to tangible figures of Greek mythology. The person acts with or against the current swelling within the soul, *syn daimoni* or *pros daimona.* It is not difficult to envision our histories with love within this context.

Nothing quite fits the original sense of the daimon better than our current emotion of love. Reflections on love can show how positive and negative aspects establish a necessary partnership in any deep psychic condition. The love demon is a force or passion that both motivates and afflicts, soothes and torments. Love is an extreme emotion and therefore requires the interaction of polarities. It will teach how to revision relationships between angels and demons.

Our love afflictions might include a dependence on others to feel valued; exclusive projection of love onto sexual vitality; a demand for continuous ecstacy; an intolerance of depressed phases; control compulsions and possessiveness; betrayals which spring from treating the beloved as a personal savior; the belief that another person can fulfill that aspect of desire that is perpetual and impossible to satisfy.

Love's demons are as important as its angels in giving character to a relationship. How shallow love would be without its jealousies, insensitivities, and impossible demands. Love becomes more flexible and complex once it has accepted imperfections and perverse longings, which are not necessarily bad. They are universal players in love's drama.

James Hillman stopped me in my tracks during a seminar when he talked about how psychotherapy focuses on love of the psyche rather than love of the other person. This idea confused, challenged, and ultimately clarified my experience with love. Hillman's statement is a paradox. Without rejecting love of the other person, we can expand our notion of love to psyche itself. Love of psyche takes the pressure off my partner. It also assumes an embrace of love's vexing ways. The emotion corresponds to the love of God, a love of life, a spiritual love that ultimately enhances our love relationships with others. Hillman helped me to differentiate different types of love and liberate the emotion from an exclusive relationship with another person. As people experienced in the ways of Eros know, we fall in love with the feeling of love and its all-consuming demons, and not just the other person who provokes these spirits in us and whose being embodies the images of love our souls carry. When we desire love, we want to be in the presence of its feelings or angels, Aphrodite and Eros, and the all encompassing mystery from which these persons emanate and return.

Although shared love objects seem to be essential to relationships, it is just as important to have private longings. Personal interests affirm the individuation of partners and celebrate differences. They expand a relationship's resources for change and renewal. In my art studios I notice how focusing psychic energy on the making of art objects expands the range of a person's soul-making. Repeatedly, people describe how caring for the soul through the making of art helps to renew their marriage or other relationships. Religious people similarly experience a renewal of faith through creative expression. We cannot expect this ongoing renewal exclusively from our partners.

Any personal interest can generate images of spiritual longing. While I was visiting Illinois, a friend told me how their famous congressman, Everett Dirksen, spent his free time cultivating marigolds. That particular flower was the congressman's Beatrice, the image of his soul's desire. He chose the marigold as a means of sanctifying his life, and no doubt he looked at the flowers in a different way than most people. He probably saw more in the flower because his soul was attuned to its nature. As with angels, any flower can become the embodiment of the soul's desire. For another person it might be a rose, orchid, or wild lily.

Collectors have highly focused objects of desire. In keeping with the nature of angels, "one" will not do for the collector. There must be many, but the plurality is a highly selective species. The same applies to artistic tastes. The world of angels is characterized by extreme individuation, such as Peggy Guggenheim's collection of modern art. I imagine her house as a temple populated with different angels in each room. The desired object becomes a fetish for the collector, and concentration increases its magical powers.

A person does not have to be wealthy to be a collector. I have known financially impoverished artists who have garnered rare libraries and art collections through friends. Even in poverty they fill their houses and surround themselves with spirits. Poor people and children show us how any object can become the focus of highly personalized tastes and desires—stones, shells, bottle caps, music. We like to surround ourselves with multitudes.

When I worked in a state mental hospital, I noticed how people without belongings ritualistically gathered objects to keep under their beds or in drawers. The objects were often unrelated to one another. It just seemed necessary to have a variety of things around. The staff labeled these people "pack rats" and saw the collecting as another manifestation of disease rather than looking at how this activity was an expression of desire and vitality: the impoverished woman who collected magazine pictures of jewelry, the man "of property" whose jacket pockets were stuffed with books, combs, and other paraphernalia that he never used.

The poet Charles Olson, who lived in Gloucester, Massachusetts, spent a period of his life trying to save historic houses in the city. His aesthetic gaze was focused on the things that most people did not see or appreciate. When he looked at a house, he imagined its history, the people who lived there, the era expressed by its design. When Gloucester houses were being destroyed by "urban renewal," Olson's writings convey a sense of lost love. The city was a reflection of the beloved image, "a magnificent angel," deeply embedded in the poet's soul. When a house was taken by the "developers," there was a sense of soul loss and depression, the same condition associated with psychic ills in archaic times.

> Moan the loss, another
> house
> is gone[1]

Gloucester became Olson's personification of divine love, his sacred object and vessel of transcendence, and he set out to save his own soul by saving the soul of the city. His discipline was poetic meditation. Every feature of the city mirrored the poet's love. This is the way the partnership with angels works. As we articulate the most particular and intimate qualities of the beloved image, we become more deeply engrossed in the angelic relationship.

In a letter to the editor of the *Gloucester Daily Times* entitled "Poet Takes a Gloucester Walk," Olson tried to convey how he senses the city's beauty and history by looking at details overlooked by most people. He described "the light on the white shapely houses too, this rarest of all paintings of this gloire of Gloucester I can look out or walk out and find." Looking out his door or taking a walk after returning from a trip, the poet approaches his home with the sensitivity of a pilgrim.

> I'm up this morning at dawn and my whole soul cries out
> again, looking out my door and seeing the early morning sun so
> differently striking the (Puritan) Hotel I better call the ancient
> Gloucester House brick—how rosy red that is brick as against
> the Mansfield's house's dark red's blood red's brick.
>
> Or I was away most of last week and on Saturday, in the
> morning, walk up again into town, cutting through Tally's to
> swing on to Main, cross over into the sun on the northerly side

and go along to post my letter at the Bob's Haberdashery box—
and up upper Hancock to my doctor's. Returning, stop in Coners
for a gingerale and then equally paced start home.[2]

The angel of the city is its unique character, which we typically
do not see, and because of this "oversight," aesthetic appreciation
of the most basic and simple things brings a fulfilling exuberance.
It is as though inside and outside worlds realize how much they
need each other in order to fully experience themselves. Exaltation
experienced while observing light outside the door of my home is
perhaps linked to an awareness of how often I pass through that
opening without seeing anything. These expressions of the physical
world activate the deep images of love that otherwise lie dormant
in the soul. Through expressions of love for things, we cultivate the
soul of the outer world and pass the sensitivity onto others.

Just as we fill our houses with desired spirits by the way we
arrange the environment, we also try to live in places that correspond to the deep longings within our souls. If we have the freedom
to choose, we select countries, regions, cities, neighborhoods, house
lots, houses, or apartments that resonate with the aesthetic needs
of the soul. It is as though the inner angels long to vibrate with the
spirits of a place.

Incidents of homesickness enable us to entertain the varied images of the homeplace of which we are often unconscious during
daily life. As the cliché teaches, "Separation makes the heart grow
fonder." The persons, things, and places that we take for granted
during our habitual lives are resanctified as beloved images through
the longing for their return. The angelic way of looking at the world
is intimately connected to the archetypal sense of illness as a loss
of soul. Appreciation of life is heightened through the eyes of loss.

I often see how a person's longing is focused on the loss of a way
of living that existed in the distant past, a lost closeness to nature
and animals, lost ties to indigenous and ethnic rituals, the lost

golden ages of culture, lost childhood and innocence. The feeling that it must have been better in an earlier time is tied to the reality of soul's way of making itself felt through the emotion of loss. The heart's pining for things past is something to be experienced as an end in itself. It fills our lives with imaginal vitality and spiritual forces. But it also involves mourning and grief and their evocations of death and the tragic dimension which deepens love and ties it to earth.

Things from the present and the past communicate with one another. Thoughts fly from the present into the past and vice versa. Imagination is the vehicle of exchange, and images are the intermediaries who pass between worlds. As with emotions, one thing evokes another in unexpected ways. The immediate image may be related to the past, in a way that can be likened to the Jungian sense of a particular image's connection to an invisible archetype, but it cannot be completely reduced to what went before.

Gaston Bachelard said that our memories of the past are echoes of the present. They express the soul's tendency to intensify a feeling by connecting it to other things. Metaphor springs from this sentiment. The poetic act binds a particular image of love with the vast and invisible spirit of the emotion. Olson bemoans the loss of a house as though it were a child, a spouse, a mythic love. His feelings for a simple thing were aligned with the forces of divine love, which are transmitted back to ordinary life through the process of imagination. He looked at common lives through the eyes of myth and history.

Through poetic imagination, the most ordinary things can become images of the soul's most profound love. There may be an element of exaggeration in this process, but the way Van Gogh paints some of the greatest masterpieces of Western art representing the artifacts of peasant life gives us cause to reconsider our relationships to things lying around the house. He made pictures of chairs, shoes, flowers in simple pots, a pipe and pouch, and modest domestic scenes that are now considered among the world's most priceless treasures.

Rather than just dismissing the example of Van Gogh on the basis of his artistic greatness and his ability to turn whatever he touched into treasured objects, we can see him delivering an aesthetic message to every person. If "the way" Van Gogh paints a simple tree makes it into a treasured image within the history of art, then the way we look at trees will do the same within the context of the personal imagination. Although we may not all be able to paint as well as he did, we can all look at things with the eyes of Van Gogh, or touch them with his sensibility for textures.

The sensitive painter knows that every aspect of the world expresses a spirit that can be cultivated and transformed into an object of beauty. The earth angel is the image that emerges as an offspring from the interaction between the person and the thing contemplated and transformed. The creative act expresses the qualities of the thing through the feeling of the artist. Van Gogh teaches us to see the beauty and vitality of the most ordinary objects when approached as images of love's desire.

The art historian Meyer Schapiro described how Van Gogh's art expressed "his exaltation before things" and how it "has helped to educate our eyes and to unloosen our feelings." In contrast to previous traditions of stiff academic realism and fantastic scenarios, Van Gogh passionately paints the commonplace. There is more movement in one of his pots of flowers than in an academic painting of a horse race. Van Gogh's pictures were an interplay between his personal exuberance and the wondrous energies streaming out from familiar objects.

We can go to an exhibition of Van Gogh's art or study a catalogue of his pictures, and then meditate on our surroundings as he did. The term *inanimate object* will no longer have a place in our vocabulary. When I do Van Gogh meditations within my house, I focus on individual things, corners, views, the changing configurations on my desks, the varieties of lights, and contemplate them with affection. These meditations on things may at times be dark and brooding, as we also see in Van Gogh's pictures. I ponder my familiar surroundings through the varieties of my moods and feelings. Invariably, they influence my spirits.

During the late 1970s a John Cage and Merce Cunningham concert taught me how to practice similar meditations with sound and movement. Cage was especially convincing as a spiritual teacher in the guise of an artist/trickster. He sat at a small table facing the audience, attached a microphone to a pencil, and used this as his musical instrument by writing on sheets of paper. His sounds interacted with Cunningham's movement. Once I surrendered to the monotony of Cage's improvisations, they became increasingly fascinating. I began to feel the different tones and tempos of scratching as though they were part of a symphony. The simplicity of the composition helped further their communication with Cunningham's movements. It was all so pure, direct, and surprisingly soulful. Cage and Cunningham were immersed in what they were doing. They loved these rudimentary expressions, and this had a strong effect on the audience.

As we work with performance art and ritual in the art studios I direct, we discover that what really matters is the commitment, the sincerity of expression, the love for what a person is doing. If these elements are present, the angels will be too. The love for the expression has to come from both the artist and those who witness it. Love generates a feeling of mystery and deep appreciation for simple things, whereas the analysis, or explanation, of an artwork lacks this sense of sanctity. The feeling of love includes dislikes and discomforts. Everything does not have to be perfect and always nice. The love for the image is a feeling of commitment to it, a willingness to stick to it, no matter how troublesome or offensive it may be. It is a complete compassion for the well-being of the other, which many are incapable of giving. It requires the ability to put my preoccupations aside for the duration of a performance.

I have learned from these performances how the most basic body movements, or the sounds of a hand tapping a table, or water being poured from a pitcher, can provoke profound feelings. Actually, it seems that the more authentic and unpretentious the expression, the more provocative it is. "The simpler, the deeper," the performances continuously tell us. Just allow yourself to be present and act instinctually while being observed by another.

It is the loving observer who creates the magic. There must be a passionate watching of something that would otherwise pass unnoticed. This is where the angel is located. In my performance art groups, witnesses do this for the actors, and in our daily life we can do it for ourselves and for the people and objects with whom we live.

John Cage demonstrated how to get excited about the most basic and familiar sounds that I typically overlook in my zeal for the "music." We do the same thing to angels. We want our sounds to be like Mozart's. Rather than seeing, hearing, and feeling them in our most personal and humble acts, we hope for grand and profound apparitions. Why not let the angels correspond to the actual spirits of our environments, let them be themselves, accept them for what they are? But instead, we have these idealized versions of our inner figures. We do the same thing to our partners through impossible demands, making them conform to our fantasies and expectations.

My method is a simple one. It loves and takes delight in the most ordinary and perverse qualities of authentic living and the images it generates. Angels are the spirits of our most intimate thoughts, feelings, and surroundings.

Soulful materialism ....

. . . and new and new and new,
that comes into and steadies my soul.
—Marianne Moore, *The Pangolin*

Freud understood the way we endow objects with psychic energy. This concentration of emotion on things and ideas is called cathexis. But Freud overlooked the countercathexis through which objects transmit their energies to people. The autonomous and expressive energy of things did not fit his scheme of psyche and its treatment, which was centered in human reason and control. If we return to the more ecological thinking of the Roman poet and philosopher Lucretius, we see that objects generate their own expressions, which fly out to people. They are loaded with unappreciated messages and influences as well as unaccessed medicines. Life is for most of us a constant interplay of unacknowledged stimulations.

Joe Skeptic says, "You're beginning to sound like Pavlov, a behaviorist in the guise of angels."

I am intrigued by the instinctual reflex, the way the physical world shapes us, the folly of human control over the elements. If God is present in everything, then Ivan Petrovich Pavlov can be imagined as a magnificent theist enthralled by the perceptible actions of the Deity. I have always had this quirky feeling that B. F. Skinner was a religious zealot. The divine purpose is in the doing, rather than what you profess. Look at the way Skinner lived, the echo of Walden in his soul, the fervent commitment to an idea. As my Irish grandmother liked to say, "God works in strange ways."

Humans have always used personal artifacts and markings to

consciously and unconsciously cultivate spiritual relationships to places. The objects function as intermediaries between persons and environments. Whenever I empty a room to work on the floor, repair a ceiling, or paint walls, I am struck by how I feel the absence of furnishings and other contents.

When moving away from a house, it seems that walking through the rooms, emptied of the familiar spirits, is the decisive ritual of passage. Taking down the pictures, packing the books, moving furniture, and then sweeping the empty room, acknowledge the change of spirits in the home. I imagine the moving trucks filled with family angels making their way to a new habitat. Similarly, we establish our psychic energy in a new home by filling it with our "things." These intermediaries, or earth angels, are the means by which we endow the house with psychic energy. They also function as conduits through which the spirits of the house enter the souls of new inhabitants.

Jewelry and family heirlooms are potent and traditional links between generations. Clothing and bodily ornaments similarly serve to mediate between our inner feelings and the energies of the outside world. Familiar and favored things are especially potent as a means of empowering or comforting their wearers. I hate to give up a well-worn wallet even though I have two new ones waiting to be used. The same applies to an old sweater or shirt. We think exclusively about our attachments to these things, but like our household animals, these things may experience deep connections to us.

My wife just gave me a new pair of slippers. I said to her, "I guess this means that it's time to throw the old ones out." They were moccasins lined with wool. I had worn them for two decades. The soles were sound, but the seams were coming apart. I reluctantly put them in the trash.

An hour later I went into the kitchen and saw that my wife had taken them out. They were sitting on the floor like old friends. I reflected on how their shape and aging had been formed through daily life with my feet. They served me well for many years. And now at the end of their useful life, they cannot adapt to another person. I am the only one who can fully appreciate their being and their history. They depend upon me for this.

My wife said, "I couldn't bear to see them in there with the milk cartons and food scraps."

"I'll find a use for them," I said.

This aspect of the earth angel can create clutter in our houses. And there are often conflicting needs in holding on to old things and preparing for the new through open space.

Value is a quality we attach to things through contact and a mutual history. Those slippers were full of soul because of our long and cozy relationship. They were my house shoes, the ones I wore through cold winters in my domestic temple, and they had a much more personal aura than the shoes I wore outside. I notice how my relations to people in the neighborhood get more intimate simply because we pass time together in the same place, acknowledge each other on the street, and occasionally speak or help one another with a problem.

I try to imagine objects and clothing as beings with which I live in an intimate association. Like any good relationship, we need time to cultivate affections for each other. This commitment keeps me from getting spread too thin or overwhelmed in my object life. I generally reflect on what I want, and do not want, to buy. Once the need has been established, I open myself to the impulses of consumerism and the pleasures of buying. The manic lust for more and more things has something to do with the world's material problems, and what we call the gross inequities in the distribution of nature's bounty.

My way does not help the economics of consumerism and the new faith that more consumption will ultimately help everyone, the idea that life on the planet will improve if everyone buys more.

Maybe they're right. Love of things and the reciprocal energies that pass between them and people may alter the world psyche. But I am suspicious. As with many medicines, too much can be harmful. Compulsive buying weakens the psychic power of objects and our relationships to them. It can become an all-consuming mania. The appeal of things no doubt generates a defense in me, an instinctual control of desire, and the inevitable pleasure that comes when I surrender and let loose in stores and restaurants, or in buying a new car or house. The release is probably that much more enjoyable because of the tantric withholding I do when it comes to buying new things. Not long ago I took my seventeen-year-old daughter on a shopping spree, and when we got home we displayed our purchases to the family like trophies after the hunt. Fresh energies were brought into the house by the new things.

One of the greatest pleasures in the lives of my four- and eight-year-old daughters is to visit the village store to buy candy and other things. My nineteen-year-old son is hooked on video rentals, my wife can't stop buying children's clothes, and I have few restraints in a good bookstore. Consumerism may be an angel in disguise when buying is in sync with a healthy love of things and a lively commercial exchange between people. During my many trips to the Old City of Jerusalem and the Arab shops along narrow lanes with wares hanging everywhere, I have felt how commerce is a deeply ingrained aspect of the soul. Shopping in the Middle Eastern bazaar puts the American mall into an archetypal perspective. The environments have changed, together with the goods and the methods of vendors, but still the buying and selling of material things is one of the most vital pulse beats of the *anima mundi*.

Angels are themselves the latest commodity in the market of fads. Marketing angels? What a contradiction, or is it the basis of the peddler's craft—the merchandising of an idea, an image?

Remember those Infinity ads that featured movement through a landscape and never showed the car? They understood the indirect and unseen ways of spirits. Maybe the advertisers are close to the soul's sensual orientation and love of mystery. They even know how to access the collective memories of a culture: James Dean wore khakis (according to the Gap ad campaign). They're essentially saying, "Angels, the images of your soul's desire, wore khakis." Rather than just looking down on the advertisers as covert persuaders, why not embrace them as expressions of soul.

But let's return to the difficulties of consumerism and how they impact on the earth angels. We tend to be so busy wanting things and acquiring new possessions that we don't give the objects a chance to influence us.

Concerned people can model faithfulness and longevity in their object relations, perhaps lessening the runaway desire for things that torments so many of us. Wealthy people might grow to desire or envy the intimate and grateful relationship that a Buddhist monk has for an article of clothing worn every day or the affection that a woman has for a bowl she made and uses with each meal. I give credit to Yankee culture on this point. There is a pure strain of aesthetic simplicity and pragmatism that runs deep in the New England soul. The true Yankee is the one who, in spite of great affluence, wears the same pair of shoes for years, drives his Ford station wagon until it dies, and keeps his favorite sweater and canvas sneakers long after the first holes appear. There are virtues in these behaviors that we miss when simply attributing them to parsimony and hanging on to the last nickel.

I am starting to moralize, and I can hear the internal critic say, "The pathologies of consumerism are also an opening to the soul. Don't try to fix things and impose yet another 'correct' standard that every one has to follow. Every desire is holy and they will never be tamed. Your moralizing doesn't work for me. I want excess, rococo angels everywhere, the Louis XIV aspect of more, and more, and more. I respect your monkishness, or is it Yankee thrift? Leave me to my extravagance and spendthrift ways. There are earth angels at work here too. I keep others working by spending. Let the money go and make its way through the world. Don't try to solve the economic problems of the planet by changing the archetypal chemistry of how people and objects relate to one another. I heard you have a middle-aged hankering for a new Harley Davidson. But you deny these objects of your soul's desire. Take a ride on excess. Let go of your frugality."

I reply, "Some say that we've each got to manage the desire. But I hate the word *manage*. It's so controlling, too much ego. How about the Epicurean standard of taste?"

"Sounds elitist," the critic says.

"That's just the label you attach to it. If you get inside the feeling, you might see that it is guided by an aesthetic sensibility as to what the soul needs. It may not want excess. Epicurus didn't. All he wanted was tranquility."

"Sounds like control," the critic replied.

I say, "Restraint has its place in a soulful life. I ride that motorcycle constantly in the imaginal realm. I may want to keep it there as an Orphic spirit."

This engagement helps me see that excess and extreme conditions are vital aspects of the soul. The life of moderation can be viewed as a defense against the extremes and their inevitable inversions. High tides are impossible without the lows. The soul thrives on peculiarities, perverse, highly individuated standards of taste, what Wallace Stevens called the "nobility" of odd imaginings.[3]

Perverse ways may have to be protected like an endangered species from the politically correct waves of conformity. So much of modern art can be viewed as an aesthetic perversion. I saw a photograph of Andy Warhol in his huge New York apartment, which looked more like a warehouse than a home. Objects that he acquired covered all of the tables, chairs, and floor space. I saw the picture just before Warhol died. It had an unforgettable impact, maybe because it was so contrary to my desires. He looked overwhelmed by the stuff. It felt chaotic.

I said to myself, "What a horrible and wasteful way to live, with your space confined by things."

I imagined the objects needing space, attention, a good dusting.

But Warhol's extravagance, his object madness and perversions, may be the reason he is who he is, while I live my bourgeois life properly caring for things. As the cliché goes, "It takes all kinds."

As soon as I move away from moralizing about Warhol's behavior, I see how his strange ways have an impact on me. They engage me through discomfort. What is most distant and repulsive strangely connects to our most unrealized inner complex. Warhol's clutter reveals my bias for order, which may be a disguise repressing my soul's longing for irregularity and pandemonium.

The picture of his apartment can be revisioned as a "postmodernist angel" helping me accept the nonlinear order of chaos and the end of ruling doctrines, the different ways of people, the extraordinary upheaval in the rooms of my adolescent children, a relaxing of my neat compulsions.

There are no natural laws of object desire. The things in Warhol's apartment might have enjoyed the atmosphere, the freedoms, the crowdedness, the sense of community. The angels are at work in every environment.

The critic speaks again: "It's interesting how you mention Andy Warhol, because I am wondering whether his paintings of Campbell's soup cans are in keeping with your sensibility for the earth angel and what you call soulful materialism."

I can't speak for Warhol's motives, but Pop Art was full of irony. Its imitations were parodies and not necessarily meditations. I don't feel a sense of reverence in the pop icons for the things of the world. The movement felt more like a cynical spoof that used the objects of popular culture as subjects for the artist's derisive wit. But like any other trend, it came and went. In the art world the treasured object was the Warhol painting that had its brief moment of fame, in keeping with his aesthetic, but I am more interested in the soup can's display on the supermarket shelf. The painting draws attention to its presence.

Pop Art was celebrated as a representation of the "new American landscape" of advertising, mass media, urban closeups, packaging, and other aspects of the contemporary environment of the 1960s as "selected, idealized, and described" by the artist.[4] This way of describing Pop Art is very close to my sense of the earth angel. But when the process is restricted to the frame of art history, it loses the angelic qualities that emit from the pure presence of the thing itself. It is interesting how modernist poetry avoided all of these "campy" trends and maintained an essentially sacred bond between the artist and the object of contemplation.

The poem sees into things with a disciplined sensitivity to the subtle spirits of their material expressions. Objects stimulate an imaginative and intimate response, as demonstrated by Djuna Barnes, who describes "a fine frying-pan that could coddle six eggs, and a raft of minor objects that one needs in the kitchen."[5] There is no irony or cleverness in this image, just affection and imaginative empathy.

Open and loving warmth toward the object may be a feminine sensibility, but it is not restricted to women, as elegantly demonstrated by William Carlos Williams, who conveys my sense of the earth angel and soulful materialism. He felt that "the poem / is a discipline" that helps us see what we already have.

In the poem "Between Walls," Williams observes the radiance of broken glass on barren ground. "Nantucket" focuses on a carefully kept room, sunlight passing through white curtains. And his signature poem, "The Red Wheelbarrow," not only brings the world to bear on the presence of a simple thing, but stresses its location in a setting of reciprocal relations with "white chickens."[6]

Williams shows how everything, no matter how lowly, carries aesthetic spirits. Poetic perception is a discipline of opening to an object's illumination. The poet serves as its speaker, as an intermediary and angel of its expression. When poets function angelically, the self is effaced as it becomes an invisible carrier, finely attuned to the object of contemplation. Poets carry the spirits of things to readers. The broken glass, the white curtains, and the wheelbarrow need creative partners if they are to move from matter to spirit. The poet similarly draws inspiration from the expressive qualities of the thing and its relations with its surroundings. This ecology of objects in a living space is not expressed by the images of Pop Art, moved from their habitats and displayed under the bright lights of a gallery.

Rudolf Arnheim says, "The more the work of art is isolated from its setting, the more it is singularly burdened with the task it used to share with its total environment." Arnheim recalls a time when objects interacted with people, served as "guiding images" and "companions" that helped us live more intimately with the material world. He sees art as a means of revival. When things are no longer a symbolic means of connecting to the broader soul of the world, we are restricted in our participation with otherness, which is the basis of the creative imagination. Arnheim says the objects "no longer speak . . . it is the eloquence of objects that makes art possible, our hope for reviving the objects now comes from the arts."[7]

The function of art becomes a shamanic journey in search of the lost soul that needs to be returned to the world. Since art is often an expression of the pathology of objects separated from a soulful ecology of matter where every physical thing has aesthetic significance, it also carries the cure. Artists everywhere have penetrated to the madness of their estrangement, and the alienation from life points toward a more soulful cooperation. The historical rise of "art," and its separation from the ecology of things, corresponds to the disassociation of soul from the physical world. The art object is a psychic symptom, an obsession, carrying the maladies of a greater complex of forces. Within this perspective, Pop Art is a strong toxin, paradoxically serving as an antitoxin, a bizarre phenomenon indicat ing our culture's departure from natural relations with things and places.

Poets have maintained a vigil with ordinary material things, always caring for their souls during difficult times. When the earth angels were disappearing, poets kept the love for them alive. Poetic reflection sustains the mysteries of people interacting with the things of the world through deep and magical levels of kinship.

I feel a big difference between the sentient gaze of the poetic soul and the brassy displays of Pop Art, sold at unnatural prices and thoroughly wrapped up in the fashions of mercantile hype. If the art of producing pictures were widely viewed as a meditation, like writing poetry, then the images as well as public attitudes toward them would change.

My reference to paintings being "wrapped up" in trends makes me think of Christo's wrapping of building and other projects where he might arbitrarily run a fence across miles of natural environment. I've always been intrigued by his events and the way they transform spaces. They've all been fascinating visual displays. But they are probably the most antithetical thing in contemporary art to my sense of the earth angel. There is so much egoism in them, and it flies on a grandiose scale. I can't imagine justifying the consumption of so much material to express a personal fantasy. The architectural extravagances of Louis XIV seem practical in comparison.

As an artist I value the transformation of environments, but I am drawn to those people who work with the natural qualities of a place, adapting themselves to the habitat. Christo's expressions seem intent on heroic domination. Raising large sums of money for these projects is a magnificent symptom of the disease afflicting the *anima mundi.* Unwittingly, the events are saying, "Wake up! Art has no place in the world. These objects don't belong. They convey a complete separation of persons and things from nature. Art only increases the alienation and pathological sensation. 'No more art' will take us to more passionate relations with all things, a radical expansion of aesthetic relations and love for objects. Despising art is the way to appreciating all things."

I have a friend who did a series of environmental constructions on beaches, below the high tide line, with things he found there. After making the work, he photographed it and waited for the sea to reclaim the materials and sweep the place back into its native condition. His expression collaborated with that of the ocean. Performance artists also construct environments in nature as sanctuaries for their rituals. I realize that Christo's constructions have a ritual aspect to them and the land is returned afterward to its natural condition, but what is it about our artistic culture that has to make such a massive and unnatural transformation? What pathology of our collective soul inhabits these provocations? Christo might be my angel of wasteful expression. As the ancient Greeks teach us, there is a god in every condition of life, good and bad.

I look out my window at the mile-long cove across the street and I imagine making a line of large iridescent orange, glow-in-the-dark buoys anchored in a twenty-four-hour display—one buoy for each hour. It excites me to imagine a string of upright orange sentinels in the historic cove lined with colonial white houses. I realize that the whole process could be approached in the spirit of a festival.

If this were Christo's project, he would probably make thousands of buoys and surround all of Cape Ann in keeping with his exaggerated scale. The project would draw attention to the environment and divisive argument. Some will say that the purpose of such an event is no less mad than ninety percent of what we do anyway in our daily lives. I am intrigued by Christo's projects, but ultimately I am more attuned to giving attention to the broken glass on cinders, to the things that already exist in a place.

My sensibility for the earth angel is closer to the way native peoples ask that we walk lightly on the earth, our presence diminished, as we honor entities other than ourselves. I identify with spiritual traditions that express themselves by modifying the land as little as possible rather than those that radically transform places. Christo's projects stimulate me to look at the world, but I prefer subtlety. I feel a similar absence of nuance in the flashy values surrounding Pop Art—which does not mean that I want polite niceties rather than offensive and unusual expressions. I am trying to get to the core of a soulful way of relating to things that does not assume that they are here on this world exclusively to serve us and our fantasies. I like to imagine myself attending to them and cultivating their well-being. I will serve them as they serve me. Our beings are reciprocal. I don't see this love for the things in Christo's environments.

And I don't know whether Warhol was loving or mocking the things he made, or whether it matters. Aside from these speculations about Warhol's intentions, or those of the critical spinmasters who interpreted his work, when I look at his oil paintings of Campbell's soup cans—cream of vegetable, turkey noodle, chili beef, scotch broth, green pea, pepper pot, and tomato—I'm intrigued with the images. I feel the same way about his *Marilyn Monroe Diptych* and his *Brillo Box* silkscreened onto a wooden cube. My impression was that Andy Warhol never projected the reverence and serious involvement with things that characterized the Dada and Surrealist movements. His manner seemed decadent and sardonic, but these qualities teach me something about dark imaginings. Ultimately, the images speak for themselves. The Brillo box is especially appealing to me. I have my personal take on it. I am engaged by Warhol's images, and this is what really matters.

This autonomy of an image is the heart of the earth angel. The image belongs to the viewer as the poem is expropriated by the reader. No significant creation has a fixed meaning. The object will take me into its being. The Brillo box does this to me. Its presence is so strong and intriguing that Warhol's intentions are irrelevant.

It is remarkable how the image of a particular thing is seized by every person who comes into contact with it, yet the things themselves cannot be given a final definition. They are like people, forever generating new responses. In practicing a soulful materialism I never take an object for granted, and I always reassess my relationship to it.

Andy Warhol cast the Brillo box before us as a thing unto itself. He deserves credit for this, and the box takes over from there. To the extent that the box is isolated from its environment, it may lead the way to the return of soul to the world. The Brillo box is sent out from the world as a messenger, an angel, whose estrangement is a call to journey home.

The enticements of water ....

Yes, as every one knows, meditation and water are wedded
for ever . . . that same image, we ourselves see in all rivers
and oceans. It is the image of the ungraspable phantom of life;
and this is the key to it all.   —Herman Melville, *Moby Dick*

I live on a body of water called Lobster Cove in Annisquam, a
village in Gloucester, Massachusetts. It's considered to be one of
two fjords on the East Coast, although greatly diminished in comparison to Somes Sound on Maine's Mount Desert Island.

For seventeen years I had a house on the other side of Gloucester in Magnolia. The city comprises most of Cape Ann and offers
different interactions between land and water. The Atlantic coast
of Magnolia is rugged, rocky, and lined with tall pines and oaks. A
short distance away in Annisquam, on Ipswich Bay, the coastline is
tidal, with radical fluctuations in water levels, miles of sandbars,
expansive marshes, and labyrinthian passages through the tidewater
channels and estuaries of West Gloucester, Essex, and Ipswich.

The vastness of the open Atlantic off Magnolia never motivated
me or the family to get out onto the water. I was content to look,
smell, and listen to the crashing waves as I walked or sat near them.
There was a sense that people belonged on shore. I imagine if the
community were more involved with life on the water, there would
be an incentive to do likewise.

Annisquam's physiognomy suggests reciprocation between
water and land. The physical characteristics of the place influence
the way life is lived within it. I am fairly regular in my habits and
meditational practices, so it is noteworthy to observe how much the

things that I do have changed since moving. The environment is the engine of my movements, and I respond to its initiatives.

Landscapes configure our spiritual impressions. They shape imaginings and transmit spirits that correspond to their structures. I've always believed that there will be a renaissance of Native American spirituality among the transplanted Europeans who built their culture without a sense of the traditions of the local pneuma of earth, sky, and waters. Indigenous spirits can never die, because they live in the expressions of the natural world.

I appear to be so attuned to the spirits of the land, waters, breezes, community configurations, and neighborhood architecture that my cosmology has radically shifted by moving across town. Having the center of the city directly east of my habitat is distinctly different from living to the south and driving north to do local business. As a New Englander, always living with the Atlantic due east, I have discovered a new orientation with Ipswich Bay to the west. Annisquam offers sunsets over the bay, something I associate with California, or an island where the relations between water and land correspond to the edges of a continent.

I am content looking at Ipswich Bay from my fixed position and don't feel an urge to travel to the other side. But when I gaze at the tidal channels, I'm drawn into them. They express close and shapely relations between water and land. I cannot resist the invitations of the labyrinth, especially when it is filled with tidal waters and lined with marsh grass. Standing before it, I am ushered into its unknown passages, its sensuous lines and curves. The scale is closer to my own place on the earth. When I enter the labyrinth, I feel an intimate interaction. The environment affirms my presence, and I am instinctively attracted to it, like a ground animal or serpent that thrives in close quarters. I feel a similar enticement when walking or skiing on a wooded path that reveals a new vista with each turn, or when driving along winding country roads. Something has me attached to its lure and line. The pull is a magnetic longing toward no place in particular. The landscape generates my action and desire to see what lies beyond the bend.

There are so many things to do on the water in Annisquam that we have been perplexed as to what kind of boat to get. My conservative aspect wants to make sure that it will be used. When my son was fourteen, he insisted on using his summer job money to buy a wind surfer. He was smitten by the image of the sport.

I said, "But you don't know how to do it yet. Shouldn't you learn first and see if it's something you like?"

Adolescent impulse prevailed against my restraint. My son bought his wind surfer, tried to get up on it two or three times, and never used it again.

We've probably all had things that we've bought on the basis of a desire not informed by experience—the kitchen gadgets and lawn games that were only used a few times before they made it to a yard sale or charity, the oil paintings and framed prints in the attic.

I have a collection of camping and hiking equipment that we used on vacations a quarter of a century ago. The stuff is so outdated that the children will probably never use it because it doesn't have a current image. It doesn't call out to them and inspire a particular action as it did to me years ago. The luster of these things has been lost because they no longer belong within the current object discourse of the recreational world. There is a forum of communication among objects and the people using them, and the old things are outside this community of interactions. But I keep the equipment carefully stored in the barn, thinking I will use it someday, but in reality I am keeping the memories of the backpacks, tent, propane stove, and lantern.

I have no desire to be in a power boat. It feels too much like driving a car, which I don't really enjoy. Besides, why inflict yet another mechanical creature on the marine habitats?

I confess my fascination with the huge Formula speedboats. The droning motors are closer to something you'd hear at the airport than the seashore. The boats group together when they anchor at a beach. They carry a distinct culture of appearances and extravagance, which is so foreign to me that it is strangely appealing. Their underworld names—*Concubine, Insanity, Skin Hunter, Mayhem II, Red Devil, Mania*—show that their owners are acutely attuned to the poetic spirits of things.

One of those boats costs more than four years at Harvard. I could never justify even a visit to a showroom. Our family has discussed a Boston Whaler with an outboard. My children say they will take care of it, but I know that like everything else outside the walls of the house, it will fall under my jurisdiction.

Do I want to care for yet another material spirit? Maybe I should get it for the children, but they're already so busy, and I feel that the boat, like the wind surfer, is more an idea than a material presence.

We discussed canoes, but I doubted that my wife and I would ever get organized enough to paddle off together with the young children and a picnic basket.

My sisters rowed in college, and I looked into ocean shells, but you can't see where you are going, and this could be a major problem, together with the outriggers for the oars, in a cozy place like ours with constant turns and boats to navigate.

While looking at canoes in Maine, I got my first look at a sea kayak. The lines of the boats, their lightness and quickness, all began to work on my imagination. On a second trip we bought a small kayak with a seat for a child. It weighs thirty-eight pounds, and I can easily carry it to the cove across the street from our house. I used the kayak almost every day, and on a third trip to Maine, I bought a larger and sleeker boat, which I also use constantly.

I found the boat that suits my spirit and the area where I live. The craft is an intermediary, a subtle and quiet presence, something that functions between me and the places to which I am drawn. Like an angelic intermediary, it is relatively invisible, a natural extension of its environment, capable of moving freely through narrow spaces.

There are also multiple benefits attached to kayaking, more than one thing happening at once, like the way Robert Frost described woodcutting as "twice warmed." I want to exercise but can't tolerate lifting mechanical devices designed solely to build muscles. I need a more indirect workout, something done outside, communing with atmospheric spirits.

I love cross-country skiing, and ocean kayaking is an archetypal kin. Both have their origins in practical transportation. They are solitary, quiet, radically low-tech, and physically rigorous moving meditations that are intimately linked to the environment. Sitting slightly below the waterline and paddling with a sense of balance in the narrow craft, extends the sensations of sight, sound, and smell.

At first I ventured into the open ocean only on calm days. I felt no control in large waves, swells, and boat wakes. The light kayak seemed inconsequential in relation to their force. As I have become attuned to the feel of the boat in different waters and less claustrophobic with my lower body confined inside the boat by a snug "skirt" around my waist and stretched over the edges of the cockpit, I have begun to enjoy the more turbulent waters. The wakes I once scorned are now opportunities for adventure. Paddling over the swells of the ocean feels like a harmonic therapy, with my whole being immersed in the rhythmic heaving of the sea. The kayak lets me gracefully float on the deep and constant breathing of the waters. It is one of the most physical ways of being in contact with the earth and its spirits.

Kayaking has expanded my intimacy with my neighborhood and my imagination of the physical world. Everything we use in daily life can be viewed with a similar appreciation. Things that we love, like my kayak, can be talismans that spread their affections to whatever we do.

As I contemplate daily life, I see that everything is done through the agency of things. I wonder if I can transfer the enticements of water to the highway? Can I convert the spirits of the beloved place to the one I despise? Can the spells of the tidal labyrinth spill over into an office? Can one form of physical vitality inspire another? Is there a contagion of the material imagination?

The creative spirit crosses all boundaries and cannot be contained in one place, one idea, one community, text, or institution. It must move from one thing to another, connecting them like the earth angels linking matter and spirit. Each realm of the creative spirit ignites others. The vitality of water heightens my sense of land and air.

An immersion in a beloved person, place, thing, or activity will arouse spirits that spread on their own accord. Any physical activity that moves the soul is a way to commune with earth angels. Water entices me, so I become an agent who radiates the spirits of enticement to other forms of life. The water and myself are participants in a larger interplay of attractions. Spirituality is an ecosystem, connected to the tonality of the earth and its elements, each one generating distinct spirits that participate in the global or cosmic play, composed of interactions between things. Rather than affixing my spiritual interests to only one part of life or one belief, the beloved object opens to the spectrum of love.

The earth angel is not a literal thing or being, but a force that moves among things. We experience it as meaningful occurrences, activities, connections, loves, and longings, but it cannot be restricted to a single place. In keeping with the classical view of angels as intermediaries between worlds, earth angels express the movement between matter and spirit, their mutual need for one another. The earth angel is the water's expression, its enticement, its spirit that activates imagination. When inspired by a material substance, I am lured by its earth angels, the qualities that attract relationship.

Our negative attitudes actually affirm the presence of spirits in things. I am quick to judge the loud, fast, gas-guzzling Formula boats, responding to them in the way a temperance advocate does to the "evil spirits" in a bottle. I don't like what the boat does to the water and to my ears, but the more I reflect on it, I see what a hold it has on my imagination. It is the provocative demon (as acknowledged in the names given to the boats by their owners) that I pair with the angel of my kayak.

The Formula boat is all engine covered by fiberglass. It is the embodiment of exaggerated technology, riding high and pounding through large waves, while the minimal kayak bobs on them and delicately makes it way. The Formula boats take me to dark and destructive powers of the sea, the unpredictable malevolence that is unseparable from its sparkling charms, the four Gloucester fishermen lost last month in a storm, the newspaper obituary in Italian that was written by a wife expressing her husband's love for the sea. The boats' powers pale before the ocean's force, Poseidon's heaving and liquid muscles.

There are separations between ourselves and anything in the physical world. Every form of matter generates the spirits of potential relationship to a soul ready to engage the imagination it carries. The Formula boat is my soul's foil, stimulating imagination as much as the beloved Kayak. Angels need their demons and cannot exist without them.

Dreams ....

The soul knows itself through the senses.
—*The Confessions of Saint Augustine*

Dreams are the primary carriers of psychic contents. They express soul's desire for images linking matter and spirit. TV dinners, credit cards, and old Packards are the earth angels of sleep that guide and entertain us with an intelligence operating outside habitual thinking. They deliver oracular messages, finely attuned to things that we overlook, and they communicate through images that exaggerate, dramatize, and offer startling perspectives on situations.

One night after my wife and I argued, I dream that *we are sitting on the hood of a small convertible sports car, speeding along with no one driving. I reach back for the wheel and try to steer, but that only makes things worse because the car appears to know its way. I think of crawling into the car and putting on the brakes, but that doesn't seem possible.*

The dream counsels about runaway and crazy argument that has a mind of its own, carrying and driving people dangerously. The bickering becomes an impossible and speeding joust for control, a sport, with the steering wheel and brakes out of reach. My wife and I are helpless, sitting on the quarrel that carries us, and physically close to each other through it all, two carpers on the car's hood. The dream is also a pure presence, an image of my wife and me careening through a life that we cannot control. The message is delivered wondrously and dramatically through the imagination of the scene. I respond to the dream with awe and feel the presence of a guardian angel in the imagery.

Last night before going to bed I realized that I had not remembered a dream for weeks. I had been very busy, and this always interferes with my reflections on nocturnal images. I find that immersing myself in the atmosphere and imagery of dreams revitalizes their place in my waking life, so I briefly looked at some dream images that I recorded from previous months and went to sleep.

I woke early in the morning with a dream, and I felt blissful connections between the dream and day world. I lay in an intermediate place between the two as I contemplated the dream. *I discover a new area in my garden, an outdoor fireplace and chimney, between my property and that of a neighbor who actually lives two houses down the street. The area is roofed and surrounded by wooden lattice and vines. There is a metal door below the fireplace, and as I open it, ashes fall out.*

A few days earlier I was at a wedding for the granddaughter of an octogenarian lady who lives between my house and the family in the dream. The house next door has gardens filled with lattice and a little studio at the back of the property where her husband used to work. He is dead now. The woman cannot freely move around her property anymore. I realize that my four-year-old daughter visited her yesterday to check in after all of the action of the wedding and a party held the day after in her garden. The neighbors on the other side of her were also at the wedding. It feels now as if the ashes in the fireplace are suggestive of the feeling after all of the fire, the transformations of the wedding. The dead husband's studio is in a place similar to the location of the dream fireplace.

My way of relating to dreams encourages a flow of connections between the nocturnal images and our day lives. There is never a single meaning or answer. The dreams draw us into a web of psyche, an ecology of soul, in which everything is related. The most subtle and apparently irrelevant details teach us to see how psyche weaves us into a tapestry of purposeful imagery.

Not only does the essential nature of the dream elude rational explanation, but its purpose is the revelation of an irrational soul-scape. An emphasis on dream meanings and answers can be a defense against dream sensation and the soul's natural ways of knowing itself. Explanations are ego's way of controlling soul. Rather than pouring the psychic contents of dreams into the hardened molds of our theories, we can appreciate the pure flow of images as they move through us at night and in our reflections on them afterward. We keep the dream fluid and sustain its imaginal life. If the soul needs sensory images in order to experience itself, as suggested by Saint Augustine, then a soulful method of responding to dreams will restrain ego's tendency to dominate.

There are techniques of control that actually try to direct the contents of dreams before they arrive. These methods oppose the essential function of the dream and soul's impingement upon ego's boundaries of experience. The way of the dream is dissolution, flow, and the constant remaking of relations between things.

The reflecting mind's desire for contact and relationship to the dream can be embraced within this flux. If we can view our associations to dreams as efforts to connect material and spiritual realms, then the process stays fluid. Soul's kinesis is sustained because the rational or reflecting mind does not try to control dreams. It desires a deepened relationship to the images that express soul's desire for intimate relations to physical things.

Let's return to my dream and interact with it through a series of connections. The purpose of my method is a kinetic process of interpretation, a stirring of possibilities rather than affixing meanings.

There are no people in the dream, only an unused and undiscovered fireplace. My art studio has been unused for months. The man who lives two houses down from me is a painter and a board member of the village hall art gallery. They keep asking me to hang pictures in their shows, and I never seem to get organized to submit anything. In a few days I will be leading art studio retreats in New Hampshire and New Mexico, and I will be surrounded by "new images," creative fires. My work is a tending of fires. I am surprised and fascinated by the fireplace in the dream. Like my studio, it is outside the house. It is time to make art, to generate fires.

I am not suggesting that my dream "means" that I have to clean out the ashes from my studio and get the fires burning again. These are simply connections that I am making to the dream. Absolute certainty is not the purpose of dream messages. Dream images stimulate us to respond to them with images. They are undisguised in their mission of infusing our lives with imagination and soul. Whatever aspects of my day life that I connect to the dream will receive the infusion of spirit, so it is helpful to make as many links as possible. The dream might inspire me to cook more often for the family, to invite the neighbors for a barbeque, to construct a lattice around my unsightly gas grill, which I have not used very often over the past year. There are endless possibilities for relationship, and this is the way of imagination. The dream image is a vast reservoir of significance, an unexplainable mystery, whose existence springs from the soul experiencing itself through the senses. But ultimately, the dream affirms the necessary partnership between material and spiritual images. In responding imaginatively to our dreams, we are simply furthering this interplay.

The stream of connections to a dream might also include links to previous dreams. The gathering of diverse dreams in memory is a community of images that are forever reconstituting themselves into personal myths and dramas. I can pair the relaxed atmosphere of the outside fireplace with my more conflicted and anxious dreams. My personal maladies often spring from excessive effort, overextension, pushing too hard, and this tendency is so different from the calm discovery of the fireplace on my property.

I have a recurring dream of *an old man trying to push a car over a hill. As soon as he nears the top, the car will no longer move. He pushes harder and harder, and in spite of the strain felt in his body and legs, there is a realization that further movement is impossible. It becomes equally difficult for him to go farther on his own. The effort has consumed him.* The dream is saying, "Relax. Take it easy. Cars go over hills on their own and not by having people push them."

The mechanical artifacts of our day life are infused with spirit through our dreams. The ubiquitous automobile of the physical world is one of the most frequent visitors in dreams, where it has become a shamanic figure. Dream cars are animated beings—allies, adversaries, and guides—who dissolve the dualism of sacred and profane. The most apparently mundane objects become carriers of potent psychic contents.

The man pushing the car has taken on its job. They have reversed roles. I was so completely focused on my identification with the man that I missed the perspective of the car. How does it feel being pushed? What about the hill, and gravity? They are players in the dream. All three of them might be gently yet decisively trying to tell the man that he is limited. They may be smiling at his mad effort, his compulsion to move the car. They are quietly joined together in a natural resistance to *his* Sisyphean aspect, chained to hopeless tasks, the futility of pushing against the hill for no apparent purpose.

"What a way to grow old," the dream says to me. The recurring quality of the dream continues, "When are you going to see yourself and let things be? I have to keep coming back to try and get your attention."

This dream is a fairly gentle caution against excessive effort. At other times when I am overdoing it, my body communicates with physical and sometimes violent protests. Children might do the same thing to parents to get their attention or rebel to have their needs considered. There truly does seem to be an angel in everything, and sometimes they vie for attention and time. We can be easily consumed by one aspect of the psyche's desire, and this interrupts the interplay with other qualities of our life—work conflicts with family, personal creation with support for others. The soul is a diverse community of needs and interests and never a single focus.

Complete concentration on one area may leave others unattended. Every bright illumination is accompanied by a shadow. When the needs of one of our intimate angels are overlooked, they shift into a more demonic or aggressive form and draw attention to their plight. If the angry demons of the waking world don't get the job done, dream figures continue the effort.

At a time when things were going more smoothly in my day life, I had a dream of *a retired man that I know. He is driving along slowly in his pickup truck.* I often see this man sitting alone or with his wife in his truck parked next to the sea. They just sit and watch the water, something I never do. I usually pass him while I'm running or driving in my car. In addition to his person, his truck is an important aspect of the dream configuration. Like him, it expresses relaxation. The "pickup" can be imagined as his angelic partner in that the two are inseparable, and within the dream world, both are equally animated. Dreams are especially helpful in showing us how objects live and contribute to the drama of psyche. Both the relaxed man and his slow-moving truck embody an aspect within my soul. They echo and reinforce the peaceful mood of contemplation.

As an artist I observe the subtle connections between my dreams and pictures. I never consciously paint images from dreams, but as I immerse myself in reflections on dreams, my paintings become increasingly infused with a dreamlike atmosphere. I am perhaps painting with the spirits and movements of the dream. The contemplation of dreams opens the day world to the psychic fields of imagination. They also help me to look at my paintings as waking dreams.

Recently, I have been making paintings of bicycle riders. My bicycle paintings are not conscious representations of dreams, but I have had recurring dreams in which I ride bikes in the sky over houses and neighborhoods. Nothing was planned as I painted these pictures, I was captivated by the image of the cycler and just stayed with him. Painting is a waking dream, a realm of earth angels, in which material and spiritual forces shape one another. I move like a cyclist in painting the pictures, quickly and freely in a way that counters my Sisyphean aspect.

I recall an old dream I had after a disappointing weekend of playing tennis. The confinements of the courts were followed by a dream in which *I cross-country-ski through a huge expanse covered with light snow in late May.* The sweeping gestures of skiing arrive to clear the congested and tight spaces of the post-tennis soul.

In addition to helping me to paint with spontaneous imagination, dreams also teach me how to enjoy the expression of a painting. If we look at paintings from a dream perspective, we can appreciate soul's desire for sensory imagery. There is a realization that we are going into a realm different from our regular operations in the day world. In my art studio retreats I find that if we begin each day by sharing dreams, their psychic energy will manifest itself in our paintings. Physical and spiritual things connect in their every detail.

Participants in the retreats feel the frustration of not being able to continue living in this way in their outside lives. A woman in a studio was deeply involved in painting from the soul. In her dream *she sits on a long couch with a man who, unlike her husband, shares her interest in esoteric things. He whispers a secret code in her ear, and she looks at an empty green rug before them. She longs for the magical qualities of the rug and knows that she cannot go there with her husband.*

The group responded to the intensity of her longing and spoke about the dream suggesting a marriage to her soul as well as her relationship to her husband. A person's deep relationship to the soul is a private and gnostic involvement that is not always accessible to others. It may be an impossible expectation to share every aspect of her soul life with her husband. The empty green rug conveys the solitary nature of the mystery. She cannot go there with other people, but the area is comforting, green, and fertile. Or she can sit on the long and comfortable couch of soulful reflection with other people who share her interests, and each one has a personal relationship with the mysteries of the empty green rug. The dream arrived to guide the woman in making the transition from the retreat group back to her daily life.

Dreams sanctify what appear to be ordinary physical things. Green rugs become carriers of the soul's mysteries. A woman in another studio dreams that *she leaves her makeup and credit cards with her aging mother before she gets into a Viking boat with two men to go onto an ominous sea.*

Another woman dreams that *a one-handed, cigarette-rolling cowboy arrives and tells her, "You can't roll gold leaf."* We made many interpretations and responses to both dreams, but ultimately they defy final explanations. They live imagistically, sustaining their most essential nature, which is fascination and imaginal enrichment. Our interpretations help us relate them to events in our lives, but we do not want to lose the irreducible vitality of the images as pure beings. As we make connections, and relationships, we do not transfer their significance to something other than themselves. But we do try in our interpretations to continue the interaction between spiritual and material things.

The most ordinary things of daily life become dream spirits. The people next door hire a crew to prune the trees between our two houses. An old garden shed and its covering of gray, weathered wood becomes visible. I am not particularly concerned about the visibility of the shed, but that night *it appears in a dream, like a being, and I contemplate its textures and lines.* I don't think there has to be more significance to my dream image of the shed than the simple fact that it made a visual impression on me in the day world. Dreams express the soul's constantly changing landscape and its insatiable desire for images. If I look only for answers and explanations in dreams, I miss the wondrous way in which they spiritualize matter.

A woman dreams that *her friend wants shrimp and is served a TV dinner*, and then the dream shifts to *her sitting in a car in a traffic jam, completely relaxed.* The most ordinary things of the world are carriers of the spirits of acceptance and tranquility. Big existential issues like destiny, our lack of control over it, and the peace in surrendering to our fate are embodied in TV dinners and traffic jams. These truths of the psyche cannot be conveyed more accurately and concretely.

Dreams also interpret our lives in the day world according to the needs of the soul. They display the feelings and energetic patterns that we cannot see by transforming them into images. The dream contents illustrate where we are in our soul life with a wit and imaginal vitality that is sheer magic. I marvel at the aesthetically stimulating way they concretize and give new twists to complex emotional situations. During the day I cut my lawn and drive my children past the house where their great grandparents lived. That night I dream that *I cut "my grass" at my grandfather's old house with his manual lawn mower, which now has a motor and cuts the grass clean and close. There is a delightful feeling of the mower getting it right.* Like a wizard, the dream combines different soul places and things into a single landscape and a feeling of ease.

I recently sold an old house that I owned for nearly two decades. I was attached to the house, and there were also vexing business complications involved in the sale, which increased the tension of the move. A week after leaving the house I dreamt that *my wife and I forgot something, and we were in the house looking for it. There is an emotional shift in the dream, and I realize that we walked in without the new owners' permission. They return with friends, and we try to hide.* The dream was full of anxiety and confusion about who owned the house, and it showed me how my soul had not left its rooms. I often think of how the body might go to a new place, but the soul does not move so quickly. The dream suggests that my soul is still living in the old house, that it is between worlds.

Two months after leaving the house I again returned to it in my dreams. *I am admiring the garden, and the new owners come out to welcome me. They take me inside and show me all of the things they have done. The feeling is relaxed, and I feel happy that they are caring for the house.* The two dreams were interpreting the way my psyche was responding to the loss. They provided the passage rites that helped me say good-bye and accept the move. It took time to accept the transition, and the dream images enacted the process.

Is it too farfetched to imagine the house having feelings about the move? The great rationalist, Saint Thomas Aquinas, believed in a vegetative soul, and like Aristotle, he felt that everything has an essential substance.

My family had been in the house for seventeen years. The children were intrigued by the new house and neighborhood, but they missed their bedrooms and the people next door. My three-year-old daughter cried at night for her room. Maybe the rooms pined for the children? At dinner we talked about the different features of the house, the things we did there, what we missed the most. The house was an expression of the soul of the family, and these informal rituals of passage in our day and dream lives helped us make the transition. The house, which lives as an angel in our imaginations, certainly had feelings about the move. It was the container of our most intimate lives for all of those years. It was the partner who was always there for us, a welcoming and comfortable sanctuary, a place for retreat and regeneration. It was generous to the family, and we reciprocated with our affections.

Fourteen months after leaving the house, I had a strikingly pleasant dream. *I am in the house making a phone call to my sister. During the call I realize that I am in the old house, and the new owner, a lawyer, is in the next room with a client. I say to myself, "Oh my God, I've done it again," trespassed into their house, using it as though it were my own. The owner approaches me, dressed in running shorts and much younger than he actually is. I apologize and explain that I still have moments of forgetting that I don't live in the house anymore. He smiles and says that he understands. I ask him if he'd like me to cut the tall privet hedge in the front of the property, which does not exist in the actual house. He says, "No. You don't have to do that. We'll take care of it."*

The man in the dream is accepting my presence in the house and my attachment to it, my intimate communications with my sister. The house is a feminine soulmate with whom I am deeply attached, and the new owner, who is "running" the place now, helps me let go of my responsibility. He is youthful in his relationship to the house, much younger than I in that particular place.

The dream continues, and *I am in the basement of the house with his wife, who shows me an old room they transformed. The basement is not at all like the actual house. It has tall ceilings and an expansive open space where a large boiler had once been. I am struck by how attractive the space is. They uncovered a huge wall space that would be excellent for a painting studio. There are some nineteenth-century wooden pegs coming out from one of the walls in the room, where there are neatly stacked, freshly painted green window shutters. I sense that the nineteenth-century man who first owned the house used this area as a workshop and that it must have been warm in winter because it is right next to the heat source.*

This second phase of the dream gets into the personal details of my relationships with the old and new houses. One of the reasons why I left the old house was the lack of adequate studio space. I made art in a ground-level room below the house with the heating system in an adjoining room. It was an attractive nineteenth-century space, but there was not enough room. It was toasty in the winter, and apparently the original owner of the house had used this area as a workplace. The green shutters and wooden pegs are features of my "new" 1830 house. During the first year, I devoted myself to working with the carpenters in transforming the house in which I now live. I stack my paintings in my studio in a way similar to the arrangement of the dream shutters. This image embodies how I had been painting shutters and other household artifacts instead of art. The wooden "shutters" had taken the place of my paintings for a few months.

The owners of my old house are executing the transformations that my soul desires and that I am actually bringing about in my new house. The things they are doing to the house are the reasons why we left. Their actions in the dream express my soul's desire, and perhaps what they are doing is a way of telling the house lodged in my psyche why I had to leave.

I feel that I have betrayed the house, my intimate companion for a generation. My dreams present the house as a love object with whom I am still psychically involved. I keep returning to the house in my dreams with a sense of guilt. My two oldest children have lived there every summer of their lives. They do not feel the same psychic bonds to the new house. A home is so much more than an asset that is bought and sold. The old house contained seventeen years of a family. I left. I keep returning in my dreams to show my attachment and to ultimately ask forgiveness for selling the repository of the family soul.

As I start to solidify my feelings around a particular story, I realize that the entire situation can be reversed. The house holds my feelings of being left behind at different times in my life. I am alone like the dream house, which carries my isolation, my need to be visited. My grandfather had a privet hedge. He taught me how to take care of gardens and houses. I miss him. I still use his hedge clippers to trim bushes. He had a workplace in his home. His house had green shutters just like mine.

I keep returning to the house of the soul and its changing scenes and inhabitants. The lost house of the dream is an embodiment of the lost soul, lost loves that activate my longing. There is also the lost love of my parents' house. My father is a lawyer, and this connects to the lawyer in the dream. I am going back to his space. I don't want to disturb him; I want to take care of his hedge and please him. These actions sound like my history with my father.

The dream house gathers so many different threads from the personal psyche and its memories, where images are forever moving in the impermanent stream of connections. One thing is always turning into another.

There are endless possibilities for relationship. The dream tells me that I had to leave, that it was OK. I don't talk enough to my sister on the phone. I miss the cozy old studio in spite of its limitations. The tall ceilings invert the actual space and its crowdedness. I actually enjoyed the repetitive job of painting shutters at the new house. The discovery of new rooms, new spaces in the soul, is a continuation of a recurring dream that has been with me for a long time.

In recent years, my dreams have shifted from the discovery of rooms in the top floor of the house with expansive views, to finding rooms in cellars. Sometimes I come upon rooms beneath rooms. This shift is like an immersion in the underworld, in the earth soul, the *anima mundi*, the feminine, creation. In the basement of my dream I meet the woman and feel that it will be a fine place to make art.

Sticking to the dream is like a group of hockey players passing the puck to one another. One move leads to another. It is the process of passing that really matters, the vitality of the interaction and the connections between players. They keep it moving. This is a radically different way of approaching dreams. We move with their kinetic and imaginal ways rather than attempt to stop them.

Our psychological reflections on dreams have for the most part focused on attaching rational meanings to dreams. As an artist who has witnessed how dreams stir creation, I am less interested in solving them and more attuned to how they activate imagination. They are earth angels who bring excitement and depth to the most ordinary things. The houses, cars, and fireplaces of the dream are the constantly changing guises of the earth angel, but they are not false appearances. They are the outward dressings of spirits who are for-

ever changing their attire, moving from one thing to another in a
flow of connections.

The movement of imagery involves a natural displacement from
one position to another. The individual psyche floats in a stream of
changing influences and directions. These shifts are essential to the
soul, and they not aberrant displacements. The vectors of the soul,
the image carriers, need to move and change. They are forces whose
nature is transformation from one place to another.

The physical aspects of the image are the essential body of the
spirit. One does not exist without the other. There is a popular idea
that angels are extraterrestrials who disguise themselves in worldly
forms. It is felt that they use material bodies and traits to appear in
the world. Exclusive emphasis on disguise, an acknowledged aspect
of dream images, keeps the angels transcendent and separate from
things that are purportedly being used for another purpose. I prefer
to marvel at the way things display their angelic beings. The spirit
of an object exists in its unique and changing presentation of itself,
and in my wonder at witnessing its presence. If I can open to the
thing's expression, and its influence on me, then I am in the realm
of the earth angels.

The dissolving of boundaries between matter and spirit assumes
a trust in the wisdom and good judgment of the psyche. Our twentieth century has been an epoch of radical positivism and strict adher-
ence to a literal sense of reality. As our understanding of
consciousness expands, we simultaneously fear madness and engulf-
ment by the images of the irrational psyche. In response to these
fears, we tighten the controls and dismiss the relationship between
day world and dream image. I have great respect for the discipline
of making distinctions between realities, and my experience has
shown that opening the images of psyche furthers, rather than im-
pedes, differentiation. The more I try to repress an existent and
necessary force, the more I increase the likelihood of psyche's overwhelming flash floods.

In cultivating dreams we discover their many varieties and the vastly different sensations they convey. Some dreams instruct me about life and give messages as to where I am out of kilter. Others amplify feelings and display psyche's unparalleled artistic powers. After hearing that Larry Bird was retiring from the Boston Celtics, I dreamed that *a huge stadium full of people holds up large cards, as they do at college football games, to make a visual pattern. The constellation of color- ful cards moves like flying "birds."* It was an absolutely wondrous feeling that correspond to Bird's graceful flights and the magic he made during his career.

My wife wants to have another child, and I resist my fifth. So she plans to bring a second dog into the family. My mother, who had eight children, is now completely disoriented by Alzheimer's disease. In my dream *I walk up to my parents' house and see my mother through the window. She gives me a huge hug and we fall to the ground hugging. The rooms are empty of furniture, just a light-colored wall-to-wall carpeting. She has a new dalmatian dog with a bluish aura. I feel that my wife would like one of those. There are other dogs in the room, and two fluffy Saint Bernard pups come to us.*

I awoke feeling wonderful. The dream filled me with spirit medicine. I lay awake luxuriating in it and easily fell back to sleep. I had had a stressful week, and the dream brought peace. Afterward I felt the connection between the pups and all my mother's chil- dren. She was never involved with animals, but she is the archetype of motherhood and she ushers in the new dog of our life. The dog we ultimately got a few weeks after the dream has spots. The dream prepares us for the new arrival in the family, and it connects the process to the depths of my mother's nurturing aura.

It is almost two years since I sold my old house. I have heard that the new owners are planting things on the property and restor- ing pine floors that were under carpets. It feels good to know that they are caring for the house and going beyond the restorations we made. But when I drive by, I see that areas of the lawn and much of the landscaping that I did have been let go. I dream that *a cluster of beautiful homes are being built around the house, and the young lawyer is now collecting antique Packard automobiles. The cars sparkle. They look like fantastic 1950s cars with fins.* The Packard was an unusual arrival since I do not deal with old cars in my daily life. My only connection to Packards is a story my father tells about his grandfather, an Irish immigrant who prospered in the leather business, having one with a chauffeur. My great-grandfather ultimately lost it all. Loss is my pervasive feeling toward the house, together with a desire that it be well maintained. I had the dream while teaching for a weekend in Wisconsin at the beginning of football season, so maybe the Packers were infiltrating my psyche. It may be that identifying the cars as Packards was an expression of the high quality that they convey, and not the literal presence of that particular car, since the ones in the dream looked more like late '50s Chevrolets and Cadillacs. I had a pleasurable feeling toward the dream and a sense of intrigue about how diligently he was restoring and caring for the cars. He was attending to something that mattered to him and not to me. My fixations on the lawn will not be his. He's involved with pine floors. The Packards are the carriers of this message.

The earth angels of dreams also carry anxiety and insecurity. I become self-conscious about my malfunctioning Swatch watch and dream of *an elegant gentleman's watch prominently displayed on his wrist.*

After attending a black-tie Boston event and a series of meetings with an impeccably dressed new dean at the college at which I wore Doc Martens, faded cotton pants, a grayish tweed jacket and gray sweater, I dreamed *the ending of a black-tie party with Teddy Kennedy in an old and slightly tattered mansion. I close stained-glass windows in need of repair. The dream shifts to me in a men's room. My gray tweed jacket slips into a toilet to my right, and my sweater is in another one to my left. I look at a prim man who works at the college with me. I feel baffled, and he smiles. There is a sense that the clothes will dry out soon.*

On the day preceding the dream, we got two feet of snow. I was constantly shoveling and feeling overwhelmed. So many things need to be done to keep up appearances, but in the dream everything just falls into the hopper. Scatology takes us into eschatology, into the death of things. There is a sense of relief in the dream, of accepting the condition of things—the old house, the condition of my clothes, Teddy's aging and my own.

Nightmares constantly challenge the belief that dream images never come to harm us. My eight-year-old daughter dreamed that *a scorpion is after her four-year-old sister. She calls 911 and no one answers. She stays on the bed and won't put her feet down on the floor.*

In the morning she was terrified of the dream. We talked about looking at the dream in different ways and how it speaks to us through feelings and fears. I said that the dream might be telling her how much she loves her little sister, and maybe she is jealous of the attention her sister gets because the scorpion goes after her. We talked about her sense of responsibility and how people do not always respond to her calls and needs for attention. I thought of how the dream might also be expressing my daughter's love of the little-child aspects within herself, or her vulnerability personified as her sister. Talking about all these ways of looking at the dream eased the fear. A sense of benign purpose replaced the oppressive onslaught. My daughter described how she had just watched a film about scorpions, and when she saw the connection between her day life and the nocturnal image, there was relief. At the age of eight she was able to embrace the disturbance of the dream as an expression of what the soul wants.

It is difficult for many to accept that the disturbing image is "the fulfillment of the soul's desire," but if we start with a belief in the psychic necessity of the image, there is a basis for re-visioning. We miss the communications of our dreams by judging them as though they are events in the day world. It may be that the treasures of the dream world use shocking appearances to protect their rarities from prosaic interpretation. As my daughter discovered, there is a tremendous relief in being able to interpret situations in different ways.

The dream can be most fully appreciated by a consciousness that corresponds to the imagination of its expression. Everything is shaped by the approach, the way of looking. By imagining dreams as angels, we ensoul and vivify them. As in any relationship, our interest will affect the other's influence on our lives. A deep commitment to the specific dream is the footing for its connections to different aspects of life. Ensouling is a reciprocal relationship. Dreams are carriers of soul, and their existence does not depend upon on our attentions, but our appreciation of their expressiveness intensifies the reciprocal experience. We ensoul one another.

The image is the fulfillment
of the soul's desire ....

The psyche is animated by a veritable hunger for images.
It wants images. —Gaston Bachelard

Sigmund Freud was on track with his wish-fulfillment theory of
dreams, but he never fully embraced the basic truth that images
made by imagination are what the soul wants. For Freud the image
was always a sign pointing to something other than itself, something
hidden. The image was a substitute for a censored wish. He put us
on the road to the soul and simultaneously obscured the way to the
simple realization that the image is the fulfillment of the soul's desire. It is the image of the grail, not the literal object, that moves
the soul.

Images from dreams, the arts, and personal reveries do function
as messengers and provocateurs, revealing unseen aspects of our
lives that need attention. They have an extraordinary ability to expand the scope of our awareness. But after many years of working
with imagery in art and therapy, I am seeing that what really matters
is the presence of the images themselves and the way they infuse
our lives with vitality. Interpretations are ways of paying attention
to images, acknowledging their existence, and becoming involved in
their worlds, but underlying every effort to relate to these figures is
the realization that the soul experiences itself through images. If
we want soul, we need imagery.

What matters is the telling of the dream and opening to its imagery. All of the different interpretive moves we make are ulti-

mately focused on the cultivation of images rather than figuring out what they mean. Our discipline keeps us in the dream and deepens our connections to the images. Therapists are skilled witnesses and guides who help construct a safe place for immersion into images that take us where we need to go. They know the way, and we follow their lead. The same thing happens when we reflect on artworks. We enter the environment of the image, which medicines and stimulates our souls. As they change, we change with them. Ensouling is not a one-way movement from persons to things. We do transmit soul to the world, but the process of animating is a reciprocal relationship between persons and things.

I see now that my methods of responding to a painting with body movement or spontaneous rituals is an instinctive effort to interpret images with images, to imagine them further and make more images. This is the way dreams interpret life, and from them we can learn how to foster the soul's longing for images. What other purpose can there be in our world's hunger for film, television, music, sports, art, household things, fashionable clothing? We get so caught up in judging the morality of these desires, or in trying to eliminate them altogether, that we totally overlook their psychological necessity. Rather than leaping to judge, we might look more compassionately at what the soul is expressing in them.

I am intrigued by Saint Augustine's confession to God that all things "are from You" simply because they exist. Augustine's notion that anything that exists is innately good, but subject to human corruption, applies nicely to how we negatively judge the way soul expresses itself through our personal creations. The harsh censor does its most potent work within ourselves.

Disturbing images challenge and ultimately affirm my belief that the soul desires the full spectrum of its imagery, what Freud saw as a perverse and polymorphous spectacle. Dreams, nightmares, childhood memories, cherished objects and places, personal artistic expressions, and idiosyncratic habits are all vital aspects of the soul's imagistic landscape.

The soul retrieves images and makes new ones in order to experience and save itself. It needs and craves all kinds, pleasing and offensive ones, angels and demons. The painter Philip Guston made self-portraits of himself as barbaric figures and said, "I tried to imagine . . . what it would be like to be evil." He described the artist as God's messenger, who sees the world for the first time, and said, "I want to paint a world as it has never been seen before."[8] In the artist's studio, the soul struggles to express its most authentic and personal imagery, like an angel who sees from provocative perspectives.

When I try to articulate what an image is, the sense of an angel is the closest I can get to its nature, which is both physical and spiritual. The image, like the angel, is a particular figure that lives within an intermediate realm. The term *earth angel* evokes this connection between matter and spirit, sensory perception and imagination.

I have a story that illustrates how people go looking for images that nourish their souls. Many "Sunday painters" visit the area around my home in Gloucester with their small easels, paintboxes, and straw hats, to make pictures of coastal scenes. A year ago I encountered one of these "artists," wearing a straw hat, at the end of my driveway as I was going out in my car. I didn't roll down the window to say hello nor make an attempt to look at the picture.

I am a painter schooled in the abstract expressionist values of the "heroic" artist who works from imagination and not literal representations of physical things. But like everybody else, I made pictures of flowers and landscapes in my adolescence, and my parents still have them hanging prominently in their house.

Looking back at my years of painting from nature, I realize how much I enjoyed making those pictures and how exciting it was to bring pleasure to my parents and other people who admired them.

There is something very significant about expressions of the soul that are "just like everybody else." In making the pictures I also realized that every painting is an interpretation, and even the most exacting "representations" are full of the artist's style and impressions.

When studying art in New York, I rejected the values of making "pretty" pictures, I obviously closed the door on an aspect of my soul's life. The adolescent pictures that I made of country houses with bridges over brooks and flowers embodied aspects of the soul's desire. As I look back at them, they evoke nostalgia and poetic remembrance. My negative feelings toward Sunday painters is connected to the rejection of this aspect of my own art. They trigger a complex I have about the purpose of art, elitist values, and the significance of my own life as an artist. Anybody can be a Sunday painter, and even though I have always felt that anybody can paint soulfully, I am still unresolved about those who make stiff, photographic "copies" of physical things. I look at the pictures and feel how much "better" they could be if there were more movement, vitality, and unusual color like we see in Van Gogh.

In reimagining Sunday painters as soul painters and witnesses to the spirits of the physical world, I do not have to abandon my critical sense of art and how I strive to improve my pictures, find my most personal style, and help my students paint with increased satisfaction. Ultimately, the easel painters are on their journey and I am on mine, and we are much closer than I realize. Each of us pursues our individual relationships with creation. My negative feelings toward them can viewed as angels, messengers who bring me closer to the most tender qualities of the soul, who protect its vulnerabilities to the moralistic and arrogant judgments of others. In these situations the angelic dimension can be imagined as the reframing of chronic attitudes.

After re-visioning my attitudes about Sunday painters, I was recently mowing my lawn on a Saturday morning. Again, I saw an easel painter on the street at the end of my driveway. He was a young man wearing a T-shirt and jeans. As I worked, I watched him out of the corner of my eye. There is a historic house on the water across the street from us, and I assumed he was painting it. As I approached him with my mower, he nodded and smiled. I kept mowing, but subtly positioned myself behind his picture to look.

He was painting our house, and the picture looked interesting. It wasn't at all like the stiff forms and unimaginative colors that I am accustomed to seeing by the roadside.

I finished my work and walked across the lawn to say hello. I admired the painting. As we spoke, I noticed a slight Castilian accent, and he said, "Few people notice. I'm Cuban, and I live in New York City."

He was visiting Cape Ann to paint "in the field." In looking at the picture I was intrigued to see how he had carefully rendered the landscaping and things that I had done to restore the structure of the house. He was painting the image of my soul's desire, my house, and he was doing it well, in keeping with the ideal, or *imago*, that I carry within myself. An easel painter was honoring one of my most personal and cherished images. The house no doubt touched something in his soul, and at that moment it was a physical and spiritual intermediary between the two of us.

Not only did the house function as an earth angel, but the incident itself felt like an angelic occurrence. The event embodied and even amplified images from my soul's life. It gave a sense of fulfillment, synchronicity, the marvelous. Angels appear in these spontaneous circumstances, small things that manifest subtle correspondences between a material event and the patterns of our psychic lives.

By imagining the angelic qualities of this incident, I affirm its connection to my personal life. But I have no need to see the presence of the artist as a supernatural appearance. It was a material event upon which I reflect with imagination. The angelic quality of the incident lies in the intimate relationship of separate things to one another. My reflections on easel painting as soulwork need not have any direct or casual relation to the artist's presence at the end of my driveway. In other words, I do not think that he was there in front of my house to complete a process through which I was going. In our self-centered and causal views of angels, we see them arriving in response to something we did, or as bestowing a favor that we need.

I don't imagine my previous actions delivering the painter to my house. For me, the angelic experience is the psychic connection made between his presence and my perception. The imagery of the outer world and the soul's desire meet for a fleeting moment in the angelic event. All of the details of the incident—the house, the painting, the artist, his easel and paints, the date, the time of day, the lawnmower, and my memories—are infused with qualities of the earth angel, which is a way of looking at them. The magic I felt in the event pervades the different images through which it is constituted. And conversely, it is the specific images, and especially his easel painting of my house, that carry spirits that stimulate my reactions. We gather together to create the event, or the event creates itself through our gathering.

The issue of agency is perhaps the most distinguishing feature between my view of angelic occurrences and conventional ideas about angels as transcendent beings with a specific purpose in mind. The latter view imagines the acts of spirits according to linear causes and effects as conceived through a particular person's outlook. I see the spirits of things existing in the world independent of my personal history and intentions. The artist visitor is on his journey. I am on mine. And my house has its own history. My sense of the earth angel is a spontaneous gathering, a meeting, for a moment treasured, when our paths intersect or our stars cross. The angelic quality is outside our control. It happens to us but also through us, and with our full participation.

The message in this event is the wonder it carries within itself. The imagery of the experience is the fulfillment of my soul's desire. Locating angels has more to do with recognizing connections and appreciating moments as carriers of satisfaction than it does with supernatural intercessions according to specific schemes. The world is constantly here for us. It is always showing the way, if we are able to read its face. And "the way" is a more complete and constant appreciation of its display. I can avoid rejecting, or even questioning, the "supernatural" by saying that every detail of our daily lives carries the divinity within itself. Its presence is not confined to special appearances.

The psychic "gathering" around my house did not stop with the easel painter incident. Shortly after his visit, a site manager who worked on a number of films made recently in our region called and asked if our house could be used to shoot a commercial. A director and film crew arrived from Los Angeles and toured the property, looking at it on a perfect October day and filling the place with "movie" spirits. It's the house that touches people with images that fulfill different desires in their souls. I see how it has a wide range of offerings. It tells many stories through the way its forms interact with the contents of a person's life.

Pathological views of experiences often invert the way images function as the fulfillment of the soul's desire. Images begin to feed the perverted wish. If people live from the perspective of fear or the need to control everything, they fit whatever they see into these schemes. They wear certain clothes and not others because of the things associated with them. An important letter is written with a particular pen because of the powers a person believes it has. Books with malevolent titles are taken off a bookshelf because their contagion is feared.

If I operate from this negative and self-enclosed view, I become suspicious about why the man at the end of the driveway is painting a picture of my house. Why does he choose my place? What is he after? Is he abducting the soul of the property? What bad influence will this have on me, on the house? And then the crew from California arrived! Is the world really after me, and my house? Fantasies about agency are again at the core of this worldview.

Paranoia is not without its imagination, but it is based on an exaggerated sense of my place in the world, and it assumes that all of the details, things, and movements in an environment are focused on me. Something like this happens in many experiences with angels when people go beyond personal rapport with the spirits of things to the conviction that they are here just for them.

The Paraclete, or spirit called to comfort and help, is present all of the time, but we lose contact with it. I feel that this loss is a natural condition of the soul. Its presence moves in and out of awareness. The call for help is an awakening to what exists and what we do not see.

Every image is somehow tied to the soul's desire to experience itself. When the earth angels are freed from our self-referential perspectives, we can approach the world once again with wonder and participate more fully in the creative interplay of the life that we make, and that simultaneously makes us. If we are able to transcend ourselves for a while, we can simply look at the way the spirits of things express themselves, acting as agents of an intelligence that we imagine through angels.

And to the person who says, "Why don't the angels visit me?," I reply:

"They do. They are everywhere and ready to be seen. You just have to look in another way."

Things to do ....

THE MALL

• Visit a mall as if you were on an Audubon tour watching for earth angels.

You might leave the binoculars at home, but a camera, especially one with a zoom lens, can serve the same purpose of framing, focusing, and taking you up close to things. A video camera gives you freedom of movement and requires less skill in its recording of images.

Focus on people's hands as they touch things. Watch the look in their eyes as they examine objects. Imagine their desires, their likes and dislikes. Whether you actually go to a mall or do this exercise in your imagination, the purpose is to help you start looking at things in new ways. How do they express themselves and fly out to you?

• Observe the objects and the aesthetics of their display in stores. Seek out things that seem most contrary to your tastes, but which you might secretly like to own and use.

• Imagine the things on display having feelings. What do *they* want? Do some people attract them more than others? What do they think about you?

• Do the same thing with a merchandise catalog. Don't take the process of ordering things literally, but look through the pages with a tantric attitude of withholding gratification. Feel the desire as an end in itself. This keeping of desire helps us understand how things act upon us, and how we relate to them. There are many things that I would like to own but do not need, cannot afford, or simply don't have the time to use, but I still enjoy my desire for them.

• Imagine something you've always wanted but never bought.

What is the appeal? Enjoy relating to it or using it in your imagination.

• Shift your focus from acquiring things to engaging objects in your environment. Bring the desire of the shopper, or the unrealized longing for the thing you've always wanted, and try focusing it on things that you take for granted. Enjoy the free play with desire by concentrating on objects you already have, and renewing their importance, the contributions they make to your life. For most people, longing is intense in shopping and we are simply transferring its spirit to what we already have. We begin to realize what we have been missing in our relationships with things, why we become victims of desire by concentrating its power on what we don't have and probably never can get. Maybe the longing will tell us that part of its nature is to stay out of reach. Enjoy this unrealizable dimension.

DREAMS

• Contemplate your dreams aesthetically; meditate on the images and dramatic scenes without trying to explain what they mean; pay careful attention to the sensory qualities of the images, the changes in action and appearances.

• Greet the dream as an angel, witnessing and receiving its expression as a wondrous appearance; spend time with the images and feelings, and don't jump to conclusions through hasty analysis.

• Realize that dreams rarely speak literally, although they do from time to time make graphic and direct statements.

• Don't judge and censor dreams according to the moral standards of the day world.

• Remember that dreams do not come to hurt you. Imagine the nightmare as an angel ruffling your feathers and helping you look at some difficult things. Be patient with these stressful dreams, and don't try to figure them out or receive their message right away. You may need time to learn how to simply relax in their presence.

Acceptance of them is in itself a major move. Once you acknowledge their significance, it may take time to find ways to coexist openly with them. As you start to see troubling images as allies, and when you are able to look at them with fascination and interest, connections to your life will be suggested.

As you accept their intimate and purposeful nature, even bad dreams become gratifying because they are attuned to the soul's movement.

• With every type of dream, the essential discipline of dreamwork involves cultivation over time. Approach the dream as a garden and not as a perfunctory message that you read and put into the trash. The dream is to be visited and revisited, contemplated from various perspectives. Some dreams come and go in a day, whereas others are always with us. The fleeting dreams are appreciated more fully if you maintain a place in your life where they are tilled and watched. Writing dreams in a journal, making pictures and poems in response to dreams, and other artistic responses are ways of cultivating and keeping dreams.

• Make as many connections between the dream and your life as possible.

• Continuously reframe the dream from the perspective of different details and elements.

• Treat your dreams with imagination; interpret images with images, soul with soul; respond to dreams with movements, sounds, creative writings, and performances that will augment their daimonic energy rather than shut it off. The artistic transformation of the dream will help you avoid excessive analysis; it will keep imaginal expressions alive and spread the psychic forces of the dream into other areas of your life.

• When responding artistically to a dream, concentrate on a particular image, situation, or feeling, and continue its imaginal movement. It is impossible to engage every aspect of a dream, and this kind of effort becomes a compulsive documentation which actually loses the spirit of the dream. It is also impossible to exactly portray a dream image or sequence of events in any kind of translation. If you remember just one image or fragment from a dream, that is enough to deeply immerse you into the oneiric spirits. Don't try to force the extraction of hidden contents. Let go of the illusion of exact rendering, which is just another attempt to capture the "ungraspable phantom" and submit it to our control. Enter the imagination of the dream through whatever door your memory provides and be carried along by it.

• Let go of any desire to explain the dream. As William Shakespeare says through Bottom in *A Midsummer Night's Dream,* "Man is but an ass, if he go about to expound this dream. . . . The eye of man hath not heard, the ear of man hath not seen, man's hand is not able to taste, his tongue to conceive, nor his heart to report, what my dream was. I will get Peter Quince to write a ballad of this dream. It shall be called Bottom's Dream, because it hath no bottom."

If I enter the realm of the dream with wonder, its significance will grow. I will always make connections to my life because, as Prospero declares in *The Tempest,* "We are such stuff / As dreams are made on."

• Imagine your dreams as intimate companions who provide wondrous experiences within the privacy of your sleep. Look at your private reverie in the day world in the same way.

• We are all familiar with spirits as we experience them in dreams, so if we want to infuse our daily life with them, we reflect upon the dream potential, the dream aspect that lives within things. Take the most common things in your kitchen—a bread board, a container of milk, a pot, a bowl of fruit, a sponge, a dirty dish—and contemplate these things as dream figures. These meditations will further the sense of the divine presence in every thing.

• The making of dream catchers and other artifacts to aid dreaming are not literal tools, but they will further your involvement with dream spirits. The same applies to constructing a simple shrine near your bed to welcome dreams. W. B. Yeats put rose petals and other things under his pillow to encourage dreams. If you make a shrine, arrange objects that connect to the particulars of your dreams. The gathering of these talismans corresponds to the gathering of the dream. Their collective presence and their freedom to make links among themselves parallels the creative spirits of dreams.

• Since physical things are often the leading characters in dreams, we inspire dreaming and become more aware of its connections to our day lives by becoming more conscious of our relations with objects. The purpose of these acts is cultivation and not control. The more we try to construct the contents of our dreams, the more they will communicate from outside these schemes, and tell us that they are not to be manipulated. They exist to let us know that we do not direct the soul. The more we try to impose our will, the more perverse the dreams will become.

• Dreams are made from the things and experiences of the physical world, and they return imagination to daily life. If you dreamed of your house, your car, an object in your environment, visit with them afterward. Return the spirits of your dream to these things through touch, visual contemplation, a simple chant, or some other physical gesture.

When you revisit the place or things of your dream—the road sign, the black asphalt, the abandoned car, the conveyor belt in the factory, the cereal section of the supermarket—you see their reciprocal existence as matter and spirit. Dreams show us how our spirits and those of the world create together.

Notes

CHAPTER 1: THROUGH THE EYES OF ANGELS

1. Jane Harrison, 1962. *Epilegomena to the Study of Greek Religion* [1921] and *Themis* [1912] (New York: University Books, 1962). Harrison approaches the human being as "essentially an image-maker" and says that religion "springs like ritual from arrested, unsatisfied desire. We figure to ourselves what we want, we create an image and that image is our god. . . . the gods are images of desire." She describes how the figures created by a community in its seasonal rites "get a kind of permanent separate life of their own and become separate beings. In this way they help to beget a kind of daimon or spirit; from being annual they become a sort of perennial though not yet immortal god" (pp. xliii–xlv).

Harrison helps me relate angels to the more ancient daimon, and she affirms my sense that the image (daimon) is the fulfillment of the soul's desire. But there is a subtle orientation in her writings toward the rationalism of her era (1850–1928). She ultimately suggests that Greek religion is a projection from the human perspective, as contrasted to James Hillman's more religious vision (tied to William Blake and others) of a divine imagination expressing itself through us. My differences with Jane Harrison are matters of nuance, which are nevertheless major in that they contrast the theophanic views of archetypal psychology and its soulful materialism, to the more dominant intellectual materialism of the twentieth century.

2. For years we have thought scientifically about the messages of dreams and other psychic expressions. We have read them as a relatively impersonal text delivered by a psyche we believed to function exclusively according to biochemical and behavioral principles. I value science but question our reliance on it as an exclusive way of knowing. The arrival of angels signals a more poetic, personal, and complex way of imagining our inner lives, a new cosmology of the psyche. The message is being personified as an angel. Even Marshall McLuhan's revolu-

tionary slogan, "The medium is the message," was articulated in relatively technical language and thoughts. If angels are messengers, then it follows that media images are angels.

When I reflect upon a thing, it offers its life to me through perceptual images that can be likened to angels. I distinguish these perceptions of things from memory images, artistic images, dream images, and archetypal images, all of which can be imagined as varieties of angels together with any other form of life, including toasters, telephone answering machines, and personal computers. Just like angels, images are elusive, manifold, incapable of fixed definition, and prone to fly around inner space. They are peripatetic entities, as suggested by the way consciousness is always shifting from one thing to another. Offspring created as perceptual images interact with the deeply lodged and purely psychic images of the individual and collective souls. The angelic way of looking at the world accepts the complex interplay while imagining life from a simple foundation of partnership and the need for others. Human beings and images depend upon one another, and creation is a participatory intelligence where even the most apparently individualistic contributions involve collaborations with a larger field, tradition, or collective mind of which we are expressions.

I do not want to say that images "are" angels, because that would place both in the life-threatening enclosure of positive definition. By approaching images "as" angels, I link the two through metaphor, and this protects each from a fixed label and preserves their ability to take on other forms and functions. I conserve the poetic and mysterious nature of the angel.

I can view the object itself as an angel and not restrict spirits to the more abstract idea of a perception. When I personify an object, there is still an interplay and a host of things happening between us.

3. James Hillman, *A Blue Fire: The Selected Writings of James Hillman*, edited by Thomas Moore (New York: Harper and Row, 1989). Hillman's many books revive the Hellenic values of giving careful attention to the gods as well as every feature of the physical world. The Greeks felt that there are gods in our diseases and dark moods, as well as our most sublime expressions and lofty places. If we are to "honor the gods," we must see their presence in everything.

When I speak of "the gods," I refer to figures of classical imagination. The divine is a mystery, and for me it is a source from which the Greek gods and other figures emanate.

4. Wallace Stevens, *Opus Posthumous,* edited by Milton J. Bates (New York: Alfred A. Knopf, 1989). Stevens says more than once in Adagia that "Poetry is not personal," but he also says that poetry is gathered from experience, that it is a "means of redemption," a love of images, "a form of melancholia," "like prayer." This sense of individual experience is religious and a way of deepening life. In Adagia he says, "The poet feels *abundantly* the poetry of everything . . . It is life that we are trying to get at in poetry." The poet's person becomes an opening to God, and not an end in itself. He says, "God and the imagination are one," and "God is in me or else is not at all."

5. Henry Corbin, "Cyclical Time in Mazdaism and Ismailism" (1951), in *Man and Time: Papers from the Eranos Yearbooks,* Bollingen Series XXX 3, edited by Joseph Campbell (Princeton, N.J.: Princeton University Press, 1983). My ideas about earth angels are inspired by Corbin's studies of Iranian-Islamic thought, Sufism, and Neoplatonism. Corbin's basic position is that "every creature is composed of his earthly part and of his celestial counterpart, his archetype or angel. Hence through every reality it is possible to discern a person—that is, to grasp this reality *as* or *in* its celestial person. The fractions of time (months, days, hours) may themselves be visualized as persons (angels and archangels whose names they bear and who are their *event*)" (p. 137).

The imagination is for Corbin the organ which creates the intermediate or imaginal realm of materials, existing between the intellect and the senses, a place where spirit and matter infuse one another with their respective qualities. He writes: "The perception of the Earth Angel will come about in an intermediate universe which is neither that of the Essences of philosophy nor that of the sensory data on which the work of positive science is based, but which is a universe of archetype-Images, experienced as so many personal presences. In recapturing the intentions on which the constitution of this universe depend, in which the Earth is represented, meditated, and encountered in the person of its Angel, we discover that it is much less a matter of answering questions concerning essences ('what is it?') than questions concerning persons ('who is it?' or 'to whom does it correspond?'), for example, *who* is the Earth? *who* are the waters, the plants, the mountains? or, *to whom* do they correspond?" (*Spiritual Body and Celestial Earth: Mazdean Iran to Shī'ite Iran*, [1960] translated by Nancy Pearson (Princeton, N.J.: Princeton University Press, Bollingen Series XCI: 2, 1977), pp. 4–5).

According to Corbin, subtlety is a condition of the earth angel: "Beneath the *appearance* the *apparition* becomes visible to the Imagination. And this is the phenomenon of the Angel, the figure which the active Imagination reveals itself to be, which it reveals to itself beneath the appearances perceived, is the figure of the Angels of the Earth. That is why terrestrial phenomena are more than phenomena . . . the beings and things, having been transmuted by the Imagination into their subtle state, are revealed as the *actions* of a personal thought, of which they are the hierurgy" (ibid., p. 29).

6. Herman Melville, *Moby Dick* [1851] (New York: New American Library, 1961).

CHAPTER 2: INTIMATE RITES

1. Tom Clark, *Charles Olson: The Allegory of a Poet's Life* (New York: W. W. Norton, 1991), p. 349.

2. Thomas Moore, *Rituals of the Imagination* (Dallas: Pegasus Foundation, 1983), p. 12. Moore's recent books—*Soul Mates: Honoring the Mysteries of Love and Relationships* (New York: Harper Collins, 1994) and *Care of the Soul* (New York: Harper Collins, 1992)—are the culmination of many years of reflecting on the imagination of ordinary life. My sense of the earth angel is closely attuned to Moore's emphasis on the sacred arts of daily living. Thomas Moore first exposed me to the writings of Marsilio Ficino, who was the subject of his doctoral dissertation at Syracuse University (Thomas Moore, *The Planets Within: Marsilio Ficino's Astrological Philosophy* [Lewisburg, Pa.: Bucknell University Press, 1982]). Ficino's *Liber de Vita* (1489) connects us to the ancient understanding of how the spirits of the earth affect the spirits of persons and communities—the power of the *anima mundi* "spreads out through all things." The reformation of the sacred sparked by Moore's books suggests that "we work on the stuff of the soul by means of the things of life" (1992, p. 184).

3. Martin Heidegger, *Being and Time,* translated from *Sein und Zeit* by John Macquarrie and Edward Robinson (San Francisco: Harper San Francisco, 1962), p. 54. Heidegger's philosophical phenomenology is another affirmation of the way in which things carry spirits unique to themselves. He says that a thing is "never a mere object." Heidegger's emphasis on how things "gather" other things into a happening, or a significant expression, corresponds to my sense of what art objects and dreams do. "Obviously a thing is not merely an aggregate of traits, nor an accumulation of properties by which that aggregate arises. A thing . . . is that around which the properties have assembled. We speak in this connection of the core of things." *Poetry, Language, Thought,* translated by Albert Hofstadter (New York: Harper and Row, 1975), pp. 22–23.

The creative movements of soul are closer to a lively social gathering than the logic of developmental stages. Like dreams, creative connections hop and abruptly jump from one thing to another, drawing diverse and previously separate phenomena into a new creative purpose that eludes analysis according to a linear sequence of causes. The earth angels are apt to move like a stream of relaxed conversation, which makes surprising and fresh connections between things and draws everyone into a spontaneous field of creation.

Heidegger's emphasis on the "thinker as poet" helps us see that many aspects of experience can only be expressed poetically. Following Nietzsche, he restores the poetic tradition of philosophical inquiry. His thoughts on the function of poetry resonate closely with Hillman's "poetic basis of mind," and the reflections of Gaston Bachelard and Wallace Stevens on the relationship between philosophy and poetry.

CHAPTER 3: THE CREATIVE SPIRIT

1. Rudolf Arnheim, *Art and Visual Perception* (Berkeley & Los Angeles: University of California Press, 1954). Arnheim defines expression as "displayed in the dynamic appearance of perceptual objects of events" (p. 445), as contrasted to "all the varieties of traditional theorizing" where there was a "disavowal of any intrinsic kinship between perceived appearance and the expression it conveyed" (p. 448). He says, "We are beginning to see that perceptual expression does not necessarily relate to a mind 'behind it'" (p. 451). Arnheim believes

that when artistic expression "depends on knowledge," it is "less direct" (p. 457). Also see: "The Gestalt Theory of Expression in Rudolf Arnheim," in *Toward a Psychology of Art* (Berkeley & Los Angeles: University of California Press, 1966).

2. James Hillman, "Image-sense," in *Spring*, 1979, pp. 152–182.

3. Rudolf Arnheim, *The Power of the Center: A Study of Composition in the Visual Arts* (Berkeley & Los Angeles: University of California Press, 1988). In place of traditional theories that approach visual experience as "nothing but an agglomeration of static things," Arnheim sees shapes and things as fields of energy and "configurations of forces" (pp. 3–4).

4. Charles Olson, Letter to Elaine Feinstein, May 1959, in *The Selected Writings of Charles Olson*, edited by Robert Creeley (New York: New Directions, 1966), p. 29.

5. Augustine, *The Confessions of Saint Augustine*, translated by Rex Warner (New York: Penguin, 1963), book 7, chap. 17, p. 154.

6. Lucretius, *The Nature of the Universe*, translated by R. E. Latham (Baltimore: Penguin, 1951), book 4, pp. 132–134.

7. Ibid., p. 153.

8. Augustine, *Confessions*, book 7, chap. 20, p. 156.

9. C. G. Jung, *Psychology and Religion* (New Haven: Yale University Press, 1938), p. 21.

10. Henry Corbin, *Creative Imagination in the Ṣūfism of Ibn 'Arabī* (1958), translated by Ralph Manheim, Bollingen Series XCI (Princeton, N.J.: Princeton University Press, 1981), p. 245.

11. Ibid., p. 200.

12. Ibid., p. 234. Among Corbin's other books are *Spiritual Body and Celestial Earth: Mazdean Iran to Shī'ite Iran* [1960], translated by Nancy Pearson (Princeton, N.J.: Princeton University Press, 1977), and *Avicenna and the Visionary Recital* [1954], translated by Willard R. Trask, Bollingen Series LXVI (Princeton, N.J.: Princeton University Press, 1988).

Although I have been deeply affected by Henry Corbin's ideas about the reciprocal relations between material and spiritual realities, there are distinct differences between his writings and what I see as the spirits of things. For me, the earth angel is a characteristic of material expression. I follow Corbin in emphasizing the mutuality of matter and spirit, but I never separate them from one another.

Corbin describes how the soul shows itself when earthly things are transfigured through active imagination, which perceives the spirit in the material form. The contemplation of concrete things engenders a transformation into "the energies corresponding to them" (1977, p. 32). But Corbin says the angelic nature is "not a material quality inherent in sensory substances" (p. 29). For him, it is the process of active imagination that reveals itself as the angel of the earth. I don't see any reason to separate active imagination from things "derived from any outer perception" (p. 11). In keeping with his dichotomy, Corbin felt that the angel of the earth is only expressed by symbolic versus representational art.

For Corbin, the angel is not the physical presence of the thing, but the image of it in the person's heart. This is fine, and I make this distinction myself, but I have no need for dualism. For me the essential statement of Corbin's writings is that the angel lives in an intermediate realm "where the spiritual takes body and the body becomes spiritual" (1981, p. 4). I accept this principle, and I am inspired by it, but I do not make hierarchical divisions between matter and spirit, inner and outer, visible and invisible. Distinctions are necessary, but they do not have to value one aspect more than another. Spirit and matter are joined in the mystery of the earth angel.

Yet Corbin's deep message doesn't so much separate visible from invisible, as it insists upon their reciprocal relations and "essential community." The dichotomy in Corbin's presentation might result from an effort to emphasize the imaginal basis of the angel in a world dominated by positive science and a literal sense of reality. His "intermediate" world of the angel can be a state of mind, as contrasted to a literal place separated from physical things. When the inner world is denied, its advocates are likely to get caught in one-sided polemics. But I cannot separate imagining from the sensory material with which I imagine. They carry real spirits, not mere appearances.

Corbin says, "To come face to face with the Earth not as a conglomeration of physical facts but in the person of its Angel is an essentially psychic event which can 'take place' neither in the world of impersonal abstract concepts nor on the plane of mere sensory data. The Earth has to be perceived not by the senses, but through the features of a primordial Image and, inasmuch as this image carries the features of a personal figure, it will prove to 'symbolize with' the very Image of itself which the soul carries in its innermost depths" (1977, p. 4).

We intimately engage the Earth in the person of its angel through the senses when they are attuned to the presence of soul. Corbin is suggesting that the outside is illusory and the true reality is to be found within. Where does this leave the physical being of the person, place, or thing that I contemplate? Sensory and spiritual experiences are wed forever, as necessary partners in reverie. When the spirit leaves the material world, we have transparent and disembodied angels.

I don't want to go so far in the direction of affirming the spirits of material things that I cast a big shadow over the inner life and what Corbin calls "the very Image of itself which the soul carries in its innermost depths." I refer to the soul's inner image of itself as an *imago*. It is in fact shaped by experiences in the material world, where physical images are formed into something distinct from them in the person's heart. As William Shakespeare says, we are the "stuff" from which dreams are made.

Inner and outer phenomena do not oppose one another. James Hillman presents "endless tandems" as an alternative to the perspective of opposition. He says, "To imagine in pairs and couples is to think mythologically. Mythical thinking connects pairs into tandems rather than separating them into opposites, which is anyway a mode of philosophy. . . . Opposition is merely one of the many modes of being in a tandem." *Anima: An Anatomy of a Personified Notion* (Dallas: Spring Publications, 1985), p. 173.

In *I and Thou* (New York: Scribner's, 1937), Martin Buber says, "All real living is meeting," and the soul's deepest desire is a longing for "cosmic connection" (pp. 11 and 25). The angel is the force of mutuality, the connection between imaginal and material experience.

13. Marsilio Ficino, *The Book of Life (Liber de Vita)* [1489], translated by George Boer (Dallas: Spring Publications, 1980). Ficino says, "The world both lives and breathes, and it is possible for us to draw its spirit" through our own spirits (p. 96). Celestial medicines are transmitted through things that correspond to them and carry imprints of heavenly rays and spirits. According to Ficino, "There is nothing so

deformed in the whole living world that it has no soul, no gift of soul contained in it" (p. 87).

14. Martin Heidegger, "The Thing," in *Poetry, Language, Thought*, pp. 167, 177. Heidegger describes the "presencing" and "thinging" of things in keeping with their "thingly" nature.

15. Brother Lawrence, *The Practice of the Presence of God: Conversations and Letters of Brother Lawrence* [1824] (Oxford: Oneworld, 1993, pp. 38 and 26.

16. Melville, *Moby Dick*, p. 472.

17. Gaston Bachelard, 1983. *Water and Dreams: An Essay on the Imagination of Matter* [1942], translated by Edith Farrell (Dallas: Pegasus Foundation, 1983, p. 17). Bachelard shows how our perceptions of the material world shape consciousness, desires, and dreams. His psychoanalysis of natural elements expands the narrow orientation of developmental psychologies that reduce everything to childhood relations with parents. Our families are part of the comprehensive formation we receive in the physical world. The realm of Eros encompasses all material things and not just sexuality. Bachelard's reflections on the imagination of matter and his studies of intimate places (homes, closets, corners, etc.) show how the earth angel is to be experienced in our most personal images and memories. "My research," Bachelard says, "is devoted to the domain of intimacy, to the domain in which psychic weight is dominant." *Poetics of Space*, translated by Maria Jolas (Boston: Beacon Press, 1994), p. 12.

Edith Cobb, in *The Ecology of Imagination in Childhood* (Dallas: Spring Publications, 1993), describes the basis of imaginal experience in the child's sense of wonder and the "perceptual interplay between self and the world" (p. 31). Adult creators "return" rather than regress to this wellspring of early imaginings and intimate memories.

18. Alan Gussow, *A Sense of Place* (New York: Seabury Press, 1971), p. 27.

19. Bachelard, *Water and Dreams*, p. 11.

20. *Gloucester Daily Times*, September 17, 1994.

21. Gaston Bachelard, *On Poetic Imagination and Reverie: Selections from Gaston Bachelard*, translated by Colette Gaudin (Dallas: Spring Publications, 1987), p. 23.

22. John Kensett, Letter to J. R. Kensett, March 19, 1842, Paris (Collection of the New York State Library, Albany, N.Y.). Quoted in Gussow, *A Sense of Place*, p. 39.

23. Herbert Read, *Icon and Idea: The Function of Art in the Development of Human Consciousness* (New York: Schocken, 1965).

24. D. W. Winnicott, Letter to Roger Money-Kyrle, November 27, 1952, in *The Spontaneous Gesture: Selected Letters of D. W. Winnicott*, edited by F. Robert Rodman (Cambridge: Harvard University Press, 1987), p. 43.

25. Bachelard, *On Poetic Imagination and Reverie*, p. 3.

CHAPTER 4: TOPSY-TURVY

1. Rudolf Arnheim, "Inverted Perspective in Art: Display and Expression," *Leonardo* 5, 1972, pp. 125–135.

2. Corbin, *Spiritual Body and Celestial Earth*, p. 29.

3. Ibid., p. 4.

4. Erica Jong, *The Devil at Large: Erica Jong on Henry Miller* (New York: Turtle Bay Books / Random House, 1993).

5. Thomas Moore, *Dark Eros: The Imagination of Sadism* (Dallas: Spring Publications, 1990). Moore encourages us to look imaginatively, rather than literally, at dark passions. If we can "preserve and follow the symptom," we may be able "to reach its soul or its gift to the psyche" (p. 149). This approach inverts the fundamental assumptions of corrective therapy. Rather than "fix" the perversion, try preserving it imaginatively, not literally, and discover what the soul desires through it. The key move to understanding the morality of this position is the ability to distinguish between the imaginal reflection and the literal act.

6. D. H. Lawrence, *Mr. Noon* (New York: Viking Penguin, 1985), pp. 316–317.

7. Ibid., p. 316.

8. James Hillman, *Insearch: Psychology and Religion* (Dallas: Spring Publications, 1991), pp. 55–56.

CHAPTER 5: EXALTATION BEFORE THINGS

1. Charles Olson, Letter of 3 December 1965, *Maximus to Gloucester: The Letters and Poems of Charles Olson to the Editor of the* Gloucester Daily Times, *1962–1969,* edited by Peter Anastas (Gloucester, Mass.: Ten Pound Island Book Company, 1992), p. 87.

2. Ibid., Letter of 12 February 1968, pp. 123–124.

3. Wallace Stevens, *The Necessary Angel: Essays on Reality and the Imagination* (New York: Vintage Books, 1951). "The imagination gives to everything that it touches a peculiarity, and it seems to me that the peculiarity of the imagination is nobility, of which there are many degrees" (p. 33). Wallace Stevens's sense of the riches of a physical world experienced through imagination is very close to my vision of the earth angel. He said, "The great poems of heaven and hell have been written and the great poem of the earth remains to be written" (p. 142). His compact collection of essays is one of the most important texts on the imagination, what he calls "the unofficial view of being," poetic or imaginal truth as contrasted to philosophical and psychological truth. Stevens, like Jean Paul Richter (*Vorschule der Aesthetik,* 1804), sees imagination as a gathering of all faculties. He does not try to show that it is more truthful than logical thought, but only wants to protect the integrity of its poetic perspective on the world (pp. 40–41).

4. Henry Geldzahler, *New York Painting and Sculpture: 1940–1970* (New York: E. P. Dutton, 1969).

5. Djuna Barnes, *Nightwood* (New York: Harcourt, Brace, 1937).

6. See William Carlos Williams, *The Collected Earlier Poems* (New York: New Directions, 1966).

7. Rudolf Arnheim, "Art among the Objects," in *To the Rescue of Art: Twenty-six Essays* (Berkeley & Los Angeles: University of California Press, 1992).

8. Quoted in an article by Nancy Stapen, "Painting as Salvation: Philip Guston Exhibit at Boston University Offers Profound Rewards," *Boston Sunday Globe,* 12 October 1994.

Index